ICT: Evaluation of Stakeholder Engagement

ICT: Evaluation of Stakeholder Engagement

Eric Dai Hague

KNOWLEDGE
BAKERS

KNOWLEDGE BAKERS

Cataloging in Publication Data--DK
Courtesy: D.K. Agencies (P) Ltd. <docinfo@dkagencies.com>

Hague, Eric Dai, author.
ICT : evaluation of stakeholder engagement / Eric Dai Hague.
pages cm
Includes bibliographical references.
ISBN 978-93-49964-54-9

1. Information technology--Research. 2. Project management. I. Title.

LCC T58.5.H34 2022 | DDC 004 23

ISBN 978-93-49964-54-9

Published by : **Knowledge Bakers**
Pune, India

Preface

Modern societies rely upon research to deal with social challenges through research and innovation (R&I) that is carried out in ICT research projects. ICT research projects are important in generating breakthrough technologies and translating these technologies into solutions for the wider society. In order to develop societally acceptable and desirable solutions, ICT research projects engage different stakeholders who play an important role in encouraging responsible outcomes. Despite the growing recognition of stakeholder engagement in ICT research projects, there is limited evidence in the literature to demonstrate its value. This gap is reflective of a general lack of discourse on qualitative evaluation of stakeholder engagement in ICT research projects. To adequately inform and support engagement activities in ICT research projects, particularly concerning the attainment of socially desirable outcomes, there is a need to understand the efficacy of stakeholder engagement.

Therefore, to address this gap, the book synthesises the literature on stakeholder engagement, responsible research and innovation (RRI) and looks at the different approaches that are used to evaluate and understand the value of stakeholder engagement in a wider research context. The synthesis is done to inform a conceptual model which is then used to unfold and analyse the value of stakeholder engagement in attaining socially desirable outcomes in ICT research projects. The proposed conceptual evaluation model informs a qualitative investigation involving a case study of four ICT research projects. Findings suggest that the efficacy of stakeholder engagement in ICT research projects, particularly with regards to the attainment of socially desirable outcomes, is predominantly based on a focused identification of stakeholders, the relevance of the form of stakeholder engagement activities and the rationale behind the engagement. Therefore, to understand the value of stakeholder engagement in achieving socially desirable and acceptable outcomes in ICT research projects, a combination of three different approaches to evaluation, including theory-based, case-based and participatory approaches, is suggested.

The book contributes to practice and theory by emphasising the vital interrelation between stakeholder engagement and the achievement of responsible outcomes in ICT R&I. The book guides better alignment of stakeholder engagement and R&I processes within ICT research projects in achieving positive outcomes for the society. It identifies specific elements of stakeholder engagement which researchers and practitioners should focus on to promote stakeholder engagement towards ensuring better R&I outcomes in ICT research. Furthermore, the research contributes to theory by looking at how evaluation theory can support understanding the value of stakeholder engagement in ICT research projects within the context of responsible research and innovation.

This book started with chapter 1 to introduce the study and set out the general idea of stakeholder engagement in ICT research projects. The chapter argued why ICT research projects were of importance to this study. In chapter 2, a review of the literature on stakeholder engagement, RRI, and evaluation of stakeholder engagement was presented to inform the development of a conceptual evaluation model that was presented in chapter 3. This was then followed by chapter 4 which detailed the research design that was used to answer the research questions. The conceptual evaluation model presented in chapter 3 provided an analytical framework that was used in chapter 5 to analyse and present the findings from the four cases that were used in this research. The findings from the four cases were then pulled together in a cross-case analysis in chapter 6. The cross-case analysis highlighted the main insights that addressed the research questions.

Finally I will always remain debtor to all our well wishers for their blessings without which this book would not have come to light.

Eric Dai Hague

Contents

CHAPTER

1

Introduction

1.1 OVERVIEW

There have been many studies conducted about the evaluation of stakeholder engagement in research (Bal *et al.*, 2013; Forsythe *et al.*, 2016; Reed, 2015) for numerous reasons including the improvement of practice and generation of knowledge (Chelimsky, 2006; Mark *et al.*, 2006). However, the approaches used vary and some are more appropriate for specific contexts of evaluation and the subject of the evaluation compared to others (Stern *et al.*, 2012; Stufflebeam and Coryn, 2014). Despite the literature on different models for evaluating stakeholder engagement in ICT research, there is still a gap in terms of qualitative models that can be used in evaluating the contribution of stakeholder engagement towards responsible outcomes in research and innovation (R&I). Considering this gap and the possibility that stakeholder engagement could strengthen the attainment of socially desirable outcomes in ICT research projects, conceptual and empirical work is needed to bridge the gap between theory and the aims of stakeholder engagement in practice. To that end, this book covers research that is aimed at addressing the gap.

In this chapter, the book begins by discussing the motivation behind this research. The research developed a conceptual evaluation model which was theoretically derived and empirically validated using a case study of four ICT research projects. The first case was Project 1 and it was about using ICT to support environmental sustainability through energy optimisation. The second case was Project 2 which was aimed at improving the use of ICT in transforming education provision in secondary schools. The third case was Project 3 which focused on the use of ICT to improve hearing aid technologies. The last case was Project 4 which was aimed at using ICT in developing a dynamic traffic management system to improve air quality.

By developing a theoretical understanding of stakeholder engagement, Responsible Research and Innovation (RRI) and evaluation, and applying the insights from four cases, this book presents an investigation exploring the efficacy of stakeholder engagement in achieving socially desirable outcomes in ICT research projects using evaluation theory and the concept of RRI.

Firstly, this chapter presents why ICT research projects are important for this research. Secondly, the chapter discusses the state of the art of stakeholder engagement in research projects including those that deal with ICT. Thirdly, the chapter introduces the need for evaluating stakeholder engagement in ICT research projects. Following this, the chapter discusses the aim of the study and the research questions that guide the study in achieving its aim. Towards the end, the chapter outlines the structure of this book.

1.2 Why ICT Research Projects are of Importance

Modern societies are relying upon research to address persistent societal challenges that affect society such as environmental sustainability (Elliot and Webster, 2017), education (Mioduser, 2015), health impairment (Haluza and Jungwirth, 2018), and social exclusion (Chen and Schulz, 2016). One type of research that is at the forefront of finding solutions to address these pressing societal challenges is ICT research. ICT research is geared to come up with new ICT methodologies and innovative solutions that address the different societal challenges mentioned above. Thus, ICT research projects are important because they facilitate and provide a platform for the generation of breakthrough technologies which translate into innovative products, processes and services for addressing the societal challenges. These innovative outputs are taken up by the wider society to deal with the different societal challenges (European Commission, 2013).

Since these technologies are intended for the wider society, it is very important that representatives from different societies are involved in the research and innovation (R&I) process. The societal challenges that lie before society will have a far better chance of being tackled if all societal actors (stakeholders) are fully engaged in the development of innovative solutions, products and services (Eden *et al.*, 2013). This is where stakeholder engagement in ICT research projects becomes of interest for this research.

1.3 Stakeholder Engagement in Research Projects

Stakeholder engagement in research projects is not a new thing. There has been lot of studies conducted on stakeholder engagement in health research projects (Olphert and Damodaran, 2007a; Pouloudi *et al.*, 2016), environmental studies research projects (de Vente *et al.*, 2016; Durham *et al.*, 2014) and technology research projects (Rahman *et al.*, 2015). In all these research projects, stakeholder engagement plays a major role in achieving specific aims towards different aspects of the research process such as financial sustainability, legitimacyof project aims, accountability and co-creation (Blok *et al.*, 2015; Bryson *et al.*, 2013; Carney *et al.*, 2009; Phillipson *et al.*, 2012a; Schenke *et al.*, 2016).

To narrow down the focus of this research, it is important to understand whether and in what way stakeholder engagement can strengthen ICT research projects. For instance, a recent conception of stakeholder engagement in research projects including those focussed on health, environment and ICT, is the one that is promoted under RRI. RRI is a concept in which stakeholders are engaged in the R&I process in order to collectively come up with socially desirable outcomes (European Commission, 2017) (see section 2.5 and 3.2). Under RRI, stakeholder engagement in research projects is envisioned to contribute towards outcomes that are societally desirable (Bauer *et al.*, 2016; Jirotka *et al.*, 2017), acceptable (Geoghegan-Quinn, 2012; Stahl *et al.*, 2014) and sustainable (Von Schomberg, 2012). The focus is on social reflection, transparency, anticipation and responsiveness in the R&I process (Jirotka *et al.*, 2017). These elements are central to RRI and have been explained further in sections 2.5, 3.2 and 3.3. In this research, the concept of RRI is simply used as a background discourse, one that states that engagement is a good thing but fails to say how it can be evaluated.

According to RRI proponents such as Sutcliffe, Owen and Stahl, some factors have led to an interest in RRI and ICT research. For example, RRI is important in ICT research to prevent adverse impacts that could result from ICT technologies such as loss of privacy and autonomy, among users (Stahl, 2013a). Further, RRI is important for ICT research because it reduces the risk of developing technologies that have irreversible consequences especially as the technologies become more complex, pervasive and difficult to understand (Sutcliffe, 2011), by bringing together different stakeholder perspectives. Therefore, it could be argued that the concept RRI has the potential to provide an important tool for evaluating and analysing the efficacy of stakeholder engagement towards the attainment of responsible outcomes of ICT research projects. RRI provide tools that can be used to inform R&I activities that are taking place in ICT research projects and therefore achieve socially desirable outcomes (Chatfield *et al.*, 2017; Rip, 2014; Stahl *et al.*, 2016).

1.4 Evaluating Stakeholder Engagement in ICT Research

Although there is ample literature on the evaluation of stakeholder engagement in ICT research projects (Bal *et al.*, 2013; Camara de Silva and Costa, 2012; Penfield *et al.*, 2014; Reed, 2015), which is reviewed in section 2.4, there seems to be a dearth in the literature on a methodological and qualitative evaluation of stakeholder engagement. This scarcity is even wider on the evaluation of stakeholder engagement within the context of responsible innovation. Recent studies on evaluation of stakeholder engagement in ICT research projects have considered the evaluation with regards to other aspects of ICT research projects such as finance (Eskerod *et al.*, 2015) and sustainability (Bal *et al.*, 2013). However, none of the ones from the literature reviewed during this research specifically looked at how stakeholder engagement contributes towards the attainment of socially desirable outcomes in ICT research projects. Other studies also tend to focus on the evaluation of stakeholder engagement in research within education (Parrott *et al.*, 2016), development (Kotvojs *et al.*, 2007) and business (Taghian *et al.*,

2015) projects while a few have discussed qualitative evaluation of stakeholder engagement in ICT research projects.

Thus, despite the vast coverage of literature on the evaluation of stakeholder engagement, there is a lack of scholarly research into the qualitative evaluation of stakeholder engagement in ICT research projects that is specifically geared towards understanding its value towards the attainment of socially desirable outcomes. One way of dealing with such scarcity is using the concept of RRI in combination with evaluation theory to understand the value of stakeholder engagement. The reason why a qualitative evaluation of the efficacy of stakeholder engagement using the concept of RRI is of significance is that it explains how stakeholder engagement could be beneficial in ICT research particularly towards responsible outcomes as discussed in section 1.3 above.

So far, the chapter has given an overview of stakeholder engagement in ICT research projects and why RRI could provide a better lens for evaluating the efficacy of stakeholder engagement towards the attainment of socially desirable outcomes in ICT research projects. Theremainder of the chapter will now discuss the study aim, research questions and the structure of this book.

1.5 Research Aim and Question(s)

The aim of this research is to understand the efficacy of stakeholder engagement in achieving socially desirable outcomes in ICT research projects using evaluation theory and the concept of RRI for its evaluation and analysis. This aim is achieved by developing a theoretical understanding of stakeholder engagement, RRI and evaluation, and applying this understanding to four cases in order to gain empirical insights from the cases with regards to the efficacy of stakeholder engagement in achieving socially desirable outcomes in ICT research projects. Evaluation theory is used to suggest ways of gaining an understanding of the efficacy of stakeholder engagement in ICT research projects (see section 2.10.1) while RRI discourse contextualises and provides an analytical lens for evaluation (see section 3.5).

Therefore, to meet the aim introduced above, the following research question is addressed in this book;

How can the efficacy of stakeholder engagement towards the attainment of socially desirable outcomes in ICT research projects be evaluated?

To answer the above research question, the study addresses the following sub-research questions;

i. What is the role of stakeholder engagement in ICT research projects?

ii. How can RRI support the evaluation of stakeholder engagement in ICT research projects?

iii. What elements are key for evaluating the efficacy of stakeholder engagement in ICT research projects?

In addressing the research questions outlined above, the book follows the structure that is outlined in the next section.

1.6 Structure of the Book

This section outlines the structure and presents the chapters of this book.

Chapter 1 introduces the book, setting out the motivation behind the research. The chapter discusses why stakeholder engagement in ICT research projects is important for this research. The chapter also introduces the need to evaluate stakeholder engagement and how evaluation theory together with the concept of RRI could provide a way of understanding the efficacy of stakeholder engagement towards the attainment of socially desirable outcomes in ICT research projects. Further, the chapter presents the research aim and the research questions that guide this study.

Chapter 2 reviews relevant literature informing the research presented in this book. First, the chapter presents a classification of projects and narrows the focus down to ICT research projects. Once this is done, it then focuses on stakeholder engagement and covers stakeholder theory. This includes a discussion about the wide-ranging rationale for stakeholder engagement in ICT research projects. The chapter then focusses on Responsible Research and Innovation (RRI) including Responsible Innovation (RI) (since these are often used interchangeably). It provides the different accounts of RRI and teases out the key conceptual features of RRI. The theoretical insights from the RRI accounts informs analytical lens that is part of the conceptual model presented in chapter 3. Further, the chapter reviews the literature on evaluation theory with a particular focus on the evaluation of stakeholder engagement. It looks at the approaches that are commonly used to evaluate stakeholder engagement in research projects and discusses three common ones that include participatory, case-based and theory-based evaluation approaches. This is then followed by a discussion of evaluating stakeholder engagement within the context of RRI. The chapter concludes by arguing that all the three approaches provide a better way for evaluating the efficacy of stakeholder engagement towards achieving socially desirable outcomes in ICT research projects.

Chapter 3 presents the conceptual evaluation model, which is a result of the review of the literature reviewed in chapter 2. The evaluation model is later validated in chapter 5. The chapter discusses the premise for developing a conceptual evaluation model that is based on a combination of the three evaluation approaches. It highlights the key elementsto focus on when evaluation stakeholder engagement in ICT research projects. Further, the chapter introduces the RRI lens, which is used as an analytical tool for evaluating the efficacy of stakeholder engagement in ICT research projects with a particular focus on the attainment of responsible outcomes.

Chapter 4 presents the research design, describing the research paradigms and discussing the research methodology that is followed in this research. It discusses the chosen research design, which is, a case study. The chapter then covers data collection and analysis methods that are employed in the case study.

Chapter 5 presents the findings from analyses of the four case ICT research projects that were selected in chapter 4. To evaluate and understand the efficacyof stakeholder engagement in ICT research, particularly towards the attainment of socially desirable outcomes in all the four cases, first the identified five key elements of stakeholder engagement are evaluated. This is followed by the application of an RRI lens to highlight how stakeholders address the crossing of R&I and collective stewardship in addressing the impact of ICT research.

Chapter 6 builds on the four case studies and synthesise the findings in a cross-case analysis. This chapter puts together the findings and analysis presented in chapter 5 that covered the four cases used in this study. In so doing, the chapter constructs an answer to the overall research question introduced in chapter 1.

Chapter 7 summarises the study and discusses its contribution. The chapter reviews the degree to which the research questions have been answered and the implications of the findings on theory, methodology and practice. It then draws conclusions, limitations of this study and offers suggestions for further research.

CHAPTER 2

Literature Review

2.1 Introduction

This chapter presents the literature review that informs this study. To begin with, the chapter gives a definition of technology projects and then classifies the technology projects in order to narrow the focus to ICT projects which are the main focus for this study. Once the literature on technology projects have been narrowed down to ICT projects, the chapter presents the literature review on stakeholder engagement in research projects with a particular focus on Information and Communication Technology (ICT) research. Thus, the chapter provides a classification of projects and then narrows down the focus to ICT research projects. This is then followed by a discussion of ICT research projects that are aimed at addressing three overarching societal challenges relating to social wellbeing, environmental sustainability and education. The chapter then turns its focus to discussing stakeholder engagement and includes a review of stakeholder theory. Under stakeholder engagement, the chapter analyses the stakeholder concept to understand who can count as a stakeholder in ICT research projects. Further, the chapter reviews the literature on stakeholder identification and analysis in research projects. Moving forward, the chapter discusses the underlying discourse on Responsible Research and Innovation (RRI) through a review of different accounts of the concept. Following that, the chapter outlines the key conceptual features of RRI to establish a lens for evaluative analysis. The chapter finishes with a review of the literature on evaluation of stakeholder engagement by looking at different evaluation approaches. These are reviewed in order to establish approaches that could be appropriate for evaluating the value stakeholder engagement in attainment of socially desirable outcomes. The RRI lens and the selected evaluation approaches informs the conceptual evaluation model that is presented later in chapter 3.

2.2 Classification of Projects

There is a vast amount of literature on projects covering different types of research projects that span across different disciplines and fields (Andreassen *et al.*, 2015;

Carney *et al.*, 2009; De Meyer *et al.*, 2002; Filippov and Mooi, 2010; Ihm and Hsieh, 2015; Olphert and Damodaran, 2007a). However, there is no universal definition of a project or a research project. Therefore, for the purposes of this study, some definitions are reviewed to find one that fits in well with how this study identifies a research project.

To start with, Turner and Müller (2003) citing Turner (1999) provide a generic definition of a project as

> *'an endeavour in which human, financial and material resources are organised in a novel way to undertake a unique scope of work, of given specification, with constraints of cost and time, so as to achieve beneficial change defined by quantitative and qualitative objectives'* (Turner and Müller, 2003, p. 1).

The definition developed by Turner (1999) could be applied to any project that takes place in a range of fields such as business, health, development, environment, education and technology. As such it is very generic and cannot be related to a specific project.

In contrast, De Meyer *et al.* (2002) defines a project as *"a unique interrelated set of taskswith a beginning, an end and a well-defined outcome"* (De Meyer *et al.*, 2002, p. 60). The definition given by the De Meyer *et al.* (2002) is rather too general and assumes that those engaged in the project can identify tasks and activities at the outset and therefore, they can provide contingency alternatives and maintain the same overall vision throughout the project. However, this is not certainly the case because projects can have uncertainties which may affect the attainment of responsible outcomes. The assumptions that underlie this definition are fair for routine and well-understood projects, but not for those that involve novel and breakthrough initiatives, which require stakeholder to rethink, reflect and adapt to different societal concerns.

Nonetheless, Turner and Muller (2003) came up with a cross-cutting definition in which they defined a project as

> *'a temporary organisation to which resources are assigned to undertake a unique, novel and transient endeavour managing the inherent uncertainty and need for integration in order to deliver beneficial objectives of change'* (Turner and Müller, 2003, p. 7).

The definition given above implies that the term project could mean a group or an organisation that is involved in dealing with a particular transaction or problem, through a reference to a visionary plan or idea. This relates well to ICT research projects because they typically involve undertaking unique and novel endeavours, for instance, to find innovative solutions for issues that affect the society. It also fits well with the attainment of responsible or socially desirable outcomes because it touches on managing uncertainty to deliver beneficial objectives of change in society. This aligns with stakeholder engagement that is used to reflect, anticipate and adapt in order to address the uncertainties that are inherent in research projects and therefore have outcomes that are beneficial to society for instance, as proposed under RRI (See sections 2.6 for a discussion of RRI).

Before getting further with the discussion of stakeholder engagement in research projects, it is important that a better understanding of projects is provided by looking at how they are classified. There has been some scholarly work to classify projects. For instance, Filipov and Mooi (2010) have classified projects into different categories such as innovation and conventional projects. In differentiating the two categories of projects, the authors focus on the characteristics of each category. Conventional projects are described as those projects that are mostly connected to, for example, infrastructure, construction and operations. On the other hand, innovation projects are described as those projects that entail a number of criteria including having an aim to develop an innovative product or service; employing innovative methodologies and approaches; leading in the improvement of innovative and learning capabilities (Filippov and Mooi, 2010, p. 8).

The classification of projects by Filipov and Mooi (2010) further classifies innovation projects as either 'technology' innovation projects or 'other' innovation projects. Other innovation project are those that are involved in innovations other than technology such as strategic processes, services and organisation (Filippov and Mooi, 2010). This classification of projects is depicted in Figure 2.1 below. The illustration in Figure 2.1 shows that technology projects including ICT research projects can also be described as either research or new product development projects.

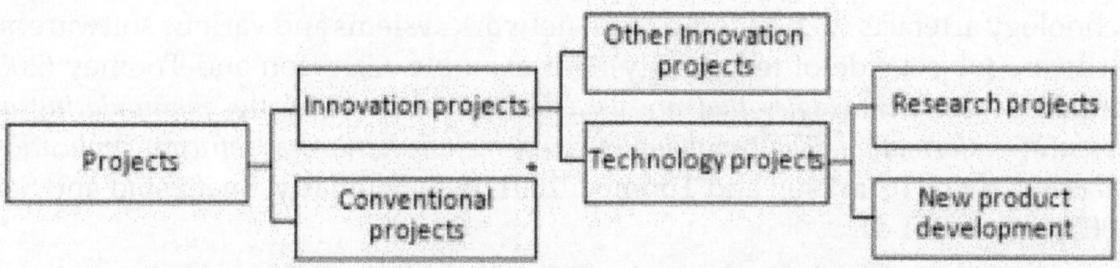

Figure 2.1: Classification of Projects with Subcategories (Adapted from Filipov and Mooi, 2010; Stosic and Milutinovic, 2014)

Although the illustration in Figure 1 tries to place different projects within categories based on characteristics, there is a weakness with this classification of projects. The weakness is in the assumption that there can be a clear line between what is termed as an innovation project, research project or a new product development project. In reality, this is not the case because the different categories can either overlap or exist within one project. An example can be seen in ICT research projects which can fit into all these categories. ICT research projects can be innovative, can involve research and can also result in the development of a new service or product, all at the same time. Therefore, the classification of projects provided in theliterature can only provide a starting point for classifying projects and narrowing the focus of the study to technology projects of which ICT research projects are a subcategory (see section 2.3). However, it fails to acknowledge the dynamic nature of projects such as ICT researchprojects in that they can embrace all the characteristics that the different authors (Entekhabi and

Arabshahi, 2012; Filippov and Mooi, 2010; Stosic and Milutinovic, 2014) have used to classify projects. It is fair to acknowledge their effort in classifying the projects since it provides a base for narrowing down the focus of this study to ICT research projects as discussed in next section.

2.3 ICT Research Projects

Building on Filipov and Mooi's (2010) classification of technology projects, Stosic and Milutinovic (2014) further classifies technology projects into research or new product development. This further classification means that technology projects can fall under a category that is researching on a particular technology such as Nano-technology, biotechnology and ICT or under a category that is developing a new product for a particular technology such as the ones exemplified above. However, for the present study, the interest is on ICT (see section 2.4). Before discussing why ICT research projects are of particular interest for this study, this section describes ICT research projects.

To describe what is meant by ICT research projects in this study, the study looks at the definition of ICT and the definition of a project discussed in the section 2.2 above. In the literature, there is no consensual definition of ICT. There are different accounts of ICT (Clarkson and Toomey, 2001; Eke *et al.*, 2015; Soeftestad and Sein, 2003; Zuppo, 2012). Some of these accounts focus on the usage of technology artefacts such as computers, network systems and various software and hardware (object side of technology). For example, Clarkson and Toomey (2001) define ICT as '*technologies that are used for accessing, gathering, manipulating and presenting information. The technologies could include hardware, software applications, and connectivity*' (Clarkson and Toomey, 2001, p. 8). Similarly, Soeftestad and Sein, (2003) define ICT as

> '*All those technologies that enable the handling of informationand facilitate different forms of communication among human actors, between human beings and electronic systems, and among electronic systems. These technologies can be sub-divided into capturing technologies, storage technologies, processing technologies, communication technologies and display technologies*' (Soeftestad and Sein, 2003, p. 2).

Further, some accounts of ICT focus on the research and methods of developing the technology artefacts (rational side of technology). For example, Eke (2012) defines ICT as *a concept that involves production and usage of scientific artefacts to convey and exchange information in various ways* (Eke *et al.*, 2015, p. 3). Zuppo (2012) also defines ICT as *the technology that facilitates the transfer of information and various types of electronically mediated communication*' (Zuppo, 2012, p. 19).

In all these definitions, it can be seen that ICT is defined based on two perspectives which are objectivity and rationality. ICT has also been defined in many ways according to context and, treatments for which it is used for (Kanematsu and Barry, 2016; Kramers *et al.*, 2014). For instance, ICT has been defined with reference to devices and networks (Kamilaris *et al.*, 2014), goods produced or their related services (Tarutė and Gatautis, 2014) and also the equipment and skills that users must have (Gatautis, 2015; Tarutė and Gatautis, 2014). However, regardless of these variations in contexts, the definition given by Zuppo (2012) is general and therefore encompasses all the different contexts that have been given by the different authors.

For example, in terms of *'transfer of information'*, this covers the devices, equipment, skills and networks that facilitate the transfer. While the *'various types of electronically mediated communication'* covers the software and techniques used to analyse and communicate information.

Therefore, taking into consideration the definition of a Project given by Turner and Muller (2003) (see section 2.2 above) and the definition of ICT by Zuppo (2012), for the purpose of this study, an ICT research project is then defined as;

> *'a temporary organisation to which resources are assigned to undertake a unique, novel and transient endeavour managing the inherent uncertainty and need for integration of technologies that facilitate the transfer of information and various types of electronically mediated communication in order to deliver beneficial objectives of change'.*

This definition is ideal for describing ICT research projects because it covers both the objective and rationale for using ICT artefacts in research projects (the temporary organisations) to deliver benefits to the society, for instance, conserving the environment (which is thechange).

Following the definition of an ICT research project, the focus now turns to different types of ICT research projects.

2.3.1 ICT Research Projects for Societal Challenges

As introduced in section 1.2 there are societal issues that need innovative solutions that can address them. For these solutions to materialise, ICT research projects are drivers for the ideas and processes that bring them about. In ICT research projects, new enabling artefacts and applications are constantly emerging, which have the potential to improve the society and address some of the pressing societal challenges met by the society nowadays (European Commission, 2013). These novel technology artefacts will continue to play an important role in providing responses to major societal challenges such as an ageing population, health and social care, sustainable energy, inclusion, education and security (Andreassen *et al.*, 2015; Bifulco *et al.*, 2016; Hilty and Aebischer, 2015; Ihm and Hsieh, 2015; Kamilaris *et al.*, 2014). On top of this, the outcomes and outputs from these projects have an impact on social behaviours, on democratic processes, economy and policies (European Commission, 2013).

In terms of the socially desirable outcomes, ICT research projects could promote mutual understanding and exchange of knowledge between stakeholders in coming up with effective transformations and solutions to some of the societal challenges (European Commission, 2017). Therefore considering the motivation of this study, ICT research projects provides a readily available arena to explore and understand how different stakeholders contribute to developing these effective transformations and solution to societal challenges.

The importance of ICT research projects has been acknowledged by authorities such as the European Union (EU) under the EU's Framework Programmes for Research and Technological Development but also by many scholars (Andreassen *et al.*, 2015; Bifulco *et al.*, 2016; Hilty and Aebischer, 2015; Ihm and Hsieh, 2015; Kamilaris *et al.*, 2014). For example, the EU has stated that ICT research is important because it enables mastering and shaping the future developments of ICTs so that the demands of the society are met. In the same light scholars have pointed out the importance of ICT research projects in the development of these technologies. Some scholars have acknowledged the importance of ICT research projects in improving society wellbeing (Ihm and Hsieh, 2015), economy (Kumar *et al.*, 2016), health (Andreassen *et al.*, 2015), productivity (Tarutė and Gatautis, 2014) and of late they has been a surge of ICT research projects that are directed towards creating a sustainable environment (Haddaway *et al.*, 2017; Hilty and Aebischer, 2015).

In all the scholarly sources, there are cross-cutting societal challenges that have been pointed as pressing for the society, and these are summarised in Table 2.1 below.

Table 2.1: Summary of Accounts on Addressing Cross-Cutting Societal Challenges with ICT Research

Societal challenge	Description	Source
Social wellbeing	This challenge is about personal life conditions and participation as a citizen, elderly, patient and consumer. Many citizens are being isolated or excluded from society due to personal issues such as ageing, gender and health impairment.	European Commission, 2013; Andreassen *et al.*, 2015; Christophorou *et al.*, 2016; Ihm and Hsieh, 2015; Faulkner and Lie, 2007; Carretero, 2015
Environmental degradation	This challenge in on environmental degradation as a result of factors such as increasing carbon emissions and climate change.	European Commission, 2013; Hilty and Aebischer, 2015; Murugesan and Laplante, 2011; Bifulco *et al.*, 2016; Boulos and Al-Shorbaji, 2014; Hilty and Aebischer, 2015; Schaffers *et al.*, 2011
Education	This challenge is about issues that hinder people to learn more effectively, acquire new skills and access to cultural resources.	European Commission, 2013; Buckner and Kim, 2014; Kreijns *et al.*, 2013; Lakkala and Ilomaki, 2015; Aflalo, 2014; De Witte and Rogge, 2014; Perera *et al.*, 2014; Kanematsu and Barry, 2016

Therefore to meet these cross-cutting societal challenges, there are different types of ICT research projects that are implemented. Hence, building on the classification given in Figure 1 above (see section 2.2) and the cross-cutting societal challenges that are found in the literature, ICT research projects are classified as illustrated in Figure 2.2 below. This further classification is important because it informs the sampling of the cases that are used in this study (see section 4.7) and further analysed and evaluated in chapter 5 of this book.

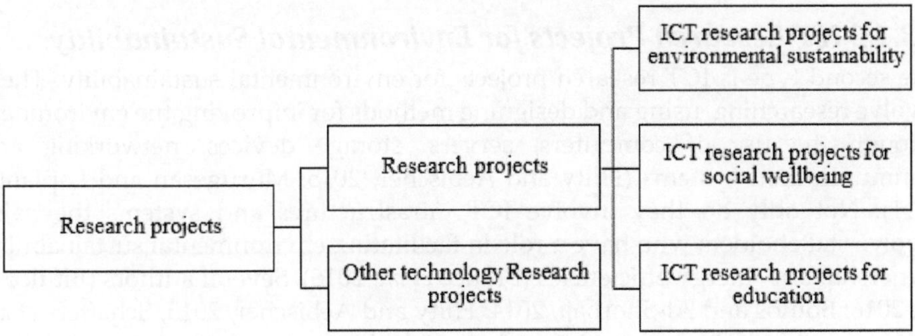

Figure 2.2: Classification of ICT Research Projects

Having illustrated the different ICT research projects that emerged from the literature as addressing the societal challenges for society (socio-economic challenges), the next sub-sections discuss the different types of ICT research projects addressing the three overarching societal challenges.

2.3.1.1 ICT Research Projects for Social Wellbeing

The first type of ICT research projects for social challenges are those that focus on social well-being. These involve researching and further developing ICTs that can be used to promote social issues such as health (Andreassen *et al.*, 2015), ageing well (Christophorou *et al.*, 2016) and inclusion (Ihm and Hsieh, 2015). These ICT research projects focus on the development of solutions that empower the individual, in a social context, to improve and manage personal life as a citizen (European Commission, 2013).

With regards to health, ICT research projects focus on how ICT can be used to manage health and disease, including disease prevention and management. In terms of ageing well Christophorou *et al.* (2016) talk about ICT research that is conducted to develop assistive technologies for supporting seniors to remain active and independent, for as long as possible, in their chosen home environment. The focus of the ICT research projects is on empowering people with age-related dependencies or disabilities to live independently, delay or avoid institutionalisation and stay active as long as possible. The solutions that may result from such ICT research projects include smart living systems and 'age-friendly' environments (Carretero, 2015).

When it comes to ICT research projects that are aimed at addressing exclusion, literature suggested those that look at ICT and inclusion based on different factors such as age (Ihm and Hsieh, 2015) and gender (Faulkner and Lie, 2007). For instance, Ihm and Hsieh (2015) talk about research that is undertaken to promote social engagement of the marginalised such as the elderly population through the use of ICT. Lastly, ICT research projects for social wellbeing involve the development of accessible ICT solutions for personalised interfaces to smart environments and innovative services for all users including those at risk of exclusion (European Commission, 2013).

2.3.1.2 ICT Research Projects for Environmental Sustainability

The second type is ICT research projects for environmental sustainability. These involve researching, using and designing methods for improving the environment through the use of computers, servers, storage devices, networking and communications systems (Hilty and Aebischer, 2015; Murugesan and Laplante, 2011). Not only do they involve ICT infrastructures and systems they also involve stakeholders who have a role in facilitating environmental sustainability, ownership and energy efficiencies (Bifulco *et al.*, 2016). Several authors (Bifulco *et al.*, 2016; Boulos and Al-Shorbaji, 2014; Hilty and Aebischer, 2015; Schaffers *et al.*, 2011) state that ICT plays a major role in reducing carbon footprints and deliver environmentally sustainable solutions.

These solutions are a product of ICT research conducted in projects where stakeholders exchange ideas and develop methodologies to tackle environmental issues. For example, until recently, there is a surge in green requirements for advancement in research and innovation that provide solutions to environmental issues either through implementation of ICT systems or communicating awareness to the society through the use of ICT (Bifulco *et al.*, 2016, p. 138). Similarly, there are initiatives in the implementation of ICT research projects that are focussing at smart cities by using the power of internet of things (IoT) to improve the quality of society's wellbeing through measures that promote a sustainable environment which is eco-friendly (Boulos and Al-Shorbaji, 2014).

The EC has also stressed the need for ICT research projects to explore opportunities for harnessing digital technologies in addressing climate change, for instance, by increasing energy efficiency and better management of resources by 2020 (European Commission, 2013, p. 66).

All these different sources of literature emphasise the role that ICT research projects play in reducing resource consumption and CO2 emissions.

2.3.1.3 ICT Research Projects for Education

The third type is ICT research projects for education. These projects play a major role in the ongoing pursuit to integrate ICT in pedagogy with an aim to improve the effectiveness of teaching and knowledge transfer in institutions (Buckner and Kim, 2014; Kreijns *et al.*, 2013; Lakkala and Ilomaki, 2015). However, there has been an argument by some authors that simply placing technology hardware into classrooms will not improve education (Aflalo, 2014). Although this is the case, the argument for ICT in education is stronger which has led to a plethora of significant ICT research projects that are enhancing the use of ICT such as computers, connectivity, or other information technologies in education settings (Buckner and Kim, 2014). De Witte and Rogge (2014) argue that the use of ICT in education has the potential to improve the efficiency and effectiveness of teaching and learning in educational settings by improving the outcomes of education and replacing traditional instruction methods with better ones through the use of ICT.

One drawback with the emphasis of the authors such as the ones above is that they limit their primary focus on the use of ICT in learning and education that takes place within institutions. However, the EC recognises the use of ICT in supporting learning and education outside educational institutions and emphasise researching on how ICT can help to foster learning and creativity in the society as a whole. According to the EC, the aim of ICT research projects is to create vibrant creative technology ecosystems and increase the capacity of citizens by providing them with better tools, capabilities and foresight (European Commission, 2013, pp. 81–84).

As mentioned earlier, the platforms for generating ideas, developing and integrating ICT in education are the research projects that exist particularly to customise learning systems that can adapt to effective use in a wide variety of diverse contexts (Perera *et al.*, 2014). As is the case with the other ICT research projects discussed in sections 2.4.1 and 2.4.2 above, ICT research projects for education also engage stakeholders who contribute to different aspects of the research. Their contribution includes building awareness, setting realistic expectations, raising support, minimising resistance and ensuring successful implementation and user adoption (Kanematsu and Barry, 2016).

So far, the chapter has presented a review of the literature regarding projects and how theyare classified. The classification has helped this study to narrow down the focus to ICT research projects that address societal challenges that are generally covered in the literature such as social well-being, environmental sustainability and education. This classification and narrowing down of the focus is useful in selecting the cases for this study (see section 4.7.1). Moving on, as stated above, ICT research projects engage stakeholders who contribute towards projects in many ways. Hence, the next section reviews the literature on engagement of stakeholders in ICT research projects.

2.4 Engaging Stakeholders in ICT Research Projects

This section reviews the literature on stakeholder engagement specifically looking at their contribution towards ICT research projects. Therefore, the section first looks at the concept of a stakeholder. It then focuses on stakeholder theory and the process of stakeholder engagement with an emphasis on stakeholder analysis and identification. Lastly, the section covers the rationale for engaging stakeholders in ICT research projects.

Stakeholders are vital in ICT research projects because of their various contributions towards the implementation of research and innovation processes. The literature discuss numerous forms of stakeholders' contribution towards ICT research projects. For instance, stakeholders are engaged in research projects to contribute to different aspects such as finance, policy-making and development of artefacts through processes such as user testing (Eskerod *et al.*, 2015; McCabe *et al.*, 2012; Phillipson *et al.*, 2012b). Of late, there has been a wave of literature on the engagement of stakeholders to contribute towards responsibility in research and innovation in projects under the notion of RRI (Bauer *et al.*, 2016; Jirotka *et al.*, 2017; Shelley-Egan *et al.*, 2017; Stahl *et al.*, 2014). Stakeholder engagement in the light of RRI is discussed further in section 2.5.

In the literature on stakeholder engagement, there are more sources from other fields such as project management, climate change and development studies (Eskerod *et al.*, 2015; Olphert and Damodaran, 2007b; Phillipson *et al.*, 2012c; Sánchez, 2015) compared to Information systems (IS) or ICT (Papazafeiropoulou and Pouloudi, 2003; Pouloudi *et al.*, 2016). Therefore, most of the literature informing this study on stakeholder engagement is adopted from the other fields to augment the literature focussed on IS or ICT. The literature reviewed gives an insight into the concepts behind stakeholder engagement and the nature of its contribution in ICT research projects. The fundamental structures and dynamics in ICT research projects are similar to that of conventional projects in other fields. As such the review, turned to business and project management literature for useful theory, concepts and tools.

Although the literature provides a basis for understanding the relations and dynamics that underlie stakeholder engagement, there seem to be different conceptions of who a stakeholder is (Pouloudi, 1999, pp. 1–2). This is discussed in the next section.

2.4.1 The Stakeholder Concept

The concept of a stakeholder has been covered by many authors in different disciplines such as project management (Sánchez, 2015), information systems (Pouloudi *et al.*, 2016) and business strategy (Laczniak and Murphy, 2012; Sánchez, 2015) and concertedly, they emphasise the relevance of stakeholders in making important decisions within entities such as ICT research projects. Historically, stakeholder concepts were inherent in the early work of system theorists such as March and Simon (1958), but it was a seminal publication from Freeman (1984) through his contribution to stakeholder theory that brought stakeholder concept to the forefront of academic research (Donaldson and Preston, 1995). The concept of stakeholder was introduced by Freeman to move beyond the shareholder-centric view of organisations. Freeman defined a stakeholder as

> *'Any group or individual who can affect or is affected by the attainment of the project's objectives' (1984, p. 46).*

Following on Freeman's seminal work on stakeholder theory and therefore the definition of a stakeholder, many scholars have provided variations of stakeholder definitions. For example, Soma and Vatn (2014) defines a stakeholder as *'an actor from society who have an interest (stake) in a specific policy issue'* (Soma and Vatn, 2014, p. 325) and Carney *et al.* (2009) defines a stakeholder as

> *'A person or an organisation that has a legitimate interest in a project or entity, or would be affected by a particular action or policy'* (Carney *et al.*, 2009, p. 2).

The definitions given above are nonetheless broad, but there is something that can be learnt from them. For instance, the first definition (by Soma and Vatn, 2014) implies that a stakeholder must have an awareness of a specific policy or research issue and crucially, an interest in its impact. The implication here is that there is an element of prior knowledge or awareness from the stakeholder. However, this first definition may be interpreted in a wider capacity to include conceivable interest which in most cases, institutions such as government and local authorities do (see section 2.3.1 for an example of the EU). Hence, from such a perspective, only a limited number of stakeholders could be deemed as having a stake in ICT research projects and therefore exclude those that do not have interest in a *'specific policy issue'*.

The second definition (by Carney *et al.*, 2009) introduces a requirement of *'legitimate interest'* from a person or an organisation who is to become a stakeholder in ICT research projects. This definition signifies that anyone with a legitimate interest in the stake of an ICT research project can become a stakeholder. With this definition, the range of stakeholders is interpreted as wide as possible considering that the interpretation of legitimate interest could be very broad. Thus, the range of those who can be stakeholders of ICT research projects is not only limited to having a stake in policy, research or innovation, but goes beyond that to include, for example, the public.

Further, there is a discussion on the differences of how a stakeholder could be identified in a project. For instance, stakeholders are defined as separate members of the public (Burgess and Chilvers, 2006), as specialists in certain areas (Jepsen and Eskerod, 2009) and even as non-human agents (Pouloudi and Whitley, 2000). Burgess and Chilvers (2006) considers citizens, government, interest groups and businesses (2006, p. 719) as stakeholders but do not put emphasis on specialists such as researchers. While Jepsen and Eskerod (2009) talk about analysing stakeholders for identification, and they point out that the analysis should go beyond the stakeholders suggested by Chilvers and Burgess (2006) and include researchers. This concurs with most stakeholder definitions since they point out that a stakeholder is one having an interest or stake in the project (de Vente *et al.*, 2016; Leventon *et al.*, 2016), which is the case with researchers. An interesting view is provided by Walsham (2010) who goes beyond the human stakeholders and suggests that non-human elements such as algorithms can also be stakeholders. This is an interesting development in stakeholder theory, but this study will only focus on the human stakeholders.

Therefore, from an ICT research project viewpoint, stakeholders may include groups or individuals such as researchers, funders, local authorities, industry players, the public and end users. These stakeholders are critical for the survival and success of the ICT research projects. This perspective is in line with instrumental stakeholder theory which provides a basic rationale for stakeholders to be engaged in ICT research projects so that they contribute towards its direction (Bailur, 2006, p. 65). Thus, for the purpose of this study a stakeholder is defined as;

> *'Any person or group who influences or is influenced by the outcomes of research and innovation in an ICT research project'*.

This definition is chosen because it is broad and inclusive. It incorporates anyone or any group that is either directly or indirectly affected by ICT research projects. It also covers those who may have interests and the ability to influence the outcomes of ICT research projects, for example, funders, researchers, industry and local authority representatives and the public.

2.4.2 Stakeholder Theory

Stakeholder theory is predominantly linked to firms and organisations. However, in this study, the theory is applied to ICT research projects because the overall dynamics such as resource allocation, power control and strategy within an ICT research project resemble those of an organisation or a firm. To begin with, there is need to understand what a stakeholder means in general and then what it means for ICT research projects. In the literature, the conceptualisation of a stakeholder is wide-ranging. This is both beneficial and troublesome when applying the theory to ICT research projects. With regards to its benefit, stakeholder theory provides a set of overarching concepts for framing a variety of decisions and issues that relate to stakeholders (Hasnas, 2013; Laczniak and Murphy, 2012; Phillipson *et al.*, 2012a). These stakeholders could also be those in ICT research projects, for instance. However, the problem is the lack of consistency in definitions and use of the theory which then results in diverse and contradictory arguments about conceptualising stakeholders of ICT research project (see section 2.4.2).

Although this is the case, the literature on stakeholder theory describes stakeholder engagement and stakeholder behaviour in ways that can also be applied to the context of ICT research and innovation (Blok, 2014; Martikainen *et al.*, 2015; Olphert and Damodaran, 2007b; Pouloudi*et al.*, 2016). For example, applying a social network perspective, the literature provides a consideration of the multiple and interdependent interactions between stakeholders that exist simultaneously in research projects (Rowley, 1997; Vandekerckhove and Dentchev, 2005). Therefore, stakeholders are conceptualised as having coalitions and direct relationships with one another towards the aims of the ICT research projects. Stakeholder theory gives a basis for understanding these relations and dynamics within the ICT research projects in light of what the projects wants to achieve.

Stakeholder theory is divided into three perspectives that include descriptive, instrumental and normative stakeholder perspectives (Donaldson and Preston, 1995; J. Kaler, 2003; Lozano, 2005). Each of these perspectives explains stakeholders in different ways. Firstly, descriptive stakeholder theory can be used in classifying and identifying the different parts of an ICT research project without assigning any value statements regarding the legitimacy of stakeholders' claims or their power (Lozano, 2005). This perspective of the theory aims to describe how stakeholders deal with other stakeholders and represent each other's interests within the research projects (Donaldson, 1999; J. Kaler, 2003). Therefore, descriptive stakeholder theory can be used to help predict the behaviour of stakeholders within ICT research projects. Also, it can be used to explain and describe certain characteristics and behaviours of the stakeholders. As an example, descriptive stakeholder theory could be used to describe the way ICT research projects are executed, the nature of stakeholder engagement within ICT research projects and how different stakeholders consider their interests in the projects.

The second perspective of stakeholder theory is the instrumental perspective. This perspective of the theory can be used to identify the networks between stakeholders and therefore the link between stakeholder engagement and the attainment of the research projects' objectives (Bailur, 2006, p. 65). With this perspective of stakeholder theory, the premise is that adhering to stakeholder engagement achieves the attainment of expected objectives (Donaldson and Preston, 1995). Thus, stakeholder engagement gives a voice to powerful and influential stakeholders which result in securing their contribution towards the success of the ICT research projects.

The third perspective is the normative stakeholder theory. This perspective to stakeholder theory goes further than the descriptive and instrumental stakeholder theories and can be used to interpret the moral guidelines for executing ICT research projects. It looks at the moral rights of any individual affected by the projects' conduct (Donaldson and Preston, 1995; Gilbert and Rasche, 2008). At the core of normative stakeholder theory, is the consideration of rights and duties of the different actors involved in the research projects and how a fair balance of concerns of these different stakeholders can be realised (Gilbert and Rasche, 2008; Lozano, 2005). With this perspective, different stakeholders should be engaged in ICT research projects so that the moral rights of the stakeholder are taken into perspective (Bailur, 2006, p. 66). As such, stakeholder engagement involves dialogue that is open and deliberative on issues of interest such as responsibility within ICT research and innovation. Stakeholder dialogue in this normative perspective applies a procedural understanding of legitimacy and a broad understanding of responsibility (Gilbert and Rasche, 2008; Habermas *et al.*, 1998).

Now that the chapter has discussed stakeholder theory, it will move on to discuss how stakeholders are engaged. For effective engagement of stakeholders, they must be analysed. This is necessary to uncover how vital is their prospective contribution for the ICT research projects, the power of the stakeholders and their possible influence towards the aims and outcomes of the research projects (Jepsen and Eskerod, 2009, p. 336).

2.4.3 Stakeholder Analysis

There are several ways of carrying out a stakeholder analysis, and most of these ways involve categorising stakeholders according to their level of interest, influence and relevance to the ICT research projects (Jepsen and Eskerod, 2009; Rahman *et al.*, 2015; Reed *et al.*, 2009). In the literature, there are some tools used to categorise and analyse stakeholders such as using the power/interest matrix, participation matrix and stakeholder maps (Bryson, 2004; Durham *et al.*, 2014; Martikainen *et al.*, 2015; Pouloudi and Whitley, 1997; Rahman *et al.*, 2015). However, the most common and basic tool for analysing stakeholders for engagement is the one that categorises stakeholders according to their influence or contribution towards the ICT research projects against their interests in the projects (Jepsen and Eskerod, 2009).

Analysing stakeholders using influence against interest as variables results in four indicative actions in terms of engaging stakeholders within ICT research projects. These indicative actions include informing, consulting, involving and collaborating with a specific group of stakeholders depending on the degree of influence and interest they have in a particular project (Bryson *et al.*, 2013; Durham *et al.*, 2014). According to Durham *et al.* (2014), the first indicative action is to inform, which entails providing the stakeholders with objective information to help them understand the issues that the ICT research Project 4s dealing with and options that are available to address them (Bryson *et al.*, 2013, p. 27). The fundamental commitment is for the stakeholders to be informed.

The second indicative action is to consult, which refers to a process through which stakeholder feedback on different aspects of the ICT research project is taken into account. The feedback could be about alternatives, analysis and decisions on how certain processes should be carried out, for instance, to mitigate harm to society (Bryson *et al.*, 2013, p. 26). The core commitment here is that stakeholders are listened to.

The third indicative action is to involve the stakeholders, and with this one, the main commitment is to work with the stakeholders. Lastly, the fourth action is to collaborate, which refers to a process where the ICT research project's stakeholders work together in different processes including decision-making (Bryson *et al.*, 2013, p. 26). With this last indicative action, the important commitment is to innovate collectively. An illustration of analysing stakeholders based on influence and interest is provided in Figure 2.3 below.

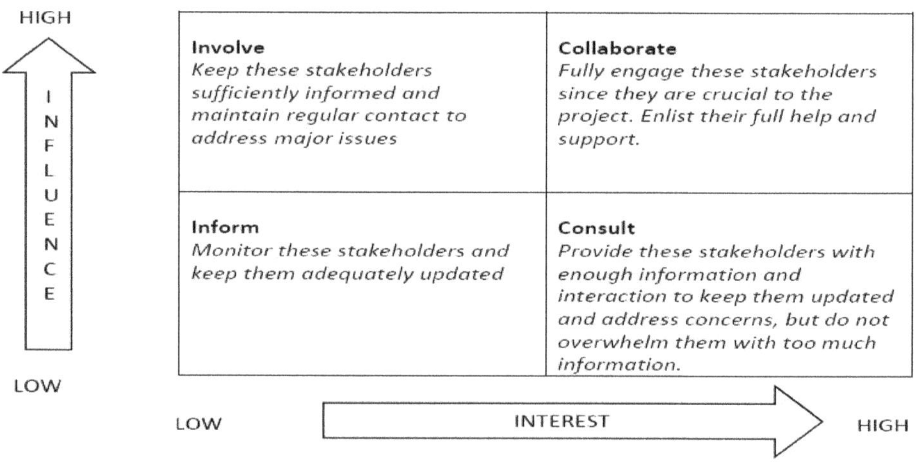

Figure 2.3: Stakeholder Analysis Matrix (Adapted from Durham *et al.*, (2014))

From Figure 3 above, the stakeholders that are in the '*collaborate*' quadrant (high interest – high influence) supply relevant resources and information, therefore, will be more beneficial to engage them in ICT research projects. These may also be greatly affected by the outcomes of the projects. The stakeholders in this quadrant are highly active and fully engaged in the projects and are effectively partners, who are in control of the direction of the innovation by contributing perspectives and resources (Bryson, 2004, p. 33). Those stakeholders in the '*involve*' quadrant (low interest – high influence) have influence that is significant for the research that is taking place in ICT research projects. These stakeholders are highly influential. Nevertheless, their interest in the research projects is low which perhaps could be either due to limited resources or capacity to engage (Bryson, 2004, p. 33).

The stakeholders in the '*consult*' quadrant (high interest – low influence) lack the capacity to notably help the research projects and contribute towards the impact of the projects. These stakeholders are supportive and may be asked for opinions or information. However, they may become influential through partnering with other stakeholders that are influential (Durham *et al.*, 2014). Due to this low influence, stakeholders in this quadrant can justifiably be excluded from the research and innovation process that is being carried out by the research projects.

Lastly, the stakeholders in the '*inform*' quadrant (low interest – low influence) have less need to be considered for engagement in the research projects especially when the resources are limited. The reason behind this is that they have little interest in or influence over research outputs (Leventon *et al.*, 2016, p. 769). However, this could be different if the research projects' are aimed at social change, for instance, behavioural change in society.

Stakeholder analysis is an essential part of stakeholder engagement which leads to the identification of which stakeholder to engage in ICT research projects. Therefore, the next section discusses stakeholder identification.

2.4.4 Stakeholder Identification

The identification of relevant stakeholders for ICT research projects is not straightforward because the research processes carried out have several phases, each of which has its stakeholders, activities, and outcomes (Pouloudi, 1999). Stakeholders can be identified by categorising them in different ways, for instance as; primary, secondary and key stakeholders (Gonzalez-Zapata and Heeks, 2015); internal and external stakeholder (Mazur and Pisarski, 2015); active and passive stakeholders (Andre *et al.*, 2012).

Focussing on categorisation as a way of identifying stakeholders is shallow because it ignores the nature of their engagement in the ICT research projects and puts emphasis on the imposed value of what the research taking place means to the stakeholders. From the literature, it comes to light that the need to place value on stakeholders is common for example, by labelling them as key stakeholders (Gonzalez-Zapata and Heeks, 2015) and passive stakeholders (Reed *et al.*, 2009, p. 1934). Similarly, Durham (2014) develops a typology of categories of stakeholder engagement that includes limited interaction, full interaction, mediator and key stakeholders as other categories that are useful in trying to identify stakeholders. In this typology, there is an attempt to differentiate the nature of engagement of stakeholders within projects, and it identifies that sometimes stakeholders can be identified for a limited engagement, and sometimes for an intensive one (Durham *et al.*, 2014, p. 23; Reed *et al.*, 2009). Although the studies by Durham *et al.* (2014)

and Reed *et al.* (2009) are specific to research projects on climate change, they however, could be applied to ICT research projects.

The Durham *et al.* (2014) and Reed *et al.* (2009) also highlight that different types of stakeholders may be engaged according to their perceived competence, their domain knowledge, expertise or whatever reason they are identified for engagement in the project at different phases of the research. Additionally, using a typology like one developed by Durham *et al.* (2014) when identifying and engaging stakeholders in ICT research projects, could clarify the level of engagement that is necessary therefore tackling the issue of unintentionally overstating or understating the level of engagement for stakeholders required by the projects.

Stakeholder identification is significant in the stakeholder engagement process because it helps the ICT research projects to scope the context for meeting its aims and achieving its outcomes (Bryson *et al.*, 2013, p. 24). If the identification of stakeholders is wrong, the developed engagement will be of no benefit to the research projects. As it is the case with all projects, each ICT research project is unique and is a construct of some issues that need to be considered. Among those issues, there is the decision-making processes, history and culture ofthe project, context and aims (Turner and Müller, 2003). These issues may affect who could be identified to be involved and not to be involved in the projects. Understanding some of these issues will ensure that the appropriate stakeholders are identified and are relevant in achieving the aim and purpose of the stakeholder engagement. Therefore, selection of stakeholders to be engaged can be subject to the potential impact and outcomes, availability of resources and the ability and willingness of the stakeholders to engage and contribute (Bunn *et al.*, 2002; Reed *et al.*, 2009).

Correspondingly, it is important to ensure effective identification of relevant stakeholders that represents those with high levels of interest in the ICT research projects and those who may have low levels of influence, in addition to strategic stakeholders with power, motivation and means to implement research outcomes. This is something that is suggested by Leventon *et al.* (2016). The author suggests that stakeholder identification that ensures effective representation, with a balance of power and influence among stakeholders, can enhance levels of mutual learning and trust between project stakeholders (Leventon *et al.*, 2016, p. 773). On the contrary, unrepresentative or restrictive stakeholder identification and selection may lead to less positive social outcomes, and may even lead to increased conflict among stakeholders (de Vente *et al.*, 2016; Reed *et al.*, 2009).

Stakeholder identification could be done in two different approaches; *ad-hoc* and *ex-ante* (Reed and Curzon, 2015, p. 24). For both these approaches, the initial step is done using secondary data sources that are used to select and map stakeholders in a systematic manner. With the *ad-hoc* approach, the process of stakeholder identification is iterative and uses feedback from newly identified stakeholders who in turn help in identifying other stakeholders. On the other hand, the *ex-ante* approach involves identifying stakeholders in advance in relevance to likely stakeholder categories for example by considering specific roles of different stakeholders such as policymakers, funders, local communities and civil society organisations. With the second approach, the categories identified can be used as a checklist to ascertain representativeness of stakeholders engaged by checking who is missing and filling in the gap as the research progresses (Reed and Curzon, 2015).

Not every stakeholder or stakeholder group needs to be involved to the same degree, or at the same time. Stakeholders may be of differing relevance at different stages of the research (Pouloudi *et al.*, 2016). By considering the relevance of the stakeholders to the ICT research Project 4t is possible to establish which might be best to contribute and which will be affected, and therefore critical to involve at a certain phase (Jepsen and Eskerod, 2009; Rahman *et al.*, 2015; Reed and Curzon, 2015).

Therefore, to understand stakeholder engagement in ICT research projects, stakeholder identification is an important area that should be considered in identifying distinct stakeholders such as the systems' developers and end-users. Without stakeholder analysis and identification, an appreciation of the contribution of these types of stakeholders would otherwise be missed since they are not included in generic stakeholder groups (Pouloudi and Whitley, 1997, p. 4).

2.5 The Rationale for Stakeholder Engagement in Research Projects

As discussed in the previous sections, one of the reasons why stakeholders are identified to be engaged in projects is based on their interests and influence (see sections 2.3.3 and 2.5.4). These two variables could also determine the justification for their engagement in research projects including those that deal with ICT. The rationale behind stakeholder engagement in projects has been discussed in literature regardless of project type (Blok *et al.*, 2015; Bryson *et al.*, 2013; Carney *et al.*, 2009; Phillipson *et al.*, 2012a; Schenke *et al.*, 2016). The reasons given in the literature are mostly generic across different types of projects whether it be a research project or a new product development project.

The underlying principle of stakeholder engagement in projects includes, amongst other issues, the following. Bryson *et al.* (2013), mentions that stakeholders are engaged in projects to add legitimacy to the research and innovation that is being carried out through the involvement of experts from a range of disciplines (p. 30). The authors add that stakeholders are engaged in projects to include the values of different people who represent the wider society or part of it (p. 31). In the same vein, Carney *et al.* (2009) note that stakeholders are engaged in projects to comply with the request made by the sponsor or funder of a particular project. An example of this could be the recent drive by the EC to involve stakeholders in responsible research and innovation (European Commission, 2017). Similarly, Schenke *et al.* (2016) and Williams *et al.* (2014) holds the view that stakeholder engagement aspires to minimise stakeholder scepticism in the research and innovation that takes place in research projects.

The examples given above are important to this study because they give a starting point to understanding the value of stakeholder engagement by depicting why different stakeholders may be engaged in research projects such as those dealing with ICT. They offer evidence that stakeholders contribute not only to the existence of the projects but also the implementation and its success towards achieving certain aims.

Although stakeholders are engaged in research projects for the reasons highlighted above, there are challenges with regards to their engagement. In research projects, some researchers see the engagement of other stakeholders to contribute towards certain aspects of the project as a constraint instead of an opportunity (Solli-Saether *et al.*, 2015). This limits the level of contribution from those engaged and impedes the benefits of stakeholder engagement highlighted above. Also, Bryson *et al.* (2013) point out that some stakeholders may lack time to engage or experience 'stakeholder fatigue', that is, they begin to feel overloaded with engagement activities which in turn negatively affects their willingness to participate and lessens the quality of their contribution.

Correspondingly, Haddaway *et al.* (2017) noted that identifying and engaging stakeholders in an unbalanced manner, probably due to poor stakeholder identification, could lead to ineffective decision making. As a result, the stakeholder engagement process becomes fruitless towards achieving the research projects' aims (Haddaway *et al.*, 2017, p. 6). The challenges given here are just a trace of the discourse on the challenges of stakeholder engagement in research projects.

So far, this chapter has reviewed the literature on stakeholder engagement in research projects including those that deals with ICT. Firstly, it classified projects with the aim to narrow down the study focus to ICT research projects. The chapter has also discussed that on a high-level, projects could be classified as innovation and conventional projects. This classification can then be further narrowed to categories of both research and new product development project. However, despite some literature on the classification of projects as presented in this chapter, the study acknowledged the limitation of such a classification and argued that ICT research projects could fall within all these different categories. Regardless, the classification provided in the literature should be considered as a starting point for defining and narrowing the focus of this study to ICT research projects.

Also, the chapter discussed the reason why ICT research projects are of interest. The literature reviewed highlighted that three overarching societal challenges could be addressed by ICT research. As a result, three types of ICT research projects were identified as aimed at addressing social wellbeing, environmental sustainability and education. These three types of ICT research projects were discussed before moving to a review of the literature on stakeholder engagement in research projects. Under stakeholder engagement, the section discussed stakeholder analysis and identification. It also looked at the rationale for stakeholder engagement in research projects and examples of the challenges that could affect stakeholder engagement. From the review, it was understood that stakeholder engagement could be beneficial to research projects including ICT research projects as suggested under the concept of RRI. Hence, the focus of the review will turn on to RRI in ICT research projects.

2.6 Responsible Research and Innovation in ICT Projects

One of the concepts that advocates that stakeholder engagement could be beneficial to ICT research projects with regards to achievement of responsible outcomes is Responsible Research and Innovation (RRI). RRI is important in research projects because it involves the engagement of stakeholders in addressing societal impacts that may result for research and innovation taking place in those projects. Seldom, the concepts of RRI and Responsible Innovation (RI) have been used interchangeably in literature with variations of definitions. However the underlying premise is the same. There has been a number of accounts of RRI (Sykes and Macnaghten, 2013) and they are discussed in the following sections.

2.7 Accounts of Responsible Research and Innovation

As stated in section 1.3, RRI is important in research projects including those that focus on ICT. RRI is essential because it provides tools that could be used to ensure that the research that is taking place in the ICT research projects achieve socially desirable outcomes. Hence, this section provides an understanding of what RRI entails through a review of different RRI accounts. The literature on RRI is still developing, and there have been two different references to the approach.

On the one hand, the concept is being referred to as Responsible Research and Innovation (RRI), and on the other, there is the omission of the term *'research'*, therefore in some literature, it is being referred to as Responsible Innovation (RI). As a result, the concept of RRI and RI have been used interchangeably in the literature with variations of definitions. However, the underlying premise seems to be the same. To avert this difference in terminology some authors such as Maia *et al.*, (2015), present it as R(R)I to show that they are primarily referring to one thing. For this study, some definitions and interpretations of RRI and RI by different proponents of the concept are presented below to understand what R(R) I entail.

In RRI, responsibility is central. Under RRI, one of the main purposes of stakeholder engagement in research projects is to support the implementation of responsibility. Responsibility for research projects, including ICT research projects, is not a new thing (von Schomberg *et al.*, 2007, p. 10). For instance, it has been previously covered in technology assessments (Burget *et al.*, 2017, p. 2; Chatfield *et al.*, 2017; Von Schomberg, 2012; von Schomberg *et al.*, 2007) and responsible development (Rip, 2014, pp. 7–8). Compared with technology assessment and responsible development, RRI is *'a broader concept, comprising ethical considerations as well as widespread governance issues'* (Burget *et al.*, 2017, p. 3). To build on approaches such technology assessments and responsible development, RRI has emerged to include governance of technological research and innovation (Wilford *et al.*, 2016).

Although the EC is the main advocate for RRI, the approach is not limited to Europe as there has been currently an attempt to promote RRI globally through a network that includes the United States of America, South Africa and China

(Chatfield *et al.*, 2017, p. 2). A current example of such initiative is the Responsible Research and Innovation Networking Globally (RRING) project which started in May, 2018 and is aimed at bringing RRI into the linked up global world to promote mutual learning and collaboration in research and innovation (RRING Project, 2018).

At the beginning, RRI was about identifying and addressing the risks and uncertainties relating to new areas of research starting with nanotechnology (Rip, 2014) and it then moved on to the environmental and health sciences (Stilgoe *et al.*, 2013). Of late, the focus has developed to include computer science, robotics, and ICT in general (Jirotka *et al.*, 2017; Shelley-Egan *et al.*, 2017; Simon, 2017; Stahl *et al.*, 2016). This supports the argument that RRI has become vital in ICT research as stated earlier. RRI aims to ensure that R&I is carried out in the interest of the society through the incorporation of methods that encourage inclusive decision making in the development of new technologies (Jirotka *et al.*, 2017). For instance, RRI could be used to create guidelines that govern or guide stakeholder engagement in order to achieve desirable outcomes from research and innovation that takes place in ICT research (Wilford *et al.*, 2016; Wilford, 2015).

Despite the infancy and continuous development of the RRI discourse, there have been some accounts for RRI in research projects, including ICT research projects (Geoghegan-Quinn, 2012; Pavie and Carthy, 2014; Stahl *et al.*, 2013; Stilgoe *et al.*, 2013; van den Hoven, 2013; von Schomberg *et al.*, 2011). These accounts have provided a starting point for both researchers and practitioners in understanding what RRI entails. To that effect, they have been used in this study for the same purpose.

To start with, the predominant definition is the one given by von Schomberg (2011) where he defines RRI as;

> *'a transparent, interactive process by which societal actors and innovators become mutually responsive to each other with a view on the (ethical) acceptability, sustainability and societal desirability of the innovation process and its marketable products (in order to allow a proper embedding of scientific and technological advances in our society)' (Von Schomberg, 2013, p. 19).*

Von Schomberg's definition emphasises on acceptability and desirability of innovative processes and products. Von Schomberg's definition could be understood as that RRI involves addressing the overall societal challenges of technology R&I by including stakeholders (who he refers to as *'societal actors and innovators'*).

Another account is developed by Geoghegan-Quinn who defines RRI as a concept which

> *'means that societal actors work together during the whole research and innovation process in order to better align both the process and its outcomes, with the values, needs and expectations of European society.' (Geoghegan-Quinn, 2012, p.3)*

The account given by Geoghegan-Quinn (2011) is very similar to one by Von Schomberg (2011). Comparable to von Schomberg's (2011) definition, the account given by Geoghegan-Quinn (2012) (on behalf of the EU) emphasises that RRI set requirements for both R&I processes and outcomes to be desirable and acceptable to the society. In Geoghegan-Quinn's account, there is also an emphasis on working together which is similar to the emphasis put forward in von Schomberg's account on themutual interaction among societal actors.

From the account of Geoghegan-Quinn (2012), the EC advances an RRI framework that includes the objectives focussing on gender equality, open access, science education, ethics, public engagement and research governance (Geoghegan-Quinn, 2012). The EU framework results from the elaboration of the account given by Geoghegan-Quinn and therefore suggest that RRI consists of six pillars which include:

- ❖ multi-actor and public *engagement* in co-creating the future by bringing together the widest possible diversity of actors, in particular, to tackle the grand societal challenges that lie before society
- ❖ *Gender* equality in the R&I process which means that all genders should be engaged
- ❖ Improving *science education,* so the language and tools of education are available to everyone for co-creation within the research and innovation process
- ❖ *Ethical* R&I to adequately respond to societal challenges
- ❖ *Openness and transparency* in R&I therefore making research results more accessible for the improvement of the process
- ❖ *Governance* models for RRI that also integrate the five other dimensions and policymakers who can anticipate to prevent harmful or unethical developments in R&I. (Geoghegan-Quinn, 2012, pp. 2–3)

The pillars of engagement, transparency, governance and ethics are closely related to the account given by von Schomberg. For example, ethics relates to the '*(ethical) acceptability, sustainability and societal desirability of the innovation process*' while the mutual interaction is closely related to transparency, engagement, governance and education. However, in contrast to von Schomberg's account Geoghegan-Quinn's account requires RRI to include gender equality, and improvement of science education. The emphasis on these two dimensions may be implied but is not explicitly discussed by von Schomberg (2011).

In comparison to the definitions given in von Schomberg's and Geoghegan-Quinn' accounts, Stahl *et al.* (2013) give a definition which is rather comprehensive and looks at RRI in terms of responsibility. Stahl *et al.* (2013) define RRI as

> *'a higher-level responsibility or meta-responsibility that aims to shape, maintain, develop, coordinate and align existing and novel R&I-related processes, actors and responsibilities with a view to ensuring desirable and acceptable research outcomes (Stahl, 2013a, p. 1).*

Stahl's *et al.* (2013) definition take into account an all-encompassing level of responsibility that could exist in ICT research projects. Not only does the definition cover responsibility in R&I-related processes, but also includes the actors involved who commit to ensure that society gets desirable outcomes. This is something that is also mentioned by both von Schomberg (2011) and Geoghegan-Quinn (2011).

On the inclusion of actors, von Schomberg talks about *'mutual interaction'* while Geoghegan-Quinn suggests *'working together'* in R&I. Further on, Stahl *et al.* (2013) talk about being responsible in R&I by referring to what they termed as a four 'P's that includes product, process, purpose and people (Stahl *et al.*, 2013, p. 203). Stahl *et al.* (2013) suggested that in order to have responsible innovation and therefore responsible outcome; attention should be given to all the four 'P's rather than the widely recognised two 'P's (product and process) of R&I. This suggestion, therefore, involves incorporating people in the R&I and purposes. People (stakeholders or actors) are important in the R&I because they can collectively consider the *"creation of better or more effective products, processes, services, technologies, or ideas that are readily available to markets, governments, and society."* (Stahl *et al.*, 2013, p. 203).

The underlying message from Stahl *et al.*'s account of RRI is that, the concept is about engaging stakeholders in achieving ethically acceptable, societally desirable and sustainable outcomes in the development and deployment of new technologies including ICT. Therefore, RRI is meant to resolve and mitigate the consequences of technological innovations on society. The creation of an idea, mitigation of consequences and collective considering of socially desirable outcomes, have some connotations of anticipatory, transparent, and reflective elements when producing those outcomes through the engagement of different actors in ICT research projects.

Another account of RRI is provided by Stilgoe *et al.* (2013). The account that is given by Stilgoe *et al.* (2013) slightly relates to the one by von Schomberg (2011) and defines RRI as;

> *'A collective commitment to care for the future through responsive stewardship of science and innovation in the present' (Stilgoe et al., 2013, p. 1570).*

This account of RRI is rather broad and therefore is open to interpretations of how RRI can be envisaged. One interpretation that can be made from this definition is that it acknowledges responsiveness in R&I process and anticipation through its reference to caring for the future. This relates to the account given by von Schomberg's (2011) definition in a way that both accounts point towards R&I that is collective (transparent and interactive) and responsive (socially desirable outcomes). Similarly, the account that is given by Stahl *et al.* (2013) also relates to the account given by Stilgoe *et al.* (2013) specifically on the premise that RRI is about being responsible and innovating responsibly, therefore relating to the concept of meta-responsibility.

Furthermore, Stilgoe *et al.*'s account mentions the need to care for the future in the present. This is something that can be interpreted and being anticipatory and reflective on present actions in the R&I process in order to come up with products that are either better or do not repeat the same shortfalls that are being experienced in the present.

The account that is given by Stilgoe *et al.* (2013) also includes the development of an RRI framework which includes four dimensions. These four dimensions of RRI align well with some of the areas that the definitions provided by von Schoenberg (2011) Geoghegan-Quinn (2011) and Stahl *et al.* (2013). All in all, they suggest that to innovate responsibly, a continuous and collective commitment that is anticipatory, reflective, deliberative and responsive is necessary. Because of this overarching nature of the dimensions the framework has been adopted in national research agendas. For instance, the Engineering and Physical Sciences Research Council (EPSRC) has used the work by Stilgoe *et al.* (2013) to suggest that RRI includes *'anticipation of potential consequences, reflection concerning the underpinnings* motivations, processes, products, *and assumptions of research, engagement with a broad range of stakeholders and acting accordingly to address the issues revealed '* (Chatfield *et al.*, 2017, p. 970).

As previously mentioned, there are also some scholars who have taken a different perspective on the concept and omitted the 'research' in their accounts and therefore use Responsible Innovation (RI) in the discourse. For example, Hellstrom (2003) has used the term *'responsible innovation'* long before the concept of RRI. Hellstrom (2003) talks about responsible innovation in the development of emerging technological systems. However, the account given by Hellstrom does not provide a clear definition of what RI is. Hellstrom's account focuses mainly on the procedures taken in R&I and ignores reflectivity which is paramount in RRI (Hellström, 2003).

The author mentions that technology and risk assessments are not enough to address the challenges posed by emerging technology system particularly with regard to the impact of 'negative synergies' between complex technologies, social institutions and critical infrastructures. Therefore, to address the limitation of the technology and risk assessments, a general framework for *'responsible innovation'*, may be carried out. However, Hellstrom admitted that he was not clear how a framework for this type of what he calls *'preventive foresight and governance of responsible innovation'* could entail (Hellström, 2003, p. 382). Despite, lack of a definition for RI, his account indicates that years before RRI was mainstream the discussion was already going on.

Van de Hoven (2013) provides an account of RI, and in this account, RI is defined as;

> *'an activity or process which may give rise to previously unknown designs either pertaining to the physical world, the conceptual world, the institutional world or combinations of these which when implemented expand the set of relevant, feasible options regarding solving a set of moral problems' (van den Hoven, 2013, p. 82).*

Van den Hoven (2013) emphatically focuses on the development of technological products rather than the results from research, therefore clearly emphasising the process. Van den Hoven argues that technology is never morally neutral so much so that it accommodates a particular conception of good at the expense of another whether intentionally or not (van den Hoven, 2013). Based on this account, RI is about making certain values explicit in order to improve the functionality and what the technological innovation has to offer to society. As an example of resolving moral dilemmas and conflicts in ICTs, van den Hoven suggests adopting a value-based perspective when designing ICT innovations. Other authors, such as Eden, Jirotka and Stahl, agree that this approach can enhance responsibility in ICT in the sense that it paves the way for incorporating value and moral considerations in ICT (Eden *et al.*, 2013; Stahl *et al.*, 2013; van den Hoven, 2013).

However, the limitation with focussing on the value-based perspective in the innovation within research, for instance, ICT research, is that those actors involved in the process can potentially miss other important aspects due to concentrating on design. In terms of ICT research projects, this account of RI fails to answer the question of what happens after the research project has passed the design phase and therefore it is not consistent with R(R)I. R(R)I in ICT research projects should be holistic rather than segmental.

Pavie and Carthy (2014) give another fairly recent account on RI and defines RI as;

> *'An iterative development process which combines a step-by-step impact analysis of a project with the imperatives of creativity stimulation throughout development phases. Social, economic and environmental performance impacts are monitored throughout the entire lifecycle, and corrective actions are anticipated accordingly through re-integration into previous development phases' (Pavie and Carthy, 2014, p. 3).*

Pavie and Carthy's definition points to monitoring impacts through the entire lifecycle of the development process through anticipation of corrective actions. At least, the account given by Pavie and Carthy shows some similarities with the RRI accounts given by the authors above in that it also emphasises anticipation and responsiveness through '*corrective actions*'. The assumption is that these corrective actions are anticipated by different actors that work collaboratively to ensure that the innovation process results in socially, economically and environmentally desirable impacts. However, the focus of Pavie and Carthy's account is mainly on the development phase of research in the business sector rather than research (Pavie and Carthy, 2014, 2013). Perhaps, this could be one of the reasons why they omitted the 'research' element from their conception.

Another, difference that can be seen from Pavie and Carthy's account of RI from the other accounts of RRI reviewed above, is scepticism with the engagement of different actors in the R&I. They refer to RI as a *'wicked problem'* because of *'its complexity due to the multitude of actors, each with their specificities and characteristics, who are involved in the process'* (Pavie and Carthy, 2014, p. 5). Pavie and Carthy further state that RI is wicked problem because it involves *'scratching the surface to solve an issue which inevitably reveals new arising issues to be addressed.'*(2014, p. 5). Whether this is a wicked problem or not, is debatable. However, one could see the revelation of new issues to be addressed as a good outcome that can help in addressing those uncertainties and hidden negative impacts of technology.

All the accounts presented above revolve around societal actors working together during the whole process of R&I to better align both the process and its outcomes with values, needs and expectations of the society although some are more explicit than the others. Nevertheless, from the above definitions of RI and RRI (R(R)I), there is some evidence that the two are fundamentally related because they all point to producing desirable outcomes from R&I that are socially acceptable.

To summarise, the different accounts given above, some areas of their focus have been tabulated in Table 2.2 below.

Table 2.2: Main Focus Areas of Key RRI Accounts

RRI account	Main focus
Von Schomberg (2011)	mutual interaction • responsiveness of all those involved • acceptability and desirability of innovative processes and products • transparent R&I
Geoghegan-Quinn, (2012) -EC	• working together in R&I • six pillars of RRI including engagement, gender equality, science education, ethics, openness and governance in R&I
Stahl (2013)	• bringing on actors, norms and activities • collective consideration of socially desirable products • higher level responsibility • anticipation - mitigation of consequences, preventing socially undesirable impacts • reflection on preconditions for successful responsibility relationships
Stilgoe, Owen and Macnaghten (2013)	• collective commitment • anticipating - caring for the future • responsive stewardship of science and innovation • Four dimensions of RRI including anticipation, reflection, deliberation and responsiveness
Van den Hoven (2013)	• emphasises design • adding moral values to designs • products of development and innovation processes and activities
Pavie and Carthy (2014)	• the anticipation of corrective actions • R&I in industry rather than research sector • engagement of different actors is a wicked problem

From the summary given in Table 2 above it can be seen that there some key differences and similarities in various accounts of RRI. On the one hand, the differences include the following;

i. There are different conceptions of RRI. Some refer to it as RRI (Geoghegan-Quinn, 2012; Stahl *et al.*, 2013; Stilgoe *et al.*, 2013; von Schomberg *et al.*, 2011) while some omit the research element from the concept and just refer to it as RI (Pavie and Carthy, 2013; van den Hoven, 2013). This could be down to some authors focussing on the practical side of 'what' has to be designed rather than researching of 'how' it can be designed in R&I.

ii. The account by EU includes gender equality and science education while the rest do not explicitly talk about these. However, some authors have slightly touched on education in the sense that they have talked about raising awareness, building capacities and encouraging mutual learning as a fundamental element of RRI (Owen *et al.*, 2013; Stahl, 2013).

iii. Some of the accounts focus on the development of technological products rather than the results from research, therefore clearly emphasising on the process (Pavie and Carthy, 2013; van den Hoven, 2013).

On the other hand, the accounts have the following similarities;

i. They all link R(R)I to ethical standards and acceptability and desirability of the outcomes. At a minimum, the accounts share the assumption that R&I need to produce socially desirable consequences and needs to omit undesirable ones to address the current societal challenges.

ii. They all call for inclusiveness in the research and innovation processes.

iii. All accounts, either explicitly or implicitly, hint towards stakeholder engagement and participation in the R&I processes, some distinguishing between innovators and societal actors. Furthermore, the accounts do not exclude any actors or stakeholders beforehand.

iv. Stilgoe *et al.*'s and Stahl *et al.*' accounts suggest that innovation processes and technology governance should be shaped according to responsibility reflections.

v. In this section, the different accounts that have been reviewed help in understanding the depth of the RRI concept. One important emphasis that is found in the discussions of RRI are the different aspects. These key aspects are a result of the main themes that each account is composed of. Subsequently, in section 2.8, these are used to establish the key conceptual features to use as an RRI lens for evaluating stakeholder engagement.

To recap the different aspects, Geoghegan-Quinn (2012) described six pillars termed as follows: engagement, gender equality, science education, ethics, open access and governance. Stahl (2013) focussed on the practical implementation of RRI and concentrated on the aspects that signified bringing together actors, norms and activities. Stilgoe *et al.* (2013) listed four dimensions that had emerged in the RRI discourses as anticipation, inclusion, reflexivity and responsiveness. This review of RRI accounts is focused on two things. First it focuses on how the aspects were described. Secondly, on how they emerged and evolved in the RRI discourses.

The different aspects are categorised and grouped together to come up with the key conceptual features of RRI that are discussed in section 2.8 below. For example, Stahl's (2013) aspect on bringing actors is grouped under '*engagement*'. von Schomberg's (2011) aspect on transparent R&I is grouped under '*openness and transparency*', and Pavie and Carthy's (2014) aspect on anticipation of corrective actions is grouped under '*anticipation and reflection*'. Some aspects suggested by

Geoghegan-Quinn (2012) for the EU framework such as gender equality and science education are not included as part of the key conceptual features for the RRI lens because they do not appear across the other accounts.

Therefore, in the end, four different conceptual key conceptual features are selected to be used as an RRI lens for analysis. These include engagement of stakeholders, openness and transparency, anticipation and reflection and responsiveness (see section 3.3). The four key conceptual features are chosen, as they appeared noticeably in the reviewed accounts and are also elaborated further by Stilgoe *et al.* (2013) and Shelley-Egan *et al.* (2017). These key conceptual features of RRI are discussed in the next section.

2.8 Key Conceptual Features of RRI for ICT Research Projects

The different accounts of RRI reviewed in section 2.7 above provide a starting point for incorporating RRI into evaluation (see chapter 3). Henceforth, this study advances some key conceptual features of RRI which could relate to research projects including ICT research projects. The study has settled for these key conceptual features because there are cross-cutting among the majority of the accounts and therefore give a concerted picture of what could be regarded as socially desirable in ICT research projects. These key conceptual features outlined below are part of the theoretical insights that, together with the empirical insights from the case study informed the evaluation of the value of stakeholder engagement.

2.8.1 Engagement of Stakeholders

The first key conceptual feature of RRI is the engagement of stakeholders. As mentioned in section 1.3, outcomes and outputs from ICT research projects have the potential to impact the society. To ensure an acceptable and socially desirable production and uptake of the outputs and outcomes of ICT research projects in society, diverse views from stakeholders should be taken into account (Shelley-Egan *et al.*, 2017, p. 11). The significance of stakeholder engagement, within the context of RRI, has been discussed by many authors (Bauer *et al.*, 2016; Shelley-Egan *et al.*, 2017; Stahl *et al.*, 2013; Stilgoe *et al.*, 2013; Sykes and Macnaghten, 2013; Wilford *et al.*, 2016). These authors agree that for a desirable uptake of outputs and outcomes of ICT research projects, an engagement of stakeholders is necessary to anticipate and reflect on the consequences of the whole R&I process (see section 2.8.3). In a nutshell, the engagement of stakeholders is key because it helps '*elucidate the social and ethical issues associated with a particular technology or application, in addition to views and concerns regarding its uptake, and potential future impacts, both desired and undesired* (Shelley-Egan *et al.*, 2017, p. 11).

2.8.2 Openness and Transparency

The second key conceptual feature that this study takes forward is openness and transparency in R&I process that takes place in ICT research projects. Shelley-Egan *et al.* (2017) on their work on RRI in the context of human cognitive enhancement, showed that openness and transparency are vital elements of responsible innovation. In agreement with Shelley-Egan et, al. (2017), Jirotka et, al. (2017) added that openness and transparency is key because it involves a balanced and meaningful discussion of research and its implications in order to facilitate stakeholders' understanding and examination of R&I that exists in ICT research projects (Jirotka *et al.*, 2017). Evidently, the importance of openness and transparency is highlighted in most studies on RRI such as those conducted by (Eden *et al.*, 2013; Stilgoe *et al.*, 2013; Zwart *et al.*, 2014)). In these studies, it is established that openness and transparency involves a variety of stakeholders to openly recognise and truthfully represent uncertainties and a lack of knowledge about different aspects of ICT research such as responsibility and sustainability.

2.8.3 Anticipation and reflection

The third key conceptual feature of RRI is that of anticipation and reflection. This feature is a combination of two aspects, anticipation as one and reflection as the other. According to Stilgoe *et al.* (2013), on the other hand, anticipation involves asking *'what if ...?'* questions to consider alternatives and what is likely to happen (Stilgoe *et al.*, 2013, p. 1570). While in agreement with Stilgoe *et al.* (2013), Shelley-Egan (2017) also points out that reflection is vital in R&I and it involves deliberating on assumptions and values underpinning R&I in support of anticipation (Shelley-Egan *et al.*, 2017, p. 13). Looking at these two examples from RRI discourses, the underlining message is that anticipation and reflection can provide valuable insights and enhance the stakeholders' capacity to act according to what they know. Therefore, in ICT research projects, anticipation might involve the assessment of unexpected and unwanted outcomes of the project while reflecting on the potential societal effects of R&I that takes place in the projects.

2.8.4 Responsiveness

The last key conceptual feature of RRI that this study advances from the literature is responsiveness. Responsiveness is key in ICT research projects because it encourages the sensitivity to the unfolding of a diversity of value positions and the absence of a consolidated knowledge for responsible innovation processes and practices. This premise is supported by Stilgoe *et al.* (2013) in that the sensitivity that is promoted by responsiveness in R&I, entails having *'a capacity to change shape or direction in response to stakeholders and public values and changing circumstances'* (Stilgoe *et al.*, 2013, p. 1573). As such, responsiveness in ICT research projects involves the consideration of how systems of innovation can be shaped so that they are as flexible and responsive as possible. Responsiveness in R&I addresses a problem that was earlier indicated by Pellizzoni (2004). Pellizzoni (2004) highlighted that despite its importance, responsiveness is sometimes neglected. The author stated that responsiveness is *'an encompassing yet substantially neglected dimension of responsibility,* (Pellizzoni, 2004, p. 557). This should not be the case. Arguably, responsiveness is crucial in R&I within ICT research projects because it builds awareness and capacity to adequately adapt and respond to changing circumstances. As such, in agreement with Stahl and Jirotka (2013), responsiveness should include the kind of social benefit that could arise from ICT research projects. Also, it should include the engagement of stakeholders in a reflexive process regarding the societal implications of their research.

In all the four key conceptual features advanced, it can be established that stakeholders are crucial within ICT research projects and therefore it is necessary to evaluate and understand their contribution towards positive outcomes of R&I within the context of RRI.

2.9 Meaning of the Features for Stakeholder Engagement in ICT Research Projects

As seen from above, there are advocates for the significance of responsibility in R&I. Since ICT research projects provide the platform on which compelling technologies are increasingly being developed through R&I, it is pertinent that the underlying assumptions of RRI are taken into consideration when implementing ICT research projects. It is important because the research being undertaken in these projects have the promise to transform the society. However, for that transformation to be socially desirable, there is pressure to involve societal actors in the ICT research projects to '*reflect on*' and consider the purposes and consequences of the R&I. As part of addressing this growing pressure, stakeholders such as researchers, industry representatives, civil society organisations and government representatives should be fully '*engaged*' in the R&I process that takes place in ICT research projects.

As mentioned in sections 3.2 above, the approaches to tackle impacts of R&I such as technology assessments within ICT research may not be enough to address widespread concerns (Jirotka *et al.*, 2017). Some of the limitations are highlighted by Simon (2016) and van den Hoven (2013) who argue that despite research processes and methodologies that implement responsibility, such methodologies as value sensitive design, privacy by design and technology foresight on their own do not address the broader concerns of R&I. Apparently, they miss out on '*anticipating*' moral concerns and accommodating them into design, sustainability, and safety at the expense of the other aspects of R&I (van den Hoven, 2013). As such, given that a bulk of R&I activities occur in ICT research projects, taking into consideration the key conceptual features of RRI suggested in section 3.3 above seems to be a better approach for understanding the value of stakeholder engagement towards the attainment of socially desirable outcomes in ICT research projects. The reason behind this is that the focus of the key features of RRI extends beyond existing research governance, policy instruments and methodologies such as technology assessment to guide R&I towards the production of socially acceptable and desirable impacts (Chatfield *et al.*, 2017).

Stakeholder '*engagement*' is central to RRI, and the literature indicates that promotion of stakeholder engagement is key in ICT research projects because stakeholders play a role in the influencing positive impacts and mitigating negative consequences of R&I in ICT research projects. As such, stakeholders should be involved in shaping innovative ideas and developing these ideas into outputs and outcomes (Bauer *et al.*, 2016). The stakeholders that are engaged in ICT research projects should *'reflect'* on their social and environmental responsibilities which then support the development of desirable, innovative outputs and outcomes. One example given by Jirotka *et al.* (2017) is that stakeholders are engaged in ICT research to ensure that there is accountability and *'transparency'* when developing new digital agents. The example given by Jirotka *et al.* (2017) is substantiated by the increasing involvement of ICT scholars and professionals to understand and address responsibility issues. In agreement with Jirotka *et al.* (2017), Stahl *et al.* (2014) indicate the involvement of philosophers and professionals to provide *'many insights into substantive moral problems as well as the theoretical underpinnings required to address them'* (Stahl *et al.*, 2014, p. 811). This is core to responsible innovation because these stakeholders, philosophers, professionals and others are engaged *'to respond to the societal challenges by guiding and designing innovations in a socially desirable and acceptable way'* (Jirotka *et al.*, 2017, p. 62).

Also in agreement with Jirotka *et al.*'s account of stakeholder engagement in ICT research, Pavie and Carthy (2014) mention that through stakeholder engagement, ICT research projects can *'anticipate'*, understand, and *'respond'* faster and more easily to impacts that affect society (Pavie and Carthy, 2014). One of the ways that stakeholders anticipate, understand and respond to impacts of ICT research projects is through stakeholder dialogue. Blok (2014) points out that stakeholders need to collaborate and engage in stakeholder dialogue on problems and downsides of R&I. Correspondingly, von Schomberg (2013) and Owen *et al.* (2013b) confirm that stakeholder dialogue is very important in R&I because it enables sharing of knowledge among stakeholders and opens up interaction to reach a consensus on the shared objectives of a research project (Owen *et al.*, 2013b). For instance, dialogue between stakeholders brings opportunities for generating new creative solutions that are beneficial for both the ICT research project and its stakeholders. Through dialogue, stakeholders become mutually responsive and share co-responsibility for the outcomes of the innovation process (Owen *et al.*, 2013b), and they pursue a harmonic stance toward R&I. As a result, they find common ground when influencing implementation of responsibility and sustainability in R&I (Blok, 2014).

In ICT research projects, the existence of the above suggestions, which are central to the key conceptual features (see section 3.3), can be used to support the alignment of R&I processes and outcomes with the needs, expectations and values of society. Therefore, within ICT research projects, RRI has the potential to highlight issues in the R&I process since it supports anticipation of consequences and encourages engagement of stakeholders in discussing the alignment of the outcomes of R&I process in relation to the values and needs of society.

So far the chapter has reviewed different accounts to gain an understanding of what RRI entails. As part of the review of the RRI accounts, the chapter highlighted the differences and similarities in the different accounts. One of the main difference was the focus of different proponents on process and outcomes of R&I. Some of the RRI proponents predominantly focus on the development of outputs and outcomes rather than the research process involved. However, despite the differences, all the accounts concertedly suggest that RRI is mainly geared towards the attainment of socially desirable outcomes and outputs. The chapter then further analysed the different RRI accounts and established key conceptual features of RRI that can be used to understand the value of stakeholder engagement towards attainment of socially desirable outcomes in research projects including ICT research projects. Therefore, to evaluate and understand stakeholder engagement in ICT research projects, the features are ideal to be used as a lens of analysis. Moving on towards understanding the value of stakeholder engagement the next sections reviews the literature on the evaluation of stakeholder engagement.

2.10 Evaluation of Stakeholder Engagement

The literature on evaluation is also important to delineate different areas on which the evaluation could focus. Therefore, this section provides an account of what evaluation entails and informs the conceptual evaluation model presented in chapter 3. It contributes towards addressing the sub-research question; *what elements are key for evaluating the efficacy of stakeholder engagement in ICT research projects?* The section discusses some reasons for conducting an evaluation. This is then followed by a succinct discussion of some definitions for evaluation to establish the meaning of evaluation in relation to this study. The section further covers different approaches to evaluation, and then three approaches that are appropriate for evaluating stakeholder engagement in ICT research projects are selected.

2.10.1 Rationale for Evaluation

There are numerous reasons for conducting evaluation. These reasons vary among different contexts for which the evaluation is called. For instance, evaluation is often required or called for by sponsors of a project or policymakers for accountability and decision-making (Stern *et al.*, 2012). Evaluation is also called for by theoreticians to generate knowledge about a phenomenon being evaluated (Mark *et al.*, 2006), and internal stakeholders for improvement or learning (Chelimsky, 2006; Mark *et al.*, 2006). This study closely relates to the rationale for evaluation given by Mark *et al.* (2006). The phenomenon or subject being evaluated is sometimes referred to as an evaluand (Smith, 2015). In this study, the evaluand is the value of stakeholder engagement in the ICT research projects with regards to attainment of socially desirable outcomes.

There is a lot said about the purpose of evaluation in research projects including those related to ICT. For example, research project funders may use evaluation to pose certain questions on the relative merit of the research and innovation which they have funded (O'Sullivan, 2012). Comparatively, evaluation may be used to ascertain the difference an evaluand such as stakeholder engagement is going to make, for example in society (Cooke-Davies, 2002; Stufflebeam and Coryn, 2014). In addition to the reasons given above, evaluation can also be used to assess society's learning, change of behaviour and success towards specified goals for instance, in ICT research projects (Klein, 2008). Therefore, in a nutshell, '*evaluation provides evidence that the research project has achieved a particular end*' (O'Sullivan, 2012, p. 520).

In general, the reasons that are given in the literature are two folds. Firstly, evaluation helps to improve practice (Schwandt, 2015; Chelimsky, 2006) and secondly, it helps to generate or improve knowledge (Mark *et al*. 2006). There is no clear-cut boundary between these two folds of which evaluation is conducted. For example, Schwandt (2015) put these together to state that it promotes learning and reflection from past work which helps stakeholders and practitioners to develop more effective projects in the future (Schwandt, 2015, pp. 31–39). It can then be argued that Schwandt's reason has elements of both improvements to practice, through reflection and improvement to knowledge, through learning. The claims by Schwandt (2015), Mark *et al*. (2006) and Chelimsky (2006) that evaluation can be used for knowledge development, accountability, decision-making and improvement on practice, again emphasises the cross rationale for evaluation in improving practice and generating knowledge.

Looking at another account for the rationale behind evaluation, Donaldson and Lipsey (2006) also suggest that evaluation has a purpose to generate or advance knowledge about social problems and their solutions (2006, p. 62). In relation to the subject matter of this research, these solutions could be a result of responsible practices and co-creation of advanced knowledge in ICT research projects. Donaldson and Lipsey's account considers evaluation as being part of developing solutions to social problems. They further state that evaluation can also act as a driver to disseminate the developed solutions. Therefore, it shows how evaluation is essential in ICT research since it can be used to understand and disseminate solutions that are borne out of stakeholder engagement in those projects through knowledge co-creation.

So far, this section has shown that the findings and information from evaluation may lead to the development of theory and social practices. One way of getting those findings is through an understanding of the lived experience of those engaged and involved in the ICT research projects (Schwandt, 2015, p. 107; Stufflebeam and Shinkfield, 2007, pp. 23–27). The next section briefly covers evaluation theory to provide a basic understanding of evaluation approaches that informed the conceptual evaluation model presented in chapter 3.

2.10.2 Evaluation Definition

This section presents the first part of an examination of evaluation theory by looking at definitions of evaluation to describe the meaning of evaluation and thereafter, section 2.10.3 presents the second part by looking at the evaluation approaches. Evaluation has been defined in many ways in the literature from a range of fields such as education, business management, project management and developmental studies. Therefore, the influential definitions for this research come from those different fields and contexts.

One of the definitions for evaluation has been defined by Weiss (1998) as;

> *'A systematic assessment of the operations and outcomes of an evaluand compared to a set of standards as a means of contributing to the improvement of the evaluand' (Weiss, 1998, p. 4).*

The definition given by Weiss (1998) emphasises that evaluation supports the improvement of an evaluand such as stakeholder engagement. Here, the assumption is that in order to assess and understand an evaluand, different elements of the evaluand such as the activities (operations) and the outcomes that result from the activities should be compared to a set of standards. These standards provide a benchmark for ascertaining whether certain objectives have been met. In the case of this study, such a benchmark could be the RRI lens of analysis that is discussed in sections 3.5.

Evaluation has also been defined by Scriven (1991);

> *'As a process that involves judgements of value, determinations of merit, worth or significance of something' (Scriven, 1991, p. 139).*

In Scriven's definition, the focus is on judgements of value. Here, evaluation involves making measured decisions or come to sensible conclusions about the merit or the significance of the evaluand such as stakeholder engagement. In light of this study, this means that in evaluating the value of stakeholder engagement, some assumptions should be made to determine its merit towards the attainment of socially desirable outcomes in ICT research projects.

Another definition is put forward by Schwandt (2000). Schwandt defines evaluation as;

> *'a technology for assigning a value to objects, events, processes, and people [...] that is built around the assumptions that evaluative information makes possible the improvement of society through the rationalisation of various kinds of social practices such as social policy and implementation of educational practices' (Schwandt, 2000, p. 215).*

Schwandt's definition is similar to Scriven's definition in that it focuses on placing value on the subject of the evaluation. However, Schwandt's definition goes further and brings in the social perspective of evaluation. Thus, Schwandt's definition does not stop on the determination of value and merit, but it also recognises that evaluation is built around assumptions that information that can be gained from an evaluation has the potential to improve society through learning.

Regardless of the reference to different fields, the definition given by Schwandt covers some elements that have been mentioned by both Weiss and Scriven. For instance, both Weiss and Scriven talks about assigning value or worth to an evaluand and so does Schwandt. However, the difference is that Schwandt elaborates further and indicates the different subjects to which the assignment can be made rather than leaving it open as it is the case with Scriven and Weiss definitions. Regarding assumptions, Weiss does not mention or implicitly indicate that assumptions could be used in the evaluation. Rather Weiss talks about evaluation as a 'systematic process' which is contrary to the accounts given by Schwandt and Scriven. Schwandt is explicit about the use of assumptions in evaluation while Scriven implicitly refers to assumptions in evaluation through the use of 'judgement' made on an evaluand.

Another definition is one provided by Stufflebeam (2003) as;

'A process of delineating, obtaining and providing useful information for judging decision alternatives' (Stufflebeam, 2003, p. 267).

The definition given by Stufflebeam mainly focuses on the use of evaluation in making decisions. Stufflebeam's definition pre-supposes that evaluation is useful when faced with different alternatives and therefore it can be used to assess the worthiness of choosing an alternative over others. This is quite limited and not directly related to the evaluation undertaken in this study.

From the sample definitions reviewed above, it can be recognised that evaluation is variably understood within the literature. Perhaps this shows how diverse is the nature of evaluation. Therefore, considering the diversity of the nature of evaluation, it is not surprising to find that no single definition has been established. However, all these definitions make a significant contribution to understanding what the evaluation of stakeholder engagement should entail. Thus, the three definitions given by Weiss, Scriven and Schwandt are more relevant to this study compared to the one by Stufflebeam.

Both definitions given by Scriven (1991) and Weiss (1998) are important to this research. The definition given by Scriven (1991) is of relevance to this study because it aims at understanding the *'value and significance'* of stakeholder engagement within ICT research projects, for example in light of responsible outcomes, through the judgements of the researcher and the stakeholders that were interviewed as part of this research (see section 6.9). Whereas the definition that is given by Weiss (1998) is also relevant to this study because it substantiates the use of an RRI lens of analysis as the standard for understanding the value of stakeholder engagement. The analysis that results from using such a lens could perhaps provide lessons on improving future stakeholder engagement concerning the attainment of socially desirable outcomes in ICT research.

All in all, the definition provided by Schwandt sums up the different elements covered in Weiss and Scriven's definitions and makes a better case for using evaluation in social perspectives such as stakeholder engagement. The fact that it rounds it up to the rationalisation of societal improvement fits in well with evaluation and the use of RRI as a benchmark.

This section has looked at the meaning of evaluation and identified the definitions that fitwell with the aim of this study. The next section further discusses approaches for conducting evaluation.

2.10.3 Evaluation Approaches

This section further reviews evaluation theory by looking at the evaluation approaches found in the literature. In the literature that was reviewed, there are 28 evaluation approaches. It is worth noting that it is not feasible in this book to describe all the evaluation approaches in detail. However, an outline of the different approaches can be seen in Appendix 2-1. This section captures the key approaches that are repeatedly covered in the literature on evaluation theory. Understanding approaches to evaluation is vital for this study because it informs the conceptual evaluation model presented in chapter 5 and therefore helps in answering the third research sub-question on *what elements are key for evaluating the efficacy of stakeholder engagement in ICT research projects?*

There is often confusion between the use of the terms 'theory' and 'approach' in evaluation (Donaldson and Lipsey, 2006; Taplin *et al.*, 2013) However, in this study the two are differentiated. Therefore an evaluation theory is understood as;

> *'A body of knowledge that organises, categorises, describes, predicts, explains, and otherwise aids in understanding and controlling an evaluation topic' (Shadish Jr. et al., 1991, p. 30).*

Whereas an evaluation approach is understood as;

> *'A broad conceptualisation about designing and conducting evaluation' (Stufflebeam and Coryn, 2014, p. 697).*

The focus of the literature reviewed on evaluation approaches is taken from the theory about social programme evaluation since this is where there is extensive coverage of these approaches (see Appendix 2-1). The evaluation approaches that are suggested in social programme evaluation theory share some ideas for evaluating stakeholder engagement activities. They share these ideas because the evaluation of social programs focus on evaluating people related practices and seek a valued understanding and improvement in the welfare of those involved (Cousins *et al.*, 2013; Nakrošis, 2014; Smith, 2015).

Despite a lack of literature that directly covers evaluation approaches in ICT research projects, the literature from other disciplines and contexts gives useful insights that can be used in ICT research projects. This claim is supported by Mark *et al.* (2006) and Smith (2015) who suggest that evaluation should employ approaches from multiple and diverse disciplines which can be used either method-by-method or as a mixed approach of evaluation to attain some knowledge about an evaluand. Therefore, it becomes imperative to review the approaches available and select those that can be used in evaluating the value of stakeholder engagement in ICT research projects in attaining socially desirable outcomes.

To that effect, the study looks at the work by Stufflebeam and Shinkfield (2007) and Stufflebeam and Coryn (2014) who collectively analyses 28 evaluation approaches that can be used in evaluation. Although the approaches suggested by Stufflebeam and Shinkfield (2007) and Stufflebeam and Coryn (2014) are given in programme evaluation literature, Stufflebeam and Shinkfield (2007) state that they can also be applied to broad range of evaluations which is similar to the suggestion by Mark *et al.* (2006) and Smith (2015). Out of the 28 approaches, the authors select approaches which are commonly used in literature such as case-based, experimental, objectives based, constructivist and utilisation focused approaches. These approaches are selected on the basis that they score high on evaluation standards such as utility, feasibility, propriety, accuracy and evaluation accountability (Stufflebeam and Coryn, 2014, pp. 230–233). A detailed discussion of these standards of evaluation is given in Appendix 2-2.

Also, some of the selected approaches by Stufflebeam and Shinkfield (2007) and Stufflebeam and Coryn (2014) match those suggested by Stern *et al.* (2012) as the most used approaches to evaluation. Comparatively, Stern *et al.* (2012) present evaluation approaches and their methodological emphasis when evaluating stakeholder engagement. However, Stern *et al.* (2012) suggest another commonly used evaluation approach that is missed out byStufflebeam and Coryn (2014) and Stufflebeam and Shinkfield (2007). The approach suggested by Stern*et al.* (2012) is the theory-based approach. Therefore, the common evaluation approaches suggested by Stufflebeam and Shinkfield (2007), Stufflebeam and Coryn (2014) and Stern *et al.* (2012) are summarised in Table 2.3 below. The evaluation approaches are presented with their methodological emphasis as suggested by Stern *et al.* (2012) and a brief description that is derived from the contributions from all authors mentioned above.

Table 2.3: Evaluation Approaches and their methodology (Adapted from Stern *et al.* (2012), Stufflebeam and Shinkfield (2007) and Stufflebeam and Coryn (2014))

Evaluation Approach	Description	Methodology Emphasis
Experimental approach	Evaluation that shows a causal relationship between participation and outcomes through a random assignment of participants to a treatment or intervention.	Quantitative
Statistical approach	Evaluation that involves examining the correlation between cause and effect or between variables and also influence of (usually) isolatable multiple causes on a single effect.	Quantitative
Theory-based approach	Evaluation that involves the identification and confirmation of causal processes or 'chains' between an evaluand and outcomes by looking at supporting factors and mechanisms at work in the context of the evaluand.	Qualitative
'Case-based' approach	Evaluation that is aimed at a comparison across and within cases of combinations of causal factors.	Mixed
Participatory approach	Evaluations involve the validation by participants that their actions and experienced effects are 'caused' by an evaluand.	Mixed
Synthesis studies	Evaluations involve assessing an evaluand through accumulation and aggregation within some perspectives such as statistical, theory-based and ethnographic.	Quantitative

The evaluation approaches shown in Table 3 above includes both qualitative and quantitative approaches. However, considering that the nature of this research, the focus is on three approaches that are relevant to a qualitative evaluation. These three include theory-based, case-based and participatory evaluation approaches.

According to Stern *et al.*, (2012) these designs can be used in evaluating impact which results from a particular intervention such as stakeholder engagement in a project. Therefore, based on these two reasons, they are ideal for consideration in evaluating the value of stakeholder engagement in ICT research projects. The following sub-sections present a review of the three approaches that are closely related to the qualitative evaluation of stakeholder engagement starting with the theory-based approach, followed by the case-based approach and finally participatory approach.

2.10.3.1 Theory-Based Approaches

The first approach to evaluation that is reviewed in this chapter is a Theory-based approach (TBA). The basis for TBA is that the assumptions and beliefs that are fundamental to an evaluand such as stakeholder engagement can be expressed in terms of a series of causes and effects (Weiss, 1997). Therefore, with TBA the evaluation looks at each component of the evaluand and uses collected data to understand how each component of the evaluand has contributed towards an intended change or outcome. With TBA the evaluation not only shows how much change has occurred but it also tells how the change occurred, therefore, highlighting areas along the line where there are failures that are affecting the intended outcomes (Weiss, 1997).

One drawback of the TBA is that there are issues in its clarity. For instance, the way the word '*theory*' is used in TBA can be confusing to some in terms of what it exactly means with regards to evaluation. Looking at the way the word '*theory*' is defined in the dictionary, the term means a set of assumptions or beliefs that are fundamental to an action or activities (Collins, 2016). Whereas in TBA, Stufflebeam and Shinkfield (2006) citing Scriven (1991) defines '*theory*' as;

'*General accounts of a field of phenomena which involves generating explanations and sometimes predictions and generalisations about an evaluand*' (2007, p.66).

In the same light, Donaldson and Lipsey (2006) mention that the use of the term '*theory*' in TBA includes a '*confusing mixture of concepts related to the notions about how evaluations should be conducted, explanatory frameworks for social phenomena and assumptions about how projects function*' (2006, p. 57).

The '*theory*' used in TBA includes '*commonly accepted assumptions*' (Weiss, 1997, p. 4). In terms of this study, these could be assumptions on which stakeholders that are engaged in ICT research projects plan and carry out their activities with regards to attainment of socially desirable outcomes, as an example.

TBA has been prevalently used in many stakeholder engagement research projects in the fields of economic development, health and education (Connell and Kubisch, 1998; Nakrošis, 2014; Rogers, 2008). However, very little was found from the literature that related to ICT research projects apart from some studies (Nash *et al.*, 2000; Scott, 2016) showing that there is an interest in using TBA in ICT or IT-related research. For instance, this emerging interest is evidenced by Scott (2016) who uses a Theory of Change (ToC). In Scott's study a ToC, which is a form of TBA, is combined with Random Controlled Trials (RCT) in evaluating stakeholder engagement in formulating policy on health IT.

In general, Weiss (1997) and (Nakrošis, 2014) mentions that TBA aims to describe the actual mechanisms that relate to desirable outcomes. In the case of this study, these mechanisms include the stakeholder engagement activities that take place in ICT research projects. For example, as an assumption, if stakeholder engagement is associated with increased ethical consideration in R&I within ICT research projects, the mechanism may be the 'consultation' and linkages might be the 'knowledge' and 'awareness' that the consultation provides. This kind of cause-and-effect process and the description of the mechanisms and their related outcomes are normally illustrated through construction of models that depicts how an evaluand work and they are used to guide the formulation of evaluation knowledge (Mayne, 2015; Shadish Jr. *et al.*, 1991; Weiss, 1997). Such a constructs are normally referred to as ToC (see sections 7.4, 8.4, 9.4 and 10.4).

2.10.3.1.1 What is a Theory of Change

In the literature, Theory of Change (ToC) is defined in a number of ways. For instance, Weiss (1997) defines ToC as;

> *'A theory of how and why an initiative works' (Weiss, 1997, p. 502).*

On the other hand, Kubisch and Connell (1998) define ToC as;

> *'A systematic and cumulative study of the links between activities, outcomes, and contexts of the evaluand' (1998, p. 2).*

Recently, Rogers (2016) defined ToC as;

> *'An explanation of how activities are understood to produce a series of results that contribute to achieving the final intended impact' (2014, p. 1).*

The cross-cutting theme in these definitions indicates that ToC can be used to evaluate stakeholder engagement by determining its intended outcomes, the engagement activities expected to achieve those outcomes and the contextual factors that may affect the implementation of activities (Mayne, 2012, p. 3).

ToC may be articulated in various ways and using different methods. There are four key approaches used to develop a ToC that is either researcher driven or Project driven (Laing and Todd, 2015; Rogers and Funnell, 2011). These approaches include;

i. A deductive approach in which the ToC is developed from existing research. This involves collating evidence from literature and existing knowledge about how the world works and simplified into steps of change.
ii. An Inductive approach in which the ToC is built from observing phenomena in action rather than relying on what is already known or assumed about how it works.
iii. A Mental approach in which the stakeholders who have their ideas about how things work are given the opportunity to express their knowledge and experience.
iv. A collaborative approach in which a ToC is co-created through collaboration between academic or evaluation expertise, that is based on

evidence from existing research and practice expertise that is based on stakeholders outlining their views of how things work.

Although there are strong advocates for TBA in evaluation such as Weiss (1997), Leeuw (2012), Mayne, (2012) and Nakrošis (2014), some notable authors of evaluation literature (Scriven, 2007; Scriven and Coryn, 2008; Stufflebeam, 2001; Stufflebeam and Coryn, 2014) have asserted that there is not much need for *theory* in evaluation. They claim that it is possible to undertake a good evaluation without a theory-based approach. Their claim is based on the premise that doing TBA is usually not feasible and it can be counter-productive if it fails. They also point out that because the assumptions used in developing theory can be different depending on who is conducting it, the results from a TBA can be very subjective and open to scrutiny and different interpretations.

This limitation is confirmed by Coryn *et al.* (2011) in their work in which they conducted a systematic review of theory-based evaluation over a ten year period from 1990 to 2009 (Coryn *et al.*, 2011). Coryn *et al.* (2011) argues against Weiss (1998) who mentions that a *theory* does not have to be true since it is based on the assumptions made by those involved in the evaluation which could be different if made by another person. The assertion by Weiss (1998) leaves the ToC open to bias and subjectivity of the evaluation findings.

However, despite this criticism, ToC is ideal in this study to show the link between the activities of stakeholders and the outcomes that depict socially desirable outcomes. The reason behind this argument is that in most cases the objectives of stakeholder engagement do not explicitly include the attainment of socially desirable outcomes in ICT research. Therefore, to effectively understand the connection between the stakeholder engagement and the attainment of such outcomes, a TBA which is based on assumptions of cause and effects sounds like a better approach to build a picture on the value of stakeholder engagement towards responsible outcomes in ICT research projects. In terms of the bias, this is addressed by using other researchers to check the analysis starting from coding all the way to the developed of ToCs.

Despite the currently ongoing academic debate about the application of TBA, Rogers (2014) and Taplin *et al.* (2013) argues that a TBA can be used to focus on the particular elements of a *theory* such as stakeholder engagement in ICT research projects. Therefore a ToC can help understand how these elements are linked to the whole story by showing linkages between activities and outcomes. According to Rogers (2014), emergent things are better evaluated using theory-based approaches such as ToC and considering that the socially desirable outcomes of stakeholder engagement in ICT research are emergent, using ToC sounds appropriate in understanding the causal links between the engagement and the outcomes that emerge from it.

2.10.3.1.2 *The premise for Considering Theory of Change in Evaluating Stakeholder Engagement*

In the literature, the two main strengths for using ToC in evaluating stakeholder engagement are surfaced by scholars (Mayne, 2012; Nakrošis, 2014; Rogers, 2014;

Sullivan, 2006 and Taplin *et al.*, 2013). Firstly, a ToC can improve stakeholder engagement by increasing the stakeholders' understanding of the intended outcomes of their engagement, the activities that need to be implemented to achieve those outcomes and the contextual factors that are likely to influence them (Connell and Kubisch, 1998; Mayne, 2016, 2001). Secondly, when an evaluation is based on a ToC, it can highlight for the stakeholders the critical outcomes they hope to achieve together with the avenues through which they expect to achieve them, which are the causal linkages between the two (Weiss, 1997; Leeuw, 2012).

Regardless of these strengths of using ToC in evaluating stakeholder engagement, there is a challenge as highlighted below.

2.10.3.1.3 Limitation of the using Theory of Change in Evaluating Stakeholder Engagement

One major drawback of ToC stems from the inability of many stakeholders to make plausible and non-contentious assumptions about linkages between their engagement activities and outcomes (Coryn *et al.*, 2011). The feasibility of the ToC is determined by the capacity of the project's stakeholders and evaluators to identify, prioritise, and then assess the key activities and contextual factors. In most cases, evaluators and stakeholders tend to look back on evaluand and then construct convincing tales of why a particular occurred or did not occur. This is a challenge in using ToC since the issues in an evaluation need to be prospectively theorised to have an effective evaluation (Connell and Kubisch, 1998).

However, in this study, this limitation is addressed by involving a participatory process that includes as wide a range of key stakeholders as practically possible. The stakeholders that were involved were given information on RRI and RI to help them make relevant assumptions to explain the R&I process and the linkages between their activities and the wider benefits, as well as how and why these activities are expected to bring benefits (see section 6.5 for a collective ToC).

2.10.3.2 Case-Based Approach

The second approach that is reviewed is the Case-based approach (CBA) to evaluation. According to Stufflebeam and Shinkfield (2014), CBA involves an in-depthexamination of the case(s) by studying, analysing and describing the case(s) as fully as possible. A case might be a project, some component of a project, a process, a situation and experiences of stakeholders. Relating to this study, a case is the ICT research project in which the stakeholder engagement in taking place. Under CBA the case's context, goals, plans, resources, features, significance, actions, needs problems and other topics are examined (2014, p. 293). There is wide use of CBA in evaluating research projects including ICT research projects with stakeholder engagement (Ondego and Moturi, 2016; Russell *et al.*, 2015). A large and growing body of literature has suggested that CBA involve preparation of in-depth descriptive evaluation information and judgemental perceptions held by different stakeholders and their conclusions within the context ofthe evaluand. Many scholars hold the view that CBA is not confined to a tightly controlled, formalised data collection and analysis, therefore, it is interpretive and connected to grounded theory and ethnography (Khan *et al.*, 2013; Northcote, 2012; Ondego and Moturi, 2016; Smith, 2015).

Although CBA is not tightly confined to formalised data collection and analysis, it does not mean that it is prone to ill decision making when evaluating. CBA can be valuablein evaluating because the information collected within a representational setting includes contextual information that can help understand the evaluand better (Stufflebeam and Shinkfield, 2007). Another important point inferred from Benbasat (1997) is that CBA is appropriate for understanding particular phenomena especially those where research, practice and theory are at their formative stages, and the experiences of actors are important in formulating practice within a context of action. In particular, the suggestion by Benbasat (1997) relates to the subject matter of the study because the theory and practice of RRI and its related stakeholder engagement in ICT research projects are still going through its formative stages. However, despite this novelty, the actions of the actors involved takes place within a context of action, and according to Mark *et al.* (2006), the context is critical in understanding the evaluand (Mark *et al.*, 2006, p. 155), which in this case is the value of stakeholder engagement.

Considering that the study uses a sample of cases (see chapters 7 to 10), using CBA is vital in learning and developing knowledge of stakeholder engagement and the attainment of socially desirable outcomes which can be generalised to other ICT research projects as pointed out by Smith (2015). Smith (2015) points out that *'case-based findings can be generalised regarding validity to the extent that one can specify similar cases of application in terms of setting, problem, evaluand, etc. Case-based findings can also be generalised to the practice of others if one can identify the conditions under which, and causal mechanisms by which, the new practice is effective" (p.71).*

However, one key limitation with CBA to evaluation is the selection of data sources. To support this criticism, Stufflebeam and Coryn (2014) gives an example of *'interview samples which can sometimes be non-representative'* (Stufflebeam and Coryn, 2014, p. 293) despite the approach being effective in contextual evaluation and understanding. In this study, this limitation is addressed by using purposive and snowballing sampling to identify and recruit interview representative participants (see section 6.9.1).

2.10.3.3 Participatory Approach

The third approach reviewed in this section is the Participatory approach (PA) to evaluation. According to Greene (2006), PA engages micro-politics of power through the involvement of stakeholders in the evaluation process (Greene, 2006, p. 125). In PA, stakeholders are involved in evaluation implementation, interpretation and putting evaluation findings into action (Cousins *et al.*, 2013; Cousins and Whitmore, 1998). As a consequence, PA involves a learning process through which stakeholders produce action-oriented knowledge about their reality, clarify and articulate their norms and values, and reach consensus about further action (Cousins and Whitmore, 1998).

The main aim of PA as an approach to evaluation is to provide agency and empowerment towards the wider ideal of social change in the distribution of power and privilege among stakeholders involved in evaluating a specific subject (Greene, 2006). As it is the case with the other two approaches, the central role of this approach is knowledge production. However, the contrasting feature is that participatory approaches '*give control of that knowledge production to the people or stakeholders who are subjects of the evaluation thereby giving them power*' (Cousins and Earl, 1992, p. 400)

Similarly to the other two approaches to evaluation reviewed above, PA has been used widely in education research projects (Brunner and Guzman, 1989; Tan *et al.*, 2009, 2013), international development (Campbell *et al.*, 2014; Pouw *et al.*, 2017) and in ICT research projects (Demiris *et al.*, 2008; Pouw *et al.*, 2017). As such, due to the wide use of the approach, there is a lot that can be learnt by this research.

Considering that the research involves participatory practices and the phenomenon of interest relates to such practices, PA is also appropriate as an approach to follow and therefore has potential to inform the model for evaluating stakeholder engagement in ICT research projects. Nevertheless, there are issues with the approach that potentially affected this research.

For instance, one of the issues with PA is the concern about who participates in the evaluation process. There is an issue of the balance of power between the evaluators and the participants and the diversity of the participants in the evaluation (Cousins *et al.*, 2013). Considering that the evaluation in this study was research-based, the responses of some of the participants was affected by the balance of power between the researcher and the key stakeholders that were needed to provide information for an effective evaluation of their engagement (Billings, 2016; Cousins and Whitmore, 1998, p. 398).

Despite the challenge mentioned above, PA is valuable in assessing stakeholder attitudes, expectations and decision-making in the research projects. The understanding of stakeholder attitudes and expectations is critical in assessing the impact and effectiveness of stakeholder engagement. Additionally, using a PA to evaluation encourages ownership of the outcomes among the stakeholders that are participating in the evaluation process (Cousins *et al.*, 2013; Cousins and Whitmore, 1998). This ownership of outcomes is fundamental to the attainment of socially desirable outcomes in R&I and therefore important to consider when evaluating stakeholder engagement in the context of RRI.

The limitations of each approach are addressed by combining evaluation approaches to address the limitations posed by one or the other as suggested by Smith (2015). As a consequence, this study embraces all these three approaches in informing the proposed evaluation model for evaluating stakeholder engagement in ICT research projects. All the three approaches will bring their weaknesses in evaluating stakeholder engagement, but each of the selected approach will address the weakness by the other, for example, the assumptions made as part of using a TBA will be made stronger by CBA's contextual outlook (see section 5.4 for a further discussion).

On one hand, as Stern *et al.* (2012) suggested, CBA and PA are well suited for this research because it is based on interpretivism (see section 4.4), focusing on the interpretation of responses of stakeholders engaged in the case studies (see chapter 5). On the other hand, this study uses TBA because it offers a means to make assumptions and beliefs that are fundamental to stakeholder engagement that can be expressed in terms of a series of causes and effects, that is, how stakeholder engagement influences responsible outcomes in ICT research projects. This helps this study to understand and evaluate the activities that occur as part of the stakeholder engagement with respect to socially desirable outcomes.

2.11 Evaluating Stakeholder Engagement within the context of RRI

Although extensive research has been carried out on the evaluation of stakeholder engagement in many contexts of research projects including those involved with ICT (Cullen *et al.*, 2007; Khan *et al.*, 2013; Reed, 2015; Rowe and Frewer, 2000), no single study exists which specifically looks at the evaluation of stakeholder engagement through the lens of RRI. Evaluating stakeholder engagement by using the RRI lens is necessary to understand how stakeholder engagement plays a role in the attainment of socially desirable and acceptable outcomes in ICT research. This will help in improving the implementation of responsible innovation in ICT research. Evaluating stakeholder engagement in light of RRI provides a reflection point for both theory and practice. This then affords stakeholders in ICT research projects to understand their role in dealing with the potentially adverse effects of R&I and hence improve on ways of dealing with them. Despite such possible benefits of evaluating stakeholder engagement within the context of RRI, the current literature has little to say about evaluating stakeholder engagementin light of RRI.

As discussed in section 2.9 of this book, RRI in ICT research projects ensures that R&I activities and outcomes should be acceptable and desirable and one way of achieving such goals is by engaging stakeholders to address the grand societal challenges that concern the society.

This then raises a need for understanding and assessing whether, and inwhat way the engaged stakeholders are likely to address these grand societal challenges. Many scholars (Billings, 2016; Greene, 2006; Cousins and Whitmore, 1998 ;) hold the view that evaluation provides an understanding of stakeholder engagement in research projects and the outcomes that result from it. Equally, evaluating stakeholder engagement within the context of RRI may be useful for understanding the outcomes that relate to the attainment of responsible outcomes and support framing stakeholder engagement in future ICT research projects. This means that evaluating stakeholder engagement in light of RRI may support understanding the activities that promote the attainment of socially desirable outcomes and the barriers that impede stakeholders' from contributing towards them in ICT research projects.

2.12 Conclusion

This chapter has given an overview of research projects and narrowed them down to those that use ICT to deal with societal challenges. When it comes to dealing with societal challenges, stakeholders play an important role therefore the chapter reviewed literature on stakeholder engagement in order to firstly, understand what the concept pf stakeholder means for ICT research projects. To that effect it covered the stakeholder engagement process by looking at the stakeholder identification. Further the chapter covered the concept of RRI which advocates the engagement of stakeholders in research to achieve outcomes that are good for society. Under RRI, the chapter looked at different accounts of RRI with an aim to determine an RRI lens that could be used to as benchmark for understanding the value of stakeholder engagement towards the attainment of desirable goals.

Towards the end, the chapter looked at the evaluation of stakeholder engagement in research projects. The chapter began by discussing the rationale for conducting an evaluation and consequently recognised the two main reasons that emerged from the literature reviewed. The two main reasons for evaluation are an improvement of practice and generation of knowledge. The latter is more relevant to this research since it aimsto understand the efficacy of stakeholder engagement with regards to the attainment of socially desirable and acceptable outcomes in ICT research projects. The chapter then reviewed commonly used definitions of evaluation and explained the meaning of evaluation in relation to this study. It then went on to present the existing evaluation approaches and selected three approaches that are ideal for a qualitative evaluation of stakeholder engagement. The three evaluation approaches that were selected and discussed include theory-based, case-based and participatory approaches. The chapter finished by arguing that in order to evaluate stakeholder engagement in ICT research projects, these three approaches should be combined to address a broader array of stakeholder engagement elements. The next chapter presents a conceptual evaluation model that was informed by the literature reviewed as an attempt to address the gap in knowledge identified thus far.

CHAPTER

3

Conceptual Evaluation Model

3.1 INTRODUCTION

This chapter presents the conceptual model for evaluating stakeholder engagement in ICT research projects. The conceptual evaluation model is aimed at understanding the efficacy of stakeholder engagement towards the attainment of socially desirable outcomes using the concept of RRI. The RRI concept allows for a methodological evaluation and analysis of the value of stakeholder engagement towards the outcomes. The model is derived from the theoretical insights from the literature reviewed in chapter 2 and is later validated through the empirical insights from the cases in chapter 5. It follows an analysis of the literature in chapter 2 which covers stakeholder engagement in ICT research projects and chapter 3 on responsible research and innovation in ICT research projects. Further, the model integrates the three approaches to evaluation discussed in chapter 2. These three evaluation approaches include Theory-based approach (TBA), with a particular focus on the theory of change (ToC), Case-based approach (CBA) and Participatory approach (PA). The main aim of the conceptual evaluation model is to construct a holistic understanding of the key elements for evaluating the efficacy of stakeholder engagement in ICT research projects. In so doing, this chapter addresses the following sub-research question: *What identifiable elements are key for evaluating the efficacy of stakeholder engagement in ICT research projects?* Hence, section 3.2 of this chapter presents the premise for developing the conceptual evaluation model. This is followed by section 3.3 which identifies the key elements for evaluating stakeholder engagement. Section 3.4 then discusses how the combination of the chosen three evaluation approaches (see section 2.10.3) is used in evaluating stakeholder engagement in ICT research projects. The section highlights that a TBA could be used to evaluate the key elements that include nature, rationale and outcomes of stakeholder engagement. The section further indicates the elements that could be evaluated using a CBA, which includes the context of the stakeholder engagement and stakeholder identification. Since the evaluation model that is proposed involves stakeholders participating in the evaluation, particularly when collecting data (empirical insights), the model also includes a PA to inform both the CBA and TBA in evaluating the five key elements identified above and discussed in section 3.3. Section 3.5 discusses the application of an RRI lens in evaluating and understanding the efficacy of the stakeholder engagement in ICT research projects with regards to achieving responsible outcomes. Towards the end of the chapter, section 3.6 presents an illustration of the developed conceptual evaluation model.

3.2 Premise for Developing a Conceptual Evaluation Model

Some existing models are used in evaluating different aspects of stakeholder engagement (see section 2.10.3), but there is a need for more options to cover those aspects that are emergent. To be more specific, there is need to seek alternative models to evaluate the efficacy of stakeholder engagement in different contexts, such as responsible innovation in order to develop theory and practice. A review of available literature on evaluating stakeholder engagement in ICT research projects yielded very little. Most of the literature focussed on evaluating stakeholder engagement in research projects in light of efficiency or quality improvement (Cullen *et al.*, 2007; Khan *et al.*, 2013; Reed, 2015; Rowe and Frewer, 2000). Some referred to the evaluation of stakeholder engagement in other research fields other than ICT, for example, evaluating stakeholder engagement in healthcare research (Esmail *et al.*, 2015).

Although these indicate evidence of a few studies on evaluating stakeholder engagement in research projects, most of published research with a stakeholder engagement dimension does not include an evaluation component (Smith, 2015). This indicates a gap in knowledge within the field of evaluation.

With regards to evaluation theory, developing a conceptual evaluation model such as the one covered in this chapter presents a nuanced way of evaluating the value of stakeholder engagement. Such a contribution is supported by Smith (2015) who mentions that '*instead of only describing current methods or comparing existing approaches, researchers should also conduct research that creates new forms of evaluation and adds knowledge about evaluation practice more generally*' (Smith, 2015, p. 71).

Further, there is also a scarcity of research on evaluating stakeholder engagement within the context of RRI, particularly in ICT research. Therefore, the developed conceptual evaluation model supplements the existing evaluation and RRI discourse and helps in addressing the scarcity of the research mentioned above. As discussed in chapter 2, stakeholders play a significant role in attaining desirable outcomes in research projects including those dealing with ICT, and their engagement towards such responsible outcomes in ICT research (see section 2.4). Therefore, an evaluation of their engagement is crucial to understand their role and learn about how their engagement could be improved.

However, stakeholder engagement is a broad phenomenon, therefore, to effectively evaluate it, its key elements have to be identified. Focussing on the key elements for evaluating stakeholder engagement will provide a more in-depth understanding and more focused approach than evaluating the phenomenon as a whole. Therefore, the next section will identify and discuss the elements that are key in evaluating stakeholder engagement in ICT research projects.

3.3 Key Elements for Evaluating Stakeholder Engagement

Evaluation provides knowledge and understanding of stakeholder engagement in ICT research projects. From the interviews (see Appendix 4-1) and the literature review for both stakeholder engagement and evaluation, five key elements for evaluating stakeholder engagement in ICT research projects are identified. As a result, to effectively evaluate stakeholder engagement in ICT research projects it is necessary to understand the following elements that are outlined in Table 3.1.

Table 3.1: Key elements for evaluating stakeholder engagement and their sources

	Key element	Indicative Source of insight
i.	The identification of stakeholders to engage in ICT research projects	• Sections 2.4.4 and 2.9 • Interview Questions 1, 2, 3, 4, 7
ii.	The context in which the stakeholder engagement is taking place	• Sections 2.5, 2.10.3.2 and 2.11 • Interview questions 4, 6, 9
iii.	The nature of stakeholder engagement activities taking place	• Sections 2.5, 2.8.1 and 2.10.3.1 • Interview questions 3, 4, 5
iv.	The rationale for engaging the stakeholders that have been identified	• Sections 2.5 and 2.10.3 • Interview questions 6, 7, 10
v.	The outcomes that result from the engagement	• Sections 2.5, 2.6, 2.10.3.1 and 2.10.3.3 • Interview questions 7, 8

Table 4 above, presents the identified key elements for evaluating stakeholder engagement in ICT research projects and their theoretical and empirical sources. These key elements are discussed below.

3.3.1 Context of the Stakeholder Engagement

In evaluating the efficacy of stakeholder engagement in ICT research projects, it is important to have an understanding of the context of the stakeholder engagement which involves understanding the details of the ICT research projects in which the stakeholders are engaged. To evaluate and gain an understanding of contextual details of the research projects, a CBA is well suited. With CBA, knowledge of the context is gained by undertaking an in-depth examination of the case(s) to study, analyse and describe the case(s) as fully as possible. This involves focussing on understanding the case's context, goals, resources, and features (2014, p. 293). In addition, evaluating the context of the stakeholder engagement involves an understanding of the setting in which the stakeholder engagement is taking place. Understanding the setting includes defining the parameters of what ICT research Project 4s aiming to achieve so that it supports the motive behind engaging the stakeholders (see section 3.2.5) with regards to the objectives of the ICT research project.

3.3.2 Identification of Stakeholders

The second element for evaluating the efficacy of stakeholder engagement is the identification of stakeholders. This is important because evaluating the process of stakeholder identification in ICT research projects provide an understanding of which stakeholders are crucial and what roles they will play in contributing towards different aspects of the projects such as the attainment of responsible outcomes. Once these roles are understood, it can help understand how these individual roles support the attainment of socially desirable outcomes, for example. Regarding the attainment of socially desirable outcomes, stakeholder engagement is paramount (see sections 2.5 and 2.8.1). Stakeholders have to be identified and assigned roles that will have influence towards the attainment of socially desirable and acceptable outcomes in the R&I process.

It is important to evaluate and gain an understanding of the process of identification together with the reasons behind the decisions made in the identification process (see Sections 3.3.3 and 3.2.5), because the evaluation provides knowledge that is used to improve future stakeholder identification and engagement efforts. This is then beneficial in effective engagement of stakeholders in achieving long-term outcomes (see section, 3.3.5) for instance, concerning socially desirable and acceptable outcomes. When evaluating this element, these aspects could be taken into account; the process of identification, range and disciplines of stakeholders (see section 2.4.3 and 2.4.4).

3.3.3 Nature of the Stakeholder Engagement

The third element for evaluating the efficacy of stakeholder engagement in ICT research projects is the nature of the stakeholder engagement. Under the nature of stakeholder engagement, the evaluation focuses on the stakeholder engagement activities or input to the ICT research projects, for example, with respect to the attainment of sociallydesirable outcomes. As mentioned in section 2.10.3.1 on TBA, it is important that the input of the stakeholders be evaluated to understand the cause and effect of their engagement in the ICT research projects.

The input of the engaged stakeholders could be the different forms of stakeholder engagement activities as highlighted in the literature in section 2.5 above. These could include knowledge co-creation, facilitating reflection on responsible innovation and bringing awareness to responsibility issues in ICT research projects. With regards to the stakeholder engagement activities, it is important to assess whether the activities are relevant in attaining the objectives of ICT research projects and are therefore in line with assumptions for engaging the stakeholders concerning a specific aspect such as attainment of desirable outcomes.

3.3.4 Rationale for the Stakeholder Engagement

The fourth element for evaluating the efficacy of stakeholder engagement in ICT research projects is the rationale for stakeholder engagement. Under this element, the evaluation focuses on understanding the motivation behind stakeholder engagement in ICT research projects. Understanding the rationale for stakeholder engagement is important because it clarifies the assumptions for engaging the stakeholders and the expectations for both the project sponsors and the stakeholders, for instance, with respect to the attainment of responsible outcomes. These assumptions could be made clear bythe responses given by the participant stakeholders, for example through interviews (see sections 2.10.3 and 4.9.1). They could also be made clear by looking at the objectives of the stakeholder engagement if they are outlined in project documents (see section 2.10.3, 3.3.1 and 4.9.2).

Once the assumptions are clear, it could be possible to spell out what the rationale for engaging the stakeholders is and how it addresses the objectives of engaging stakeholders towards achieving certain outcomes. There are numerous examples given on what the rationale for stakeholder engagement could be in ICT research projects (See Sections 2.5 and 2.9). For instance, from the perspective of socially desirable outcomes, the rationale for engaging stakeholders may be based on the assumption that stakeholders are engaged to pre-empt societal concerns and provide innovative suggestions to the dilemmas of R&I in ICT, and therefore it could be beneficial for the long-term outcomes of the ICT research projects. Thus, to understand how the long-term outcomes are achieved through stakeholder engagement, there is need to understand why the stakeholders are engaged in the first place and the expectations for their engagement, for example.

3.3.5 Outcome of the Stakeholder Engagement

The last element for evaluating the efficacy of stakeholder engagement in ICT research projects is the outcome of the stakeholder engagement. Evaluating this element provides an understanding of the less tangible results which may include ownership of solutions, responsible technology diffusion, stakeholder capacity building and enhanced democracy within the processes of R&I. Within the context of RRI, they may also cover the inclusion of diverse ideas and perspectives on responsible innovation, mutual learning and increased sustainable innovation (see sections 2.5 and 3.2).

So far, this chapter has discussed the premise for developing a conceptual evaluation model for evaluating the efficacy of stakeholder engagement in ICT research projects. The chapter has also outlined the five key elements for evaluating stakeholder engagement in ICT research projects. The section that follows discusses thecombination of the evaluation approaches that are part of the conceptual evaluation model presented in this chapter.

3.4 Combined Approaches for Evaluating Stakeholder Engagement

Many studies (Cullen *et al.*, 2007; Khan *et al.*, 2013; Reed, 2015; Rowe and Frewer, 2000) suggest that evaluation is vital in understanding and assessing the importance of stakeholder engagement. However, to gain a holistic understanding of the importance of stakeholder engagement, particularly in the attainment of socially desirable outcomes, a combination of the evaluation approaches suggested in the literature (see section 2.10.3) is recommended. Hence, the conceptual evaluation model covered in this chapter involves a combination of three approaches that have been highlighted in chapter 4 which are TBA, CBA and PA.

Firstly, applying TBA in evaluating stakeholder engagement is useful to understand the nature of stakeholder engagement. Under the nature of stakeholder engagement, TBA supports an understanding of the form of stakeholder engagement activities and the barriers that affect effective stakeholder engagement within the ICT research projects (see section 3.3.3). TBA is also used to understand the rationale for stakeholder engagement in the ICT research projects. Using TBA, assumptions made by the stakeholders and the evaluator(s) are used to understand the rationale of stakeholder engagement. These assumptions are informed by beliefs of those participating in the evaluation (see section 3.3.4). Thus, the assumptions made under a TBA include that there are a series of causes and effects of stakeholder engagement. The causes can be expressed in terms of engagement activities (input) that are related to a particular aspect, for instance, responsible innovation and the effects can be expressed in terms of the related outcomes that result from those engagement activities. Under TBA, the evaluation looks at the causal linkages between the nature of stakeholder engagement and the outcomes which is often shown as a ToC.

Secondly, CBA is used to understand the context of the stakeholder engagement. This approach is used to understand the contextual information about the ICT research projects, which are the cases in which the stakeholder engagement is taking place (see section 3.3.1). CBA is also used to evaluate the stakeholder engagement process, specifically gaining an understanding of the identification of the stakeholders that are engaged in the ICT research projects (see section 3.3.2).

Lastly, PA is valuable in understanding the stakeholders' attitudes, expectations and assumptions in ICT research projects. PA is ideal because the conceptual evaluation model developed involves the participation of stakeholders that are engaged in the case ICT research projects. As part of understanding their engagement, stakeholders are expected to provide information that validates that their actions and experiences affect the outcomes of stakeholder engagement in the ICT research projects. Therefore, the stakeholders in the ICT research projects are involved in the evaluation and learn from it. As a result of PA's capabilities to facilitate learning and being informative, the other two approaches are also informed and supported by PA.

Additionally, PA is valuable because the data collected for understanding the stakeholder engagement and building the related *'theory'* (as in TBA's theory of change) involve stakeholders that are engaged in the ICT research projects. Therefore, the use of PA facilitates a learning process through which stakeholders produce action-oriented knowledge about their engagement with respect to the attainment of socially desirable outcomes and how they can further understand their role towards the outcomes. The knowledge gained through the use CBA and PA is then conveyed by the use of TBA which expresses the series of causes (activities) and effects (outcomes) of the stakeholder engagement in a ToC which is informed by the assumptions of all that are involved in the evaluation. Thus, the combination of approaches provides a wider understanding of stakeholder engagement in ICT research projects.

There are merits for combining the three approaches to evaluate stakeholderengagement in ICT research projects. The use of CBA compliments TBA by providing a rich understanding of the context in which TBA is being employed. Also, CBA helps to define the construct validity, that is, the degree to which the constructed theory confirms what it claims to be representing, in a way that makes sense to stakeholders in the case projects (Stern *et al.*, 2012). For that reason, CBA contributes towards building the *'theory'* and validates the ToC.

Another merit for a combined approach to evaluating stakeholder engagement is that it helps to examine the validity of the evaluation outcome through triangulation. For example, Donaldson and Lipsey (2006) advocate embracing a diversity of evaluation approaches as a way forward with evaluation due to different circumstances and characteristics of the issues that the evaluation is being subjected to. The authors argue that combining approaches gives the flexibility that is necessary to cover diverse perspectives in evaluating an evaluand such as stakeholder engagement. As pointed out earlier, this means that when developing and expressing a *'theory'* using TBA, CBA and PA can be used to determine if the *'theory'* is plausible.

All these three approaches, will individually bring their weaknesses together, but at the same time, each will address the weakness brought in by the other. This is why the conceptual evaluation model combines TBA, CBA and PA to capitalise on their features and address the limitations of each of the approaches by exploiting the strengths of the other.

To sum up this section, Figure 3.1 below shows the five key elements for evaluating stakeholder engagement and the evaluation approach that primarily addresses each of them. Therefore, figure depicts a confluence of three approaches for evaluating stakeholder engagement in ICT research projects.

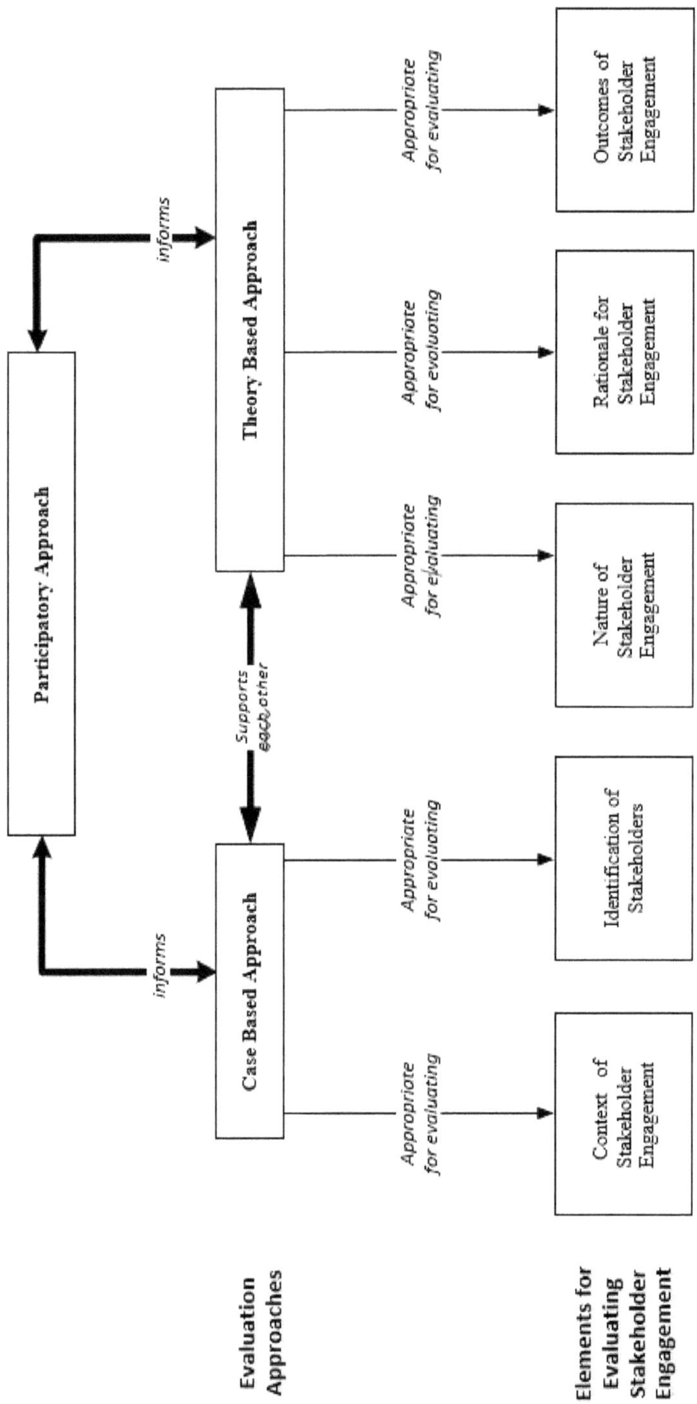

Figure 3.1: Confluence of Approaches in Evaluating Stakeholder Engagement

Figure 3.1 above shows the connection between the three evaluation approaches. It illustrates that both CBA and TBA support each other in evaluating and gaining an understanding of the five elements for evaluating stakeholder engagement in ICT research projects. The figure also indicates that the two approaches, TBA and CBA are informed by a PA and vice versa. However, the figure illustrates that although all the three approaches can be used in evaluating stakeholder engagement, specific approaches are more suitable for particular elements for evaluating stakeholder engagement than the others due to their features, strengths and limitations. For example, a CBA is more appropriate in evaluating the context of stakeholder engagement compared to outcomes of stakeholder engagement which is better understood by using a TBA.

This section has argued why the conceptual evaluation model includes three evaluation approaches. It has analysed the three approaches to evaluating stakeholder engagement and has argued that for a holistic and triangulated evaluation of stakeholder engagement in ICT research projects, three approaches should be combined. Since the developed conceptual evaluation model is specifically aimed at evaluating the efficacy of stakeholder engagement in ICT research projects towards the attainment of socially desirable outcomes, the following section brings in a perspective that relates to responsible innovation in the evaluation by discussing the application of an RRI lens.

3.5 Applying the RRI Lens

As discussed earlier, stakeholder engagement is paramount in the attainment of socially desirable outcomes. When it comes to socially desirable or responsible outcomes, RRI is at the forefront in promoting R&I that translates into such outcomes. Therefore, in order to understand the efficacy of stakeholder engagement in attaining the outcomes, it is important to evaluate it in the context of RRI (see sections 2.9 and 2.11). Evaluating stakeholder engagement in the context of RRI provides knowledge and also facilitates learning and reflection on how stakeholder engagement can effectively support the attainment of socially desirable and acceptable outcomes in ICT research projects. Thus, integrating RRI theory to the evaluation of stakeholder engagement, *viz.* applying the RRI lens, provides a novel way of understanding stakeholder engagement in ICT research projects.

Applying the RRI lens in evaluating stakeholder engagement in ICT research projects involves relating the four key features of RRI (see section 2.8) to the different key elements for evaluating stakeholder engagement identified in section 3.3 above. The application means exploring stakeholder engagement through the lens of RRI by looking for and providing practical examples of its implementation through an evaluative analysis. The reason behind applying the RRI lens in evaluating stakeholder engagement in ICT research projects is twofold. Firstly, it addresses a gap in knowledge and practice in evaluating the stakeholder engagement in the attainment of socially desirable outcomes in ICT research projects. Secondly, applying the RRI lens in the evaluation of stakeholder engagement highlights how stakeholders address the increasingly crossing of R&I and collective stewardship in addressing impacts of ICT research.

To recap, the RRI lens that is applied in evaluating stakeholder engagement comprises of the following features that are summarised in Table 5 below and have been discussed in detail in section 3.3 of this book.

Table 3.2: Features of the RRI lens for Evaluating Stakeholder Engagement

Key RRI feature	Brief description and necessity
Engagement of stakeholders	This about involving a wide range of actors at an early stage in the R&I process that is being implemented in the ICT research projects. This includes the deliberation and decision-making to yield more useful and higher quality knowledge and expertise. Under this feature, the identification of stakeholders to engage and when to engage them is crucial since it determines the breadth of stakeholder disciplines, backgrounds, perspectives and expertise.
Openness and transparency	This involves communicating in a balanced, meaningful way the methodologies and methods used in the ICT research projects, the results and outcomes of the processes that are being implemented in the projects and implications of the projects. It looks at enabling open stakeholder scrutiny and dialogue. Applying this feature assesses the visibility and understanding of responsible research and its related issues within the R&I process in the ICT research projects.
Anticipation and reflection	This involves envisioning impacts and reflecting on the underlying assumptions, values, and purposes to better understand how R&I that is being implemented in the ICT research projects shape the future. This is important in evaluating stakeholder engagement because it provides valuable insights and increases the stakeholders' capacity to act on what they know and make improvements if necessary.
Responsiveness	This is about being able to modify ways of thought and behaviour in response to changing and emerging circumstances, knowledge, views, norms and perspectives. This is crucial in the evaluation because it aligns actions with the needs expressed by stakeholders and society as a whole. Thus, responsiveness is a prerequisite for adaptive change. As part of RRI, responsiveness is about having a capacity to change or shape existing routines of thought and behaviour but also the overarching structures and systems in response to new insights, changing circumstances, and stakeholder values.

The Table 3.2 above summarises the four key features of RRI that emerged from chapter 3 and describes what each feature relates to when evaluating stakeholder engagement. For instance, in applying 'engagement of stakeholders,' the evaluation provides knowledge to support an understanding of how the stakeholders were identified and what sort of roles they play as part of their engagement in the ICT research project, for example, with regards to responsible outcomes.

Thus far, the chapter has covered the premise for developing a conceptual evaluation model and identified the key elements for evaluation stakeholder engagement. Also, the chapter has discussed why evaluating stakeholder engagement should combine three evaluation approaches. It has also discussed the application of an RRI lens to evaluate stakeholder engagement in ICT research project. Having looked at all the above, the chapter now brings everything together to illustrate the developed conceptual model for evaluating the efficacy of stakeholder engagement towards the attainment of socially desirable outcomes in the section that follows.

3.6 The Conceptual Evaluation Model

In the conceptual evaluation model illustrated in Figure 3.2 above, three evaluation approaches have been adopted, PA, CBA and TBA. Using a PA, the model involves stakeholders who provide essential information used in the evaluation. PA informs the two approaches that are CBA and TBA and vice versa in generating knowledge from the stakeholders (see section 3.3). The knowledge generated is then used for learning and reflection by different stakeholders that are engaged in the ICT research projects.

In addition to the three evaluation approaches, the model includes five key elements for evaluating stakeholder engagement. The first element relates to understanding the context of the engagement and therefore uses CBA to understand boundary for the engagement, expectations and views of stakeholders on their engagement and their awareness about the issues that they are engaged for. The second element also uses a CBA to evaluate the identification of the stakeholders that are engaged in the ICT research projects. In evaluating this element, CBA helps in studying, analysing and describing the stakeholder identification process.

The conceptual evaluation model incorporates the three evaluation approaches that were deemed appropriate for evaluating stakeholder engagement (see section 4.4). It also includes the five key elements for evaluating stakeholder engagement in ICT research projects (see section 3.3). The model indicates the evaluation approaches that are appropriate for each of these five key elements based on the characteristics, strengths and limitations of the approaches (see section 4.4) and the focus of the elements (see section 3.3). Further, the model includes an RRI lens which is applied to the five key elements to understand the significance of stakeholder engagement in ICT research projects towards responsible outcomes (see section 5.4). For illustration purposes, Figure 3.2 below is provided to depict the developed evaluation model.

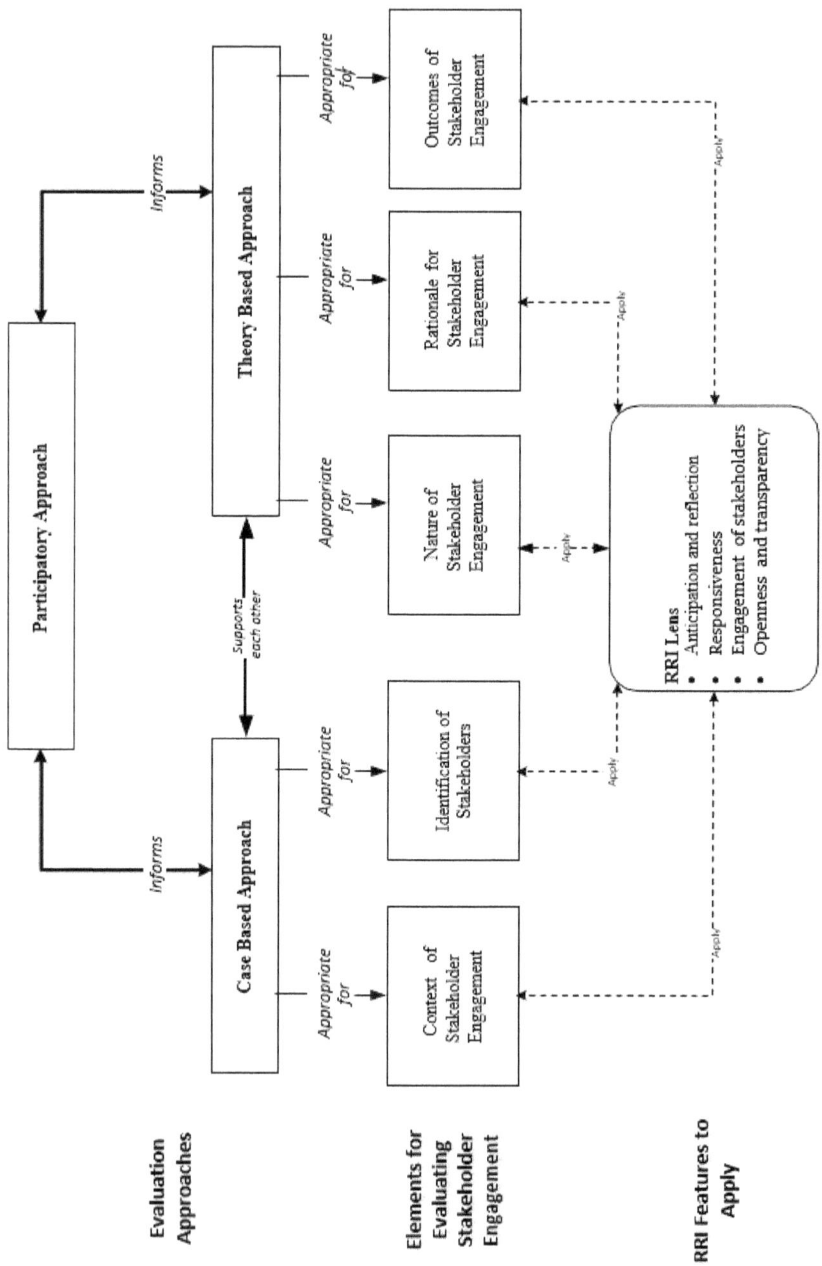

Figure 3.2: Model for Evaluating Stakeholder Engagement within the Context of RRI

Figure 3.2 above, also indicates that TBA is appropriate for the third, fourth and fifth elements for evaluating stakeholder engagement. Under the third element, the approach is used to understand the nature of stakeholder engagement and how it has contributed towards outcomes that are socially desirable. With the fourth element, TBA is used to make and understand the assumptions and beliefs that stakeholder engagement can cause effects that manifest within ICT research projects and therefore understand the motivation behind engaging stakeholders. Lastly, with regards to the fifth element, TBA is used to understand the assumed outcomes of stakeholder engagement and provide a link between the nature of stakeholder engagementand the outcomes, for instance, the socially desirable outcomes.

Since the conceptual evaluation model that is presented in this chapter is mainly intended for evaluating the value of stakeholder engagement towards responsible outcomes, it also includes an RRI lens which is an application of the four key RRI features (see sections 2.8 and 3.5) to the suggested five elements for evaluating stakeholder engagement. As stated earlier, this involves relating the four key RRI features in the evaluation process in order to understand the efficacy of stakeholder engagement with regards to responsible outcomes and how it supports the attainment of socially desirable and acceptable outcomes in ICT research projects.

Using the developed conceptual evaluation model, a theory of change (ToC) could then be constructed to describe and explain the influence of stakeholder engagement on the attainment of socially desirable outcomes in ICT research projects. The construction of the ToC fromthis evaluation model is based on the assumptions made from the stakeholder engagement. For example, the assumption could be that once the rationale for engaging stakeholders is understood, then relevant stakeholders necessary to address that rationale should be identified for engagement. If the identification is right, the stakeholders then undertake different forms of engagement activities which then result in intermediate outcomes that later translate into long-term socially desirable outcomes.

3.7 CONCLUSION

This chapter began by discussing the premise for developing a conceptual model for evaluating stakeholder engagement. It argued that there be a gap in knowledge on evaluating the efficacy of stakeholder engagement towards the attainment of socially desirable outcomes in ICT research and innovation. The chapter then identified five key elements for evaluating stakeholder engagement in ICT research projects. The chapter then argued that to effectively evaluate stakeholder engagement in ICT research projects, three evaluation approaches that include PA, CBA and TBA should be combined. These combined evaluation approaches could then be used to understand the five key elements for evaluating stakeholder engagement depending on the appropriateness of the approach. Further, the chapter discussed that to evaluate stakeholder engagement with regards to attainment of socially desirable or responsible outcomes, the evaluation model should include an application of an RRI lens which is made of four key features of RRI. The chapter then suggested using a ToC to explain the influence of stakeholder engagement in ICT research projects towards achieving socially desirable outcomes. The next chapter presents the research design that was used in this study to answer the research questions.

CHAPTER 4

Research Design

4.1 Introduction

This chapter describes the research design used to answer the research questions that were introduced in chapter 1 of this book (see section 1.5). Research involves a systematic process in which a subject carries out rigorous, methodical scrutiny with the aim of getting results or answers to a problem (Creswell, 2012; Denscombe, 2010). Thus, this chapter describes the systematic process that was used to answer the research questions which are outlined in section 1.5. The chapter starts by describing the composition of a research paradigm in section 4.2.

This is then followed by section 4.3 which presents a review of research paradigms that are commonly used in research: positivism, interpretivism and critical research. Section 4.4 then situates the study based on the review of the research paradigms. Further, section 4.5 justifies why the study applied a qualitative research design. In section 4.6 the chapter then presents some potential research strategies to ascertain their suitability for this study. The section then concludes by arguing that doing case studies is the ideal strategy to gain knowledge that answers the research questions. The rest of the chapter describes how the case study isapplied in this study. Thus, section 4.7 highlights the data collection methods that are appropriate for the case study. Then, section 4.8 discusses how cases were selected for inclusion in the study. The section further presents the unit of analysis used in the study, and then in section 4.9, the chapter describes the data analysis used in this study by discussing the application of thematic analysis, including the coding involved in the analysis process.

4.2 Composition of Research Paradigms

Research paradigms involve the underlying perceptions, beliefs and assumptions about nature and knowledge of reality that influence the design of the research process (Given, 2008, p. 408). They describe ways in which data concerning phenomenon should be collected, analysed and used (Feilzer, 2010). Research paradigms consist of three components that include ontology, epistemology and methodology (see Figure 4.1 below). These three components are all important in shaping up the research design for this study (Creswell, 2012) and are briefly discussed in the following subsections.

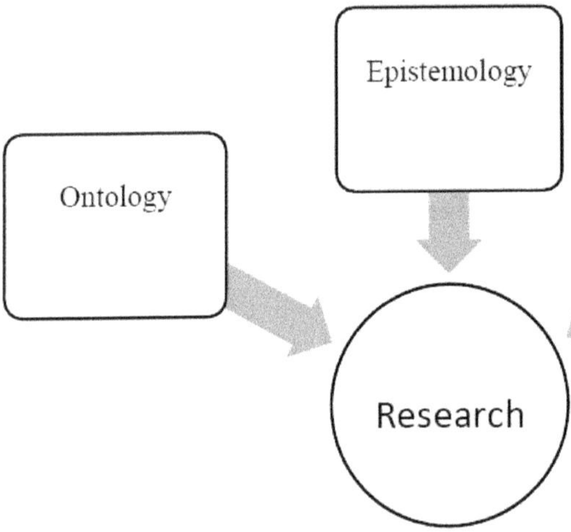

Figure 4.1: Composition of a Research Paradigm

4.2.1 Ontology

Ontology is defined as the science of being, and it focuses on nature of reality (Blaikie, 2010, 2007). As such ontology is a system of belief that reflects an individual's interpretation of what constitutes a fact. In this study, the researcher gives out views, makes claims or assumptions on the nature of reality which determine his ideas, insights and conclusions on the value of stakeholder engagement in ICT research projects within the context of responsible outcomes.

However, to come up with an appropriate research design, two central ontological views are considered, and they include objectivism and subjectivism. With objectivism the assertion is that social phenomena and their meanings do not depend on social actors for their existence, meaning that reality is independent of human consciousness (Blaikie, 2007; Bryman, 2004, p. 22). On the other hand, with subjectivism, the assertion is that social phenomena are a result of perceptions and actions of those social actors concerned with the existence of the phenomena. The main difference between the two ontological views is that, with objectivism, meaning is *"integral to the phenomenon"* while with subjectivism, meaning is *"related to phenomena as part of the reality"* (Bryman, 2004, p. 23). This means that with objectivism, the meaning of reality in a phenomenon is independent of social actors while with subjectivism the meaning of reality, that is to say, how reality is constituted and how it is understood, is found in experiences and interpretations of social actors (Blaikie, 2007, p. 109). Given these points, finding the meaning of reality within research can be achieved in different ways depending on the researcher's ontological view.

With regards to this study, the ontological view is that of subjectivism rather than objectivism because the engagement of stakeholders in ICT research projects relates to the stakeholders' actions experiences and interpretations that exist within their lived lives. For this reason, to evaluate the value of stakeholder engagement, this study involves an interpretation and understanding of the experiences of those engaged in the ICT research projects.

4.2.2 Epistemology

With respect to attaining knowledge, despite the different views and beliefs of reality (ontology), there is need to have a method of gaining knowledge from the world around. This is part of epistemology which is understood as the science of analysing the way human beings comprehend knowledge about what is perceived to exist (Blaikie, 2010, p. 93). Epistemology addresses the question of how one can arrive at a true cognition of a phenomenon (Beckerand Niehaves, 2007). Thus, epistemology can be described as that which deals with how the nature and reality of knowledge can be acquired (Blaikie, 2007, p. 180). Hence, to develop knowledge about the subject of this study, there is need to understand how information is comprehended to answer the research questions introduced in section 1.5 of this book. For that reason, epistemology is important for understanding what the stakeholders in the cases (see section 4.7) know in an attempt to acquire and build on the knowledge. This shows the inter-dependency between ontology and epistemology in that the assumptions made about the nature of reality inform the ways of acquiring the knowledge of that reality. This is why it is important in research to understand the relationship between the two when it comes to the generation of knowledge.

It is important to realise that although epistemology explains how knowledge is gained, there are differences on how to get concepts and knowledge (Blaikie, 2007, p. 113). Therefore, it is worth pointing that epistemological views can fall either under rationalism or empiricism (Markie, 2015). These two epistemological views look at the limits of one's thoughts and knowledge. These two epistemological views are briefly introduced below.

4.2.2.1 Rationalism

In rationalism, the stance is that reasoning influences the way the world is seen, and knowledge is acquired. With this view, the belief is that knowledge of reality can be acquired independent of people's experiences – *a priori* (Markie, 2015). With rationalism, there is a belief that knowledge of a phenomenon is acquired by intuition, that is, people were endowed with knowledge of truth from the beginning, and they use that truth in understanding knowledge of reality.

4.2.2.2 Empiricism

In contrast, with empiricism, the belief is that there is no existence of innate knowledge and it expresses that knowledge can be gained through experience. With this view, the belief is that people attain knowledge of the subject dependent upon experience - *a posteriori* (Markie, 2015). With empiricism, knowledge is gained through experience or observations hence the term empirical research.

Given these points, this study follows the epistemological view of empiricism. As a consequence, the knowledge that informed this study is gained through understanding experiences of the stakeholders that are engaged in the projects *a posteriori.*

This subsection has described epistemology. The following subsection considers the last constituent of research paradigms in research, which is, methodology.

4.2.3 Methodology

In research, methodology is defined as a system of principles which underlie the structure of how we investigate the world together in relation to the assumptions and beliefs behind the way we see the world (Scotland, 2012). Methodology substantiates the way knowledge (epistemology) is generated within research and describes the perception of reality (ontology) by considering the concepts and theories which underlie the understanding of the world. Hence, it determines the research strategy and method(s) to be used (Leedy and Ormrod, 2010, p. 12).

In this study, the decision on the research design starts with a consideration of the research paradigm that informs the study which is discussed in the section that follows.

4.3 Research Paradigms

Since this research relates to ICT research projects, which are part of information systems (IS), the focus of the research paradigms discussed in this book are those that are frequently mentioned in the literature on IS research (Asghar, 2013; Kelliher, 2011; Myers and Klein, 2011; Oates, 2006; Orlikowski and Baroudi, 1991; Stahl, 2013b, 2007). Research paradigms are a fusion of a person's epistemological and ontological beliefs, concepts, values and methodological assumptions (see section 6.2) that construct the way one views the world or reality (Guba *et al.*, 1994; Oates, 2006). Many IS researchers (Baskerville and Myers, 2004; Myers and Klein, 2011; Orlikowski and Baroudi, 1991; Walsham, 1993) have described positivism, interpretivism and critical research paradigms in relation to the IS research field.

Epistemologically, positivism and interpretivism are the most popular opposing key paradigms which cover a range of stances (Baskerville and Myers, 2004; Oates, 2006; Orlikowski and Baroudi, 1991; Walliman, 2006; Willis, 2007). In addition to these two paradigms, a third paradigm is described in the literature. This third paradigm, critical research, (Given, 2008, p. 734; Myers and Klein, 2011; Stahl, 2008; Willis, 2007, p. 95) takes a midstream position. In this section, all three paradigms are reviewed.

4.3.1 Positivism

Positivism is used to apply methods of natural science to social phenomena (Smith, 1983) where the facts can be found only through measuring what is observable (Oates, 2006). The paradigm uses scientific laws in explaining what is observable and measurable (Trochim, 2006). Positivism takes an ontological position that presupposes that reality is objective and is controlled by the systematic study of the natural world through experimentation and observation. Also, positivism assumes that reality exists independent of human behaviour and is not an artefact of the human mind (Stahl, 2007). Under these circumstances, positivism assumes that the existence of the social world is objective and validity of knowledge is based on observation and empirically measured experience through quantitative methods (Blaikie, 2007).

In relation to this study, the disadvantage of this paradigm is that it ignores the subjective roles of stakeholders in the ICT research projects. These roles are important in understanding and constructing the social reality that results from their engagement. Also, positivism fails to consider the social context and conditions that influence the representation of social ideas and action (Blaikie, 2010; Fagan, n.d.; Orlikowski and Baroudi, 1991).

In evaluating the value of stakeholder engagement, both the researcher's role and the activity of the stakeholders (participants) are of vital importance in generating knowledge through the interpretation of their experiences and social interaction. In addition, stakeholder engagement is a subjective construct that can pose problems to quantify and measure. Therefore, positivism would not be ideal for answering the research question because stakeholder engagement is a social construct that is subjective rather than objective. However, although this is the case, positivism could have been suitable if the study aimed to look for objective causes and results of stakeholder engagement in ICT research projects. For example, positivism could be ideal for studying trends and patterns of stakeholder behaviour in ICT research projects and understand correlations between different variables that are external to the stakeholders' opinions, but this is not the intention of this study.

4.3.2 Interpretivism

The second research paradigm is interpretivism. This paradigm is related to the notion that the existence of reality is subjective and is a social product that is constructed by people (Oates, 2006). The basic assumption underlying interpretivism is that reality cannot be understood independent of social actors that construct and make sense of that reality (Orlikowski and Baroudi, 1991). In interpretivism, knowledge is acquired through understanding the meaning of social actions and people's experiences (Kelliher, 2011). Hence, knowledge is a result of a social construction of people's consciousness, shared meaning and language (Myers and Klein, 2011) which form different interpretations to their experiences. With interpretivism, the researcher can understand the different interpretations and meanings of the social world under study through the language of the participants to describe the social process (Myers and Klein, 2011) and activities that go with it. Thus, to evaluate and understand the value of stakeholder engagement with regards to the attainment of socially desirable outcomes, the study explores the social construction that exists within ICT research projects with reference to RRI. For instance, as part of the evaluation, there is an understanding of the process and rationale behind the stakeholder engagement through an exploration of the activities, perceptions and expectations of the stakeholders within ICT research projects in light of responsible innovation through an interpretation of the language used.

4.3.3 Critical Research

The third paradigm is critical research. This paradigm revolves around the assumption that reality has structures that dominate our experiences and it consists of objective properties (Myers and Klein, 2011; Oates, 2006). As such, critical research does not refute objectivity. However, it *'retains the idea that knowledge can be objective by defining objectivity, not in terms of correspondence with an independent reality, but rather in relation to the explication of the shared patterns of culturally and historically developed understandings'* (Given, 2008, p.734). Critical research paradigm aims at critically examining the social reality by critiquing existence of social processes and systems, looking at conflicts and contradictions and enabling people to find ways of overcoming them (Oates, 2006; Orlikowski and Baroudi, 1991).

In critical research, there is a belief that the social world can be constructed and reconstructed through people's actions and reflection (Willis, 2007). Critical research intends to change the social status quo, overcome marginalisation that stems from alienation, domination and injustice in the social system therefore promoting emancipation (Myers and Klein, 2011; Stahl, 2008).

Critical research opposes positivism by advocating that the researcher and participants have a role in emancipation and that they have a role in social changes. For instance, in this study, this could be achieved by creating awareness and an understanding of the social influence of stakeholders that are engaged in ICT research projects on society and suggest ways of ensuring that this influence is beneficial to society (Orlikowski and Baroudi, 1991). Thus, critical research paradigm rejects that social problems can be solved using technical solutions. In short, critical research enables the exploration and understanding of the restrictions that result in a status quo and encourages a radical change in social actions (Kvasny and Richardson, 2006; Orlikowski and Baroudi, 1991).

In a way, evaluation of a social process such as the stakeholder engagement has potential to enable people to find ways of overcoming irresponsibility and improving responsible research and innovation in ICT research. For instance, stakeholders can learn and improve on practice according to the knowledge they get from the evaluation. This relates to this study, and therefore the paradigm is useful in answering most of the research question specifically in understanding the rationale for engaging stakeholders.

So far this chapter has discussed the composition of a research paradigm and discussed three research paradigms. To recapitulate what the chapter has covered so far, Table 4.1 below shows a summary of research paradigms and their composition.

Table 4.1: Summary of Research Paradigms

Paradigm	Ontology (reality)	Epistemology (knowledge acquiring)	Methodology (way of finding)
Positivism	There is an objective reality, and we can understand it through the laws by which it is governed.	Positivism employs a scientific discourse derived from the epistemologies of objectivism and empiricism. Positivism holds that knowledge is acquired *a posteriori*.	Experimenting, surveying, statistical analysis
Interpretivism	The existence of reality is subjective and is a social product.	Knowledge is acquired through understanding the meaning of social and contextual understanding of people's experiences	Interpretation of narratives, interviews, observations
Critical research	Reality exists and has been created by directed social bias.	Knowledge is acquired through critiquing existence of social processes and systems, looking at conflicts and contradictions and enabling people to find ways of overcoming them	Critical analysis, historical review

4.4 Situating the Research

Following the discussion on research paradigms covered in sections 4.2 and 4.3 above, this study is situated on the following philosophical stance. Ontologically, since stakeholder engagement is a social construct, the reality in this study is subjective (see section 4). Regarding epistemology, this studyaims to gain knowledge about how stakeholders that are engaged in ICT research projects contribute towards those projects with regards to responsible outcomes. This knowledge is gained through understanding the participants' experiences and therefore, gained through the collection and analysis of primary data based on those experiences. Hence, this study is an empirical research (see section 4.2.2.2). The engagement of stakeholders in ICT research projects involves social interactions among those identified for the engagement. Thus, this should be regarded as a social phenomenon that ties in with interpretivism (see section 4.3.2).

However, evaluating the value of stakeholder engagement in ICT research projects, particularly in light of responsible outcomes, has connotations of critical research. The knowledge gained from the process can be viewed as promoting an ideal status quo which encourages a responsible innovation in ICT research projects. The mere fact that there is an engagement of stakeholders in itself is an emancipation process because it gives a voice to those engaged. Thus, the study finds the two paradigms described herein, relevant and therefore to avoid hindering the robustness of the study in answering the research questions, the study follows a pragmatic stance to combine the two, interpretivism and critical research. In doing so, the study distance itself from sticking to one specific paradigm and the methodology relating to it. This position is based on the following assumptions;

- ❖ Paradigms could be interpreted as prescriptive and as requiring particular research methods and excluding others. In that sense, basing this study on one paradigm can constrain intellectual curiosity and creativity, blind the researcher to aspects of social phenomena, or even new phenomena and theories and limit imagination (Feilzer, 2010, p. 3).
- ❖ Taking a pragmatic stance sidesteps the contentious issues of truth and reality.

The pragmatic stance taken in this study, accepts philosophically, that there are singular and multiple realities that are open to empirical research and positions this study toward contributing to solving practical problems in the "real world" (Creswell and Plano Clark, 2011, pp. 21–23) which is in tandem with responsible innovation in ICT research projects. As a result, a pragmatic stance allows the researcher to be free of mental and practical constraints imposed by the forced choice of a specific paradigm (2011, p. 26).

Having discussed the positioning of this study, the next section discusses the two main categories of research and indicates the one to which this study belongs.

4.5 Qualitative and Quantitative Research Dichotomy

Research is broadly categorised into qualitative and qualitative types of research (Silverman, 2013). As part of discussing the research design of this study, a brief outline of each type is given. With qualitative research, the emphasis is on finding meaning, conceptualisation and describing things through reference to metaphors, symbols and experiences (Silverman, 2013). In contrast, with quantitative research, the emphasis is on counts and measure of things (Creswell and Plano Clark, 2011). Although, theoretically there is this distinction between the two types of research, in practice the line of separation is blurry (Creswell and Plano Clark, 2011; Mingers, 2001; Smith, 1983). Quantitative research often involves some qualitative aspects and vice versa. This means, although one may be dominant in a chosen research design, the other should not be ruled out.

However, although this is the case, in most cases there is a domination of one research type than the other. In the case of this study, the aim is to explore the value of stakeholder engagement in ICT research projects, particularly within the confines of RRI. This exploration involves delving deep in understanding the actions and intricacies that may be interpreted as stakeholder engagement in relation to the attainment of socially desirable outcomes in ICT research projects. The interpretation involves the construction of meaning based on the interaction with stakeholder participants and their activities to find meanings and description of their contribution in light of RRI. As such, a qualitative research design is ideal for answering the research question(s) introduced in section 1.5 as opposed to a quantitative approach which could be ideal if the aim was *'to measure some existing variables'* (Creswell and Plano Clark, 2011, p. 46) of stakeholder engagement.

Having mentioned that this study falls within the qualitative type, several research strategies could be followed, and these are reviewed in the next section.

4.6 RESEARCH STRATEGIES

Research strategies enable the researcher to explore how to gain knowledge (Creswell, 2012). The philosophical assumptions discussed in the sections 4.2, 4.3 and 4.4 of this chapter were useful in determining the research strategy for this study. That is why it was important to discuss the research paradigms in the previous sections because of the connection between the two. In order to address the research questions aptly, it is essential that an appropriate research strategy is identified.

For the purpose of this study, five common qualitative research strategies were recognised from the literature (Creswell, 2007; 2012; Denscombe, 2010; Oates, 2006; Yin, 2015; Goulding, 2005; Baskerville and Myers, 2004 and Strauss; Lewin, 1946; and Corbin, 1998). There are summarised in Table 4.2. These are case study, phenomenology, action research, ethnography and grounded theory.

Table 4.2: A Summary of Common Qualitative Research Strategies

Research strategy	Description
Case study	An issue is explored through a case within a bounded system or multiple bounded systems (cases) over time (Yin, 2015).
	Involves multiple sources of data, therefore, giving an in-depth understanding of the case.
	The analysis involves a description of themes or issues, and the results can be organised as a chronology, analyses across cases, as a contrast and compare task or be presented as a theoretical model (Creswell, 2007).
	Uses multiple sources of data to conduct an in-depth research (Creswell, 2007; Oates, 2006).
Phenomenology	The researcher provides a description of several individuals for their lived life experiences. It assumes that a commonality exists as participants experience a phenomenon or a situation (Creswell, 2012, 2007).
	The main goal is to maximise the understanding of different immediate experiences. Therefore, it can be seen as a critical reflection on conscious experience and is designed to uncover the important features of that understanding (Goulding, 2005)

Research strategy	Description
Action Research	It involves a reflective process (Oates, 2006) Problems are solved by individuals working together normally with an aim to improve practices and solve social problems (Lewin, 1946). Emphasises collaboration between the researcher and the participants in solving problems that affect society, therefore, requiring the researcher's active role in the research fieldwork (Baskerville and Myers, 2004).
Ethnography	The focus is on an entire cultural group of participants It involves the description of patterns for people's shared values, beliefs, and languages in a culture-sharing group of participants through fieldwork (Creswell, 2012; Oates, 2006) The data is collected to aid the understanding of cultural processes and culture (Creswell, 2012; Oates, 2006)
Grounded Theory	It involves an iterative process of data collection and analysis that is used to develop or discover a theoretical explanation for a phenomenon (Creswell, 2012). Theory is discovered through generating conceptual themes or categories and their properties from data, thereby aiding the researcher in capturing the relevant aspects of the problem or phenomena under research (Strauss and Corbin, 1998)

Based on the review of the research strategies summarised in Table 7 above, an appropriate strategy is chosen. The research strategy is chosen based on *'its feasibility and suitability in answering the research question*(s)' (Denscombe, 2010, p. 4). It worth mentioning that although a research strategy is chosen, the line between one strategy and another is blurry therefore some of the features of one strategy can be evident in another (see sections 4.6.1 and 4.6.2). For instance, a case study strategy may involve using some features or the whole of grounded theory to develop atheory (Creswell, 2012).

4.6.1 Case study

This study aims to evaluate the value of stakeholder engagement in ICT research projects using the RRI lens. The evaluation involves collecting and analysing views and perceptions of stakeholders in ICT research projects. This study uses a casestudy research strategy because it is ideal for investigating stakeholder engagement that exists in a *'real-life context within a boundary'* (Yin, 1994, p. 23). This real-life context is the ICT research projects in which these stakeholders are engaged (see section 6.7). Therefore, a case study strategy fits in well with the overall aim of the study and it has the potential to answer the research question succinctly. Case study strategy is used in describing the context and understanding how stakeholders contribute to socially desirable outcomes in ICT research. The case study strategy gives the participants (stakeholders) an authoritative and in-depth explication of their views on how they think or interpret their engagement in ICT research projects in light of responsible innovation without the researcher's control.

Another consideration is that doing case studies gives the flexibility to '*use different data collection methods which aids triangulating the sources to validate the findings of the study*' (Yin, 2003, p. 99). In this study, data were collected through interviews to understand stakeholders' experiences and through documents to understand the context of stakeholder engagement.

Although the case study strategy is considered ideal, one of the argument against the use of the strategy is that the findings from the case studies cannot be generalised to other contexts (Creswell 2007). Firstly, this study argues that this should not be an issue because transferability is important in a qualitative study than generalisability (Ponelis, 2015, p. 538). Transferability concerns the extent to which the findings from one study are relevant to other contexts. Probably, what is learnt from this case study is not limited to specific cases used. The argument is that the findings can be used reflectively in gaining an understanding of stakeholder engagement in other settings where the findings might be relevant. Secondly, although the issue of generalisability is not so relevant in qualitative research more than in quantitative research (Gomm *et al.*, 2000), this is nevertheless addressed by using multiple cases (Yin, 2003) which are identified in section 4.7 below. The multiple case projects have a variety of contextual factors for stakeholder engagement, and therefore findings could be applied to other ICT research projects that are related.

The other argument against case study as a strategy is that there is a concern on the issues with reliability and validity of findings from case studies (Kelliher, 2011, p. 123). In the case of this study, this concern is addressed by combining data sources (see section 4.9).

4.6.2 Other Research Strategies not used

4.6.2.1 Phenomenology

Phenomenology would help this study to gather 'deep' information and perceptions of stakeholders in ICT research projects regarding their engagement in light of RRI. This information could be gathered through inductive qualitative methods such as interviews, discussions and participant observations, and then representing the information from the perspective of the research participants (Groenewald, 2004; Trochim and Donnelly, 2006). Hence, phenomenology would be ideal for understanding stakeholders' subjective experiences, gaining insights into stakeholders' motivations and actions with regards to their contribution while engaged in the ICT research projects. Also, as part of the process of inquiry in phenomenology, data collection requires that stakeholders involved in this study should be willing and able to express themselves about their experiences fully. They should do this without the researcher giving leading questions regarding preconceived beliefs and opinions, in what is termed as 'bracketing' (Groenewald, 2004, p. 12). Bracketing would be a problem in this study because the evaluation of stakeholder engagement towards the attainment of socially desirable outcomes of ICT research using the concept of RRI is a novel phenomenon. Therefore, to effectively address the research question in this study the direction of the research should be led by the researcher's opinions and preconceived ideas of the subject. Without bracketing, it would take a long time to arrive at data that could be interpreted as information that answers the research question and informs the developed evaluation approach (see chapter 3). As such, phenomenology is not ideal for this study, however in analysing the findings, some of the data analysis techniques used in phenomenology are used (Creswell, 2007; Goulding, 2005). For instance, coding (see section 4.12).

4.6.2.2 Action research

Action research would require the researcher to be fully involved in ICT research projects and taking an active role in the engagement processes taking place while at the same time collecting data that would help understand the phenomenon under research (Lewin, 1946). This research strategy would require the researcher to be fully immersed in the ICT research projects and research within the setting where the phenomenon is being studied (Baskerville and Myers, 2004, pp. 331–333). However, this would be a problem in relation to this study due to the timing of identified cases and the study period for the researcher. Also, this strategy is very time consuming, and it would not allow multiple cases to be studied with the available time. Therefore, this would not have been a suitable strategy because the researcher would not have followed the basic requirements of action research to gain useful insights.

4.6.2.3 Ethnography

Ethnography would help in understanding the cultural dynamics that occur within ICT research projects and as part of it understand the contribution of the stakeholders that are engaged in the projects within the context of RRI. Also, this would help in understanding the dialogue that exists among stakeholders particularly about RRI in ICT research projects (Creswell, 2012; Oates, 2006). For instance, ethnography would help this study to explore the terms used by the stakeholders when discussing and deliberating on activities that entail RRI and the range of views that stakeholders have about responsible research and innovation in ICT research projects. However, as it is the case with action research, ethnography requires a longer duration in the studying the ICT research projects. As a result, there could be an issue with continuous access to particular ICT research projects to explore stakeholder's engagement within context.

4.6.2.4 Grounded Theory

Grounded theory is discussed in the literature as both a research strategy and a data analysis method. As a data analysis method, grounded theory can be used in other research strategies to analyses data. This involves the researcher constantly looking for the emergence of certain words and phrases that highlight an important issue and assigns a code to them in a process called coding (Allan, 2003). In this study, some data analysis techniques that are used in grounded theory are to analyse the interviews with stakeholders. From the interview transcripts, a thorough analysis is conducted to have an interpretation of the said 'words' about stakeholders' experiences and opinions on stakeholder engagement within the

ICT research projects. Although all this sounds relevant, as a research strategy, grounded theory is not suitable because it involves developing new theory using an inductive data analysis approach (Charmaz, 2011). Grounded theory requires the researcher to research with a blank mind about the phenomena of interest, that is, without knowledge of prior research and a defined research question (Charmaz, 2014; Goulding, 2005; Suddaby, 2006). This is contrary to the approach used in this study since it uses a hybrid approach that combines deductive and inductive data analyses (see sections 4.12.1 and 4.7.2 below). In this study, there is the use of some preconceived knowledge that informs that analysis of the data collected. Also, to understand stakeholder engagement in ICT research projects, it is important that the context and stakeholder engagement process be taken into consideration a priori. The nature of this study is exploratory rather than theorising. Therefore, the strategy is not ideal.

4.7 Selection of Cases

In this study, the ICT research projects to be included as cases must be in a setting that involves academia in ICT research. The research has to be tailored to improve society by tackling at least one of the issues that affect society such as education, exclusion, environmental degradation and health impairment. This provides a clear boundary of the projects and the context within which the projects take place. Furthermore, the research projects should be relevant for this study in conceptualising the evaluation of the efficacy of stakeholder engagement with respect to attainment of socially desirable outcomes in research and innovation. Relevance is established by the association of the research projects with different features of RRI that surfaced in the discussion of RRI (see sections 3.3 and 2.5). In addition to these prescriptive reasons, practically, the cases were to be included based on accessibility and the time available to conduct the research. Therefore, they should have at least a UK partner that can be accessible by the researcher within the means of resources available for the study.

4.7.1 Identifying ICT Research Projects

Ponelis (2015) mentions that randomly selecting cases is neither necessary nor preferable but the relevance of the cases to the research questions rather than representativeness should be the criterion for the selecting cases (Ponelis, 2015, p. 540). Using this line of reasoning, this study employs purposive sampling as well as snowball sampling (Patton, 2002). Access to the projects and therefore the stakeholders engaged in the projects was an important consideration in the selection of cases. As a result, following Hartley's (1994) argument that contacts in industry, academia, and friends can help to establish a list from which cases can be selected (Hartley, 2004, p. 367) potential cases were obtained using a purposive and snowball sampling strategies (Silverman, 2013) using:

i. Personal networks and word-of-mouth referrals

ii. ICT research projects associated with the researcher's university.

Academics at the researcher's university were consulted and asked to suggest ICT research projects that met the selection criteria. Ten potential cases were recommended (see Table 4.3 below). From the suggested cases those that met the criteria described in section 6.7 above and had information that was rich enough to answer the research question were selected. The cases identified were as shown in Table 4.3 below.

Table 4.3: Suggested ICT related research projects

Project	Project Title	Social challenge	Aim	Accessibility
A	Affective Computing for Augmented Communication	Health	To improve the communication channels and social connections of children with a degenerative disease through the of use Brain and Neural Computer Interface (BNCI)	No
B	Brain Computer Interfaces	Health	To link Brain/Neural Computer Interaction (BNCI) technologies with other novel and emerging types of ICTs. to develop technologies that would support severely disabled users	No
C	ICT-enabled system for Management of Chronic Organ Condition	Health	To establish how ICT can beused for patients suffering from a chronic organ related condition	No
D	Smartspaces	Environmental degradation	To use ICTs to support environmental sustainability through energy optimisation	Yes
E	Hypatia	Gender/ Education	To foster gender inclusivity in STEM subjects such as ICT.	Yes
F	Digilit	Education	To determine and improve the use of ICT in transforming education provision in secondary schools	Yes
G	3D Tune-In	Health impairment	To use ICT to improve hearing aid technologies	Yes

Project	Project Title	Social challenge	Aim	Accessibility
H	Michelangelo	Health impairment	To exploit ICT and other technologies in assessing and treating the Autistic Spectrum Disorder in children in a more "natural" home environment where non-obtrusive techniques will be used	No
I	I-Traq	Environmental degradation	To use ICT in developing a dynamic traffic management system to improve air quality	Yes
K	Renewable Energy	Environmental degradation	To develop a web-based technology that will be simple to use and beneficial for the public in terms of potential costs if they invest in solar panels	No

Applying the criteria described above projects D, E, F, G and I were selected because these were accessible out of the ten relevant cases. Access to Projects A, B, C, H and K was problematic either because the contacts that were given did not respond to emails or none of the contacts was available to participate in this research. For clarity, the projects that were selected have been renamed as follows;

- Project D will be referred to as Project 1
- Project F will be referred to as Project 2
- Project G will be referred to as Project 3
- Project I will be referred to as Project 4
- Project E will be referred to as Project 5

The researcher acknowledges that the selected ICT research projects may not represent all ICT research projects. However, they were sufficient as a sample for this study, considering the limited resources at the researcher's disposal such as time. Also, the cases were sufficient for the study because there was diversity in the aims of the cases. The selected cases are covered succinctly in chapters 5 of this book.

4.8 UNIT OF ANALYSIS

This study focuses on exploring the value of stakeholder engagement in ICT research projects in light of responsible outcomes. To effectively understand the value of stakeholder engagement in cases identified in section 4.7 above, the research involves two levels of analysis. The first level is analysing the individual

ICT research projects and the second level is analysing individual stakeholders engaged in these projects. Each level of analysis provided data that was used in the case studies (see sections 4.9.1 and 4.9.2).

4.9 Data Collection Methods

As discussed in section 4.6.1, a mix of data collection methods is used to increase the validity of this research. Miles and Huberman (1994) suggests that validity and triangulation can be achieved by combining data sources and methods. Therefore this section discusses the data collection methods considered in the study. The section starts with those that are relevant in exploring the unit of analysis discussed in section 4.8 above.

4.9.1 Interviews

The data collection aimed to evaluate the value of stakeholder engagement in ICT research projects with regards to responsible outcomes. The study opted for semi-structured interviews to keep the interviews focused but also to provide room to explore new and relevant issues that emerge during the interview concerning stakeholder engagement and responsible innovation. The interviews enabled the study to gain an understanding of the research topic from the interviewees' perspective and understand the stakeholders' knowledge, views, experiences and interpretation of their engagement (Cassell and Symon, 2004, pp. 12–15). This exploration was fundamental in evaluating the value of stakeholder engagement since the participants gave answers that were subjective and therefore produced new themes that would not have otherwise emerged if a different data collection method was used.

With the semi-structured interviews, the researcher used a list of questions as shown in the interview schedule in Appendix 4-1. The researcher was at liberty to change the order of the questions in response to the direction which the interview was taking. The questions and responses were flexible and open-ended (Denscombe, 2010). The interview schedule was guided by themes that were pre-conceived (inductive) to answer the research questions as shown in Table 4.4 below.

Table 4.4: Connection between themes, research questions and interviews

Theme	Research question	Interview question No.
Context of the stakeholder engagement	(i) and (iii)	1, 3,4,6,9
Stakeholder identification	(i) and (iii)	1, 2, 3,4
Nature of stakeholder engagement	(i), (ii) and (iii)	3,4,5,6,
Outcomes of stakeholder engagement	(ii) and (iii)	4,5,7,10
Rationale for stakeholder engagement	(i), (ii) and (iii)	4,5,7,8,10
RRI application	(ii)	7,8,9,10

Semi-structured interviews were ideal because they gave the researcher a continuous coverage of the identified themes which are relevant to answering the research questions without restricting the participants' responses to predetermined answers.

As it is with any other data collection method, semi-structured interviews have drawbacks. Interpreting data is often problematic because of the issue with the subjectivity of the interpretation (Patton, 2002). This is overcome by implementing a clear data analysis procedure (see section 4.12) that compliments the research design (see section 4.6).

To support the semi-structured interviews, the literature reviewed in chapters 2 and 3 were used by the interviewer to as background information. As an example, when asking the participants about their role within the ICT research project, the suggestions given in the literature about stakeholder engagement (see section 2.66) and RRI helped the research in questioning the participants.

4.9.1.1 Interviewee selection process

Using purposive sampling, the researcher identified key informants that were engaged in the selected ICT research projects (see section 6.7). Once the key informants were identified, the researcher then employed snowballing sampling. The key informants suggested potential participants that would be available, accessible and willing to talk about their opinions and experiences. This sampling technique proved effective due to the limited number of case projects and participants who could serve as sources of primary data. This proved successful because the key informants that were identified showed willingness to assist with the research. Once these were contacted, theyfurther suggested other stakeholders that might also be valuable to the research.

The process was iterative, involving continual sampling, collection and analysis of data from the selected cases. This iterative process informed the next stage of the sampling until thematic saturation was achieved whereby no new ideas or concepts with regards to their engagement emerged (Coyne, 1997, p. 628; Wilmot, 2005). This relates to the explanation given by Silverman (2013) that in qualitative sampling, the issue is not how many cases are enough to give confidence but how the cases are selected to answer the research questions and their relevance to the research area. Thus, the size of the sample was not predetermined at the beginning of the study but was a result of the thematic saturation which gave confidence that the research question would be answered with the collected data.

4.9.1.2 Interview approach

Interviewees were identified from March 2016 then contacted byemail and telephone to arrange dates and places to conduct the interviews. The researcher sourced 45 email addresses of different stakeholders who were engaged in the selected five case ICT research projects (see section 4.7.1). However, despite having access to case Project 5, and identifying five potential participants (stakeholders), they eventually stopped responding to emails when they were asked to arrange a time for interviews. Therefore, Project 5 was not used as part of the study. In total 20 interviews were conducted: ten for the Project 1, three for the Project 2, two for the Project 4 and five for the Project 3 (see chapter 5). Once the time and places for interviews were arranged, the researcher obtained the interviewees' consent for participating in the study and being recorded during the interview. The consent form that was used can be seen in Appendix 4-2.

The interviewees were informed of the aim of the study and what topic will be explored during the interviews. Once the stakeholders were interviewed, their identities were anonymised and given an identification (ID) code. The code was a combination of the project code and an interview sequence number. A table with a participant code was also developed in case there was a need to trace the interviewee. The table included the interviewee's initials, date approached and date interviewed (see Appendix 4-3).

During the interviews, the researcher gave the interviewers five minutes to read the tentative interview questions to give them a snapshot of what will be explored. Each interview began with an introduction of the research topic which was then followed by semi-structured questioning. The set of tentative questions used in the semi-structured interviews is shown in Appendix 4-1.

The interviews were mostly conducted face to face. However, due to the availability of the respondents, some interviews were carried out online by using Skype software.

All interviews were recorded using voice recording software. The interview recordings were then transferred to a secure data storage drive which was only accessible by the researcher. The researcher commenced the transcription and data analysis straight after the first interview, and it continued to run concurrently with subsequent interviews as data was collected.

The researcher continued with data collection until no new insights were gained and the data started to repeat itself. The data collection progressed until the researcher was convinced that the findings were enough to meet the objectives of this study, therefore answer the research questions.

4.9.2 Document Review

In addition to interviews, this study also reviewed documents to complement the data collection. The documents included project reports, web pages and published articles from project websites, Google Web, Google Scholar and the De Montfort University library database. The data in documents provided information for understanding the context of the stakeholder engagement. The document review provided an understanding of the research projects' settings by accessing relevant information about the projects such as its aims, procedures, approaches and outcomes. This was important in understanding the contextual background of the stakeholder engagement. Also, considering the limited resources such as time and finance, document review was a cost-effective method of getting data and therefore answering research questions as shown in Table 4.5 below.

Table 4.5: Connection between Themes, Research Questions and Document Review

Theme	Research question	Type of document
Context of the stakeholder engagement	(i) and (iii)	Web pages, project reports
Stakeholder identification	(i) and (iii)	Webpages, project reports
Nature of stakeholder engagement	(i), (ii) and (iii)	Published articles
Outcomes of stakeholder engagement	(ii) and (iii)	Project web pages, published articles
Rationale for stakeholder engagement	(i), (ii) and (iii)	Published articles
RRI application	(ii)	

Further, documents provided secondary data that formed the basis for some of the research by looking at existing literature. Using a literature review, the researcher had a picture of the status quo with regards to stakeholder engagement and how it is evaluated in ICT research projects. The literature was reviewed to get underlying knowledge of how the evaluation of stakeholder engagement is conducted with regards to other aspects of ICT research projects other than responsible research and innovation. Looking at existing work on stakeholder engagement and evaluation of stakeholders' participatory processes gave the researcher a starting point.

4.9.3 Other Data Collection Methods not used

As suggested by Yin (2003), observations and questionnaire surveys are also commonly used in case study research strategy (2003, p. 100). However, these were reviewed and left out as explained below.

4.9.3.1 Observations

With regards to this study, observations could have helped the researcher to understand and get an insight into the stakeholder engagement process by observing the dialogue and collaborative activities that were taking place among stakeholders. It would have certainly provided some data but not comprehensive enough for an in-depth understanding of the phenomena. Also, some of the case projects were used in this study after they were completed and there was no observable activity left which meant that the exploration and understanding of stakeholder engagement would have been difficult to study using observations. Therefore, this method was not adopted as a data collection method for this study although it could have possibly be used as a complementary source of data collection.

4.9.3.2 Questionnaire survey

Questionnaire survey is ideal for saving resources such as money and time since the researcher can access a large number of respondents and the responses can be easily analysed using systematic analysis methods with very minimal bias (Denscombe, 2010). However, the drawback with using questionnaire surveys is that they offer less flexibility in answering the questions which can result in answers that lack depth and validity (Denscombe, 2010, p. 157). In this study, there was a need to gain an in-depth understanding of stakeholder engagement. However, questionnaires would not have been ideal to provide the level of depth required to answer the research question. With this drawback in mind, the researcher did not use this data collection method.

4.10 Pilot Case Study

A pilot case study was conducted from September 2015 to February 2016 as can be seen in pilot study timeline that is provided in Appendix 4-4. The pilot case study was conducted to assess the applicability of the methodology that is employed in this study. During the pilot case study, the researcher tested the interview questions, the structure of the interview guide and the format of the interviews. From the pilot case study, the researcher was able to get reaction and feedback from the interviewees. The pilot was conducted on Project 4. Project 4 was selected for the pilot study because of the stakeholders that were involved in the project were the first to show willingness to take part. Three potential interviewees agreed to take part, but only two were interviewed because the third one cancelled the interview.

The researcher prepared a case study protocol which was used as a guide during the data collection phase of the pilot case study. The protocol included a description of the problem, what motivated this study and the intended outcome. The protocol also covered the study design. The study design covered the criteria used to identify the case for the pilot. In addition, it described the data collection and analysis methods for the pilot study. Furthermore, the pilot case study protocol covered how data was to be managed which included secure data storage, transcription and confidentiality. Towards the end, the pilot study protocol described the timeline, quality assurance and how the results of the study would be disseminated.

The pilot study tested the method followed in approaching the potential participants. No major changes were made as a result of testing since participants indicated that they were satisfied with the approach used. The pilot was useful in improving the structure of the interview. The pilot study was also useful in amending the phrasing and format of certain questions. This included identifying overlapping questions and unclear questions. The interview schedule was initially focussing on asking the stakeholder about their understanding of responsibility in technology research and innovation projects and how they contribute towards it. The pilot study revealed that interview participants were more conversant and comfortable to focus on the key research themes as shown in Table 10 (see section 4.9.1) rather than on responsibility because the concept was ambiguous. The ambiguity of responsibility as a concept rendered it difficult for the interviewees to give clear and straightforward answers. As such the study adopted an interview guide based on the main themes identified in the literature review which are outlined in Table 10 above (see section 4.9.1)

4.11 Ethical Consideration

As part of this study, the researcher followed the ethical research procedures of De Montfort University (DMU) before and during the study. Documentation was completed to gain ethical approval for conducting research. The researcher was open and transparent to the participants. The study participants were provided with an information sheet indicating the aim and objectives of the study. Furthermore, the researcher sought consent from the participants for their participation and use of their anonymised data (see Appendices 4-2 and 4-3).

So far, the chapter has discussed the research paradigms, research strategies and the data collection methods. In so doing, it has positioned the study as following a pragmatic stance that is based on the interpretivist and critical research paradigms. The chapter has also mentioned that the study employs a case study research strategy which involved semi-structured interviews and document review for collecting data from the four cases that were selected for the case studies. Moving on, the section that follows will now consider data analysis.

4.12 Data Analysis

Data analysis involves extracting, transforming, and modelling data for the discovery of useful and constructive information (Sandelowski, 2000). The information resulting from the data analysis is used to support the developed contribution of this study. To answer the research questions presented in chapter 1 of this book, the data collected for this research was analysed using a thematic analysis discussed in the section.

4.12.1 Thematic Analysis

Thematic analysis involves the search of themes that emerge from data as a description of a phenomenon (Fereday and Muir-Cochrane, 2006). This type of qualitative data analysis is used to research classifications and present themes relating to the collected data. A theme is a pattern that is realised from data and at a minimum describes, organises and interprets aspects of a phenomenon (2006, p. 4).

Thematic data analysis was ideal for analysing data in this study for the following reasons.

- Firstly, its aim of analysing narrative materials fits in well with the data that was collected from the interviews.
- Secondly, thematic analysis works well with the interpretivism perspective that is adopted in this study.
- Lastly, the thematic analysis process was ideal to ensure that the context of the

- Phenomena was not missed which could have been the case if another analysis technique such as content analysis was used. The latter concentrates on themes drawn from the frequency of occurrence of certain words and concepts which is not deep enough to understand stakeholder engagement in the context of RRI.

Thematic analysis can either be deductive or inductive (Fereday and Muir-Cochrane, 2006). In the inductive thematic analysis, the themes that emerge are closely linked to the data since the assumptions made are data-driven. Therefore, the analysis occurs without attempting to fit the data into a pre-existing frame. On the other hand, in the deductive thematic analysis, the themes that emerge are linked to a preconceived frame that was determined prior to analysis. Contrary to inductive thematic analysis, the deductive thematic analysis is theory-driven and is limited to a pre-conceived frame (Fereday and Muir-Cochrane, 2006, pp. 2–4).

This study used a hybrid thematic data analysis approach suggested by Fereday and Muir-Cochrane (2006). With the hybrid thematic data analysis, the study used both inductive and deductive thematic analysis (2006, p. 4). The hybrid approach was used because the study employed pre-defined themes to give the researcher a startingpoint for the coding process and define the focus of the research within a pre-definedframe (see Appendix 4-5). The analysis then continued with the emergence of new themes from the data that was collected through the interviews as mentioned in section 6.9.1 above.

This approach is more pragmatic than using one approach to thematic data analysis because it used both the raw data from interview transcripts (empirical data) and literature (theory) toward the identification of overarching themes that captured the phenomenon of stakeholder engagement in ICT research projects as described by participants in the study.

The data analysis was done in two folds; firstly, within each case ICT research project and then across all the case projects by synthesising the data from the four cases.

4.12.2 Application of Hybrid Thematic Analysis within case projects

In applying a hybrid approach to thematic analysis, the researcher used a deductive thematic analysis to define broad code categories a priori (Fereday and Muir-Cochrane, 2006, p. 84) based on the conceptual evaluation model that was driven by theory from the literature and the research questions. The broad categories include; "context of stakeholder engagement", "stakeholder identification", nature of engagement" rationale for stakeholder engagement", "outcomes engagement" and "RRI application".

These broad code categories formed the pre-defined coding template where codes were written and identified by a code label and description of what the theme concerns. Another researcher was invited to code a sample of transcripts to test the reliability and applicability of the codes to the raw data (from interview transcripts), by following the predefined codes. The coding results were compared, and no modification to the predefined coding frame was required.

The codes from the pre-defined coding template were then applied to the text in transcripts with the intention of identifying meaningful fragments of text. The transcripts were entered into Nvivo software, and the codes developed for the code manual were entered as nodes. Therefore, the text was coded by matching the codes with fragments of data that was deemed representative of the code. At this stage of the process, the analysis of the text was guided but not restricted by the predefined codes. During the coding of the interview transcripts, inductive codes were allocated to the fragments of data that described a new theme realised in the text. These emerging codes were either different from the predefined codes, or they expanded the predefined codes. For illustration purposes, codes relating to 'outcomes of stakeholder engagement are shown in Figure 4.2 below.

Figure 4.2: Codes emerged under Outcomes of stakeholder engagement

The codes were then connected, and themes identified based on the similarities and differences between data that emerged at this stage of the data analysis. The previous stages were scrutinised to ensure that the clustered themes were representing the assigned codes and initial analysis. In Nvivo, this clustering was done by putting similar nodes in sets as illustrated in Figure 4.3 below which shows the sets for the broad theme of 'stakeholder identification'.

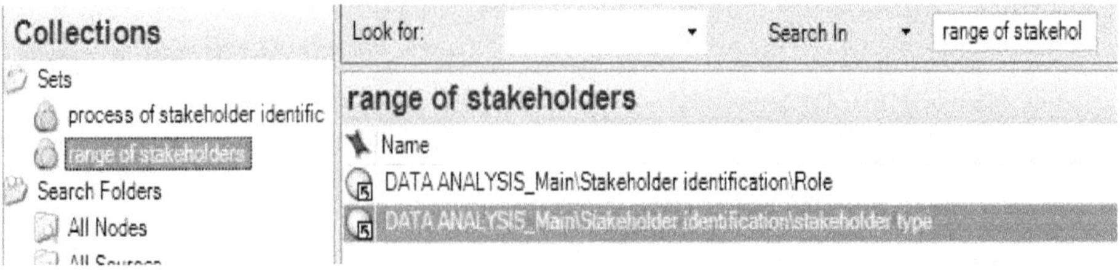

Figure 4.3: Code clustering for themes under stakeholder identification

From the illustration, it can be seen that there are two themes that resulted from the codes under this broad category which were 'process of stakeholder identification' and 'range of stakeholders'. The theme 'range of stakeholder' emerged as a result of clustering the nodes/codes under 'role' and 'stakeholder type'. This was an iterative process until the clustered themes were given short phrases describing their meaning that underpinned the theme (Fereday and Muir-Cochrane, 2006).

Once the themes were established they were analysed based on the analysis which informed the conceptual evaluation model presented in chapter 3 to evaluate stakeholder engagement in the case ICT research projects. The analysis involved assessing the five key elements for evaluating stakeholder engagement (see section 3.3) through the use of a lens of RRI (see section 3.5). The analytical illustration followed in analysing data from each ICT research project is shown in Figure 4.4 below.

Analytical illustration

Part 1:Evaluation of the Key Elements for Evaluating Stakeholder Engagement

Key elements for evaluating		**related themes**
i.	Context within which stakeholders are engaged	
ii.	Identification of stakeholders	
iii.	Nature of stakeholder engagement	
iv.	Rationale for stakeholder engagement	
v.	Outcomes of stakeholder engagement	

Part 2: Applying the RRI lens

Key conceptual feature of RRI		**related themes**
i.	Engagement of stakeholders	
ii.	Anticipation and reflection	
iii.	Openness and transparency	
iv.	Responsiveness	

Figure 4.4: Analytical illustration

4.12.3 Cross-Case Projects Analysis

Next, the results of the analyses of the four individual case projects were synthesised by conducting a cross-case analysis which is discussed in chapter 6. Using the layout provided by the analytical illustration (see Figure 9 above) the value of stakeholder engagement in light of responsible innovation was evaluated in individual cases. The cross-case analysis then involved comparisons to seek out what was common and what was particular in the case projects (Ponelis, 2015, p. 543). These were then discussed in relation to the existing literature on stakeholder engagement, RRI and evaluation as presented in chapter 2. The analysis across the case projects concluded by synthesising the main findings together to answer the research questions introduced in chapter 1.

4.12.4 Other Data Analysis Methods not used

4.12.4.1 Narrative analysis

Narrative analysis focuses on how stories from participants are told to help in explaining the way in which the participants think and are organised within groups. The main focus is to reconstruct stories from participants who are subjected to different contexts and experiences for instance by comparing accounts of two or more people (Grbich, 2012; Smith, 2000). This method of data analysis could have been ideal if this study was mainly collecting stories from stakeholders about their experiences in their engagement. In that case, narrative analysis could have given the researcher an insight into how stakeholders structure their dialogue and communication in relation to achieving responsible outcomes in ICT research projects. However, this would have missed out on essential knowledge extracts that could support the research in answering the research questions sufficiently. Therefore, this type of data analysis was not ideal for the research.

4.12.4.2 Discourse analysis

Discourse analysis is a method of analysing a spoken interaction that includes all types of texts. These types of text consist of media that are written and visual (Grbich, 2007, p. 146). In discourse analysis, the emphasis is on how people produce and make sense of their ordinary daily social interactions, for instance by looking at the way they use their language in situations (Berg *et al.*, 2004). Therefore, with discourse analysis, the researcher not only analyses conversation but also takes into consideration the social context in which the conversation occurs. This includes taking account of previous conversations, and power relationships.

Discourse analysis could have helped to identify and track the balance of power and influence among stakeholders that are engaged in ICT research projects through their dialogue and actions in relation to responsible innovation. However, the main aim of this study is neither to understand the power balance among stakeholders within ICT research projects nor to look at the marginalisation of certain stakeholders when engaging them in projects. Thus, this data analysis type was not adopted.

4.12.4.3 Content analysis

Content analysis is the procedure used to extract and categorise desired verbal or behavioural data from a body of material with an objective to identify specified characteristics of the material for classification, summarisation and tabulation (Berg *et al.*, 2004; Smith, 2000). Using content analysis data could be analysed on two levels. The first one is where data is analysed on a descriptive level, in other words, an enumerative level where the focus is on frequencies and description of data. The second one is where data is analysed on an interpretative level where the focus is on developing codes from data (Grbich, 2007, p. 111). The difference between the two is that the former simply aims at finding out 'what is the data' within the content while the latter looks at finding out 'what was meant by the data?'

Content analysis could have been ideal to use in this study, for instance, if it was involved with large sets of existing documentation and was looking to find meaning from the dominance or frequency of particular words or else data descriptions that are related to the topic of this study.

Also, due to the nature of the research question, using this type of analysis could have resulted in misinterpreting stakeholder responses by over-relying on descriptive features such as word frequencies and word counts rather than getting an in-depth analysis of the data that is collected from respondents. With this in mind, the research did not adopt content analysis for analysing the data that was collected.

4.13 Chapter Conclusion

This chapter has described the research design that is used in this study to answer the research question(s) formulated in chapter 1. The chapter commenced by discussing research paradigms which led to settling for a pragmatic stance that combines interpretivism and critical research as ideal for understanding the value of stakeholder engagement in ICT research projects in light of responsible outcomes. The chapter also mentioned that the overall research design is of a qualitative nature. The chapter then discussed and reviewed some research strategies that are used in qualitative research and indicated that the research followed a case study strategy. The chapter argued that a case study strategy was ideal because it enables an in-depth analysis of stakeholder engagement and it significance towards responsible innovation within a real-life context, that is, the ICT research projects. Furthermore, the case study research strategy was chosen because it allows the use of mixed methods, which supports triangulation. Henceforth, it enhances the validity of the findings and the use of pre-established theoretical proposals underlying the conceptual evaluation model that was presented in the previous chapter and later applied in chapter 5. The chapter went on to present different data collection methods and pointed out that semi-structured interviews and document review were appropriate for this study. In addition, the chapter presented different data analysis methods and discussed the analysis method that was used in this study which was a hybrid approach to thematic data analysis. The next four chapters will present the analysis of the individual case ICT research projects.

CHAPTER 5

Evaluation Findings

5.1 Introduction

This chapter presents the findings from an analysis of the four cases that were part of the case study for this research. The four cases includes Projects 1, 2, 3 and 4 which were selected in The case analysis aims to evaluate the efficacy of stakeholder engagement towards the attainment of socially desirable outcomes in the four case projects. The analysis follows the analytical illustration presented in section 4.12.2. In sections 5.2, 5.5, 5.8 and 5.11 the chapter presents the analysis of the five key elements for evaluating stakeholder engagement in Projects 1, 2, 3 and 4 respectively. The analysis is based on the conceptual evaluation model presented in section 3.6. The chapter also covers an application of the RRI lens in the four projects to understand the efficacy of stakeholder engagement within the context of RRI. The application of the RRI lens is covered in sections 5.3, 5.6, 5.9 and 5.12. Further, the chapter includes Theories of Change (ToCs) for Project 1, 2, 3 and 4 in sections 5.4, 5.7, 5.10 and 5.13 respectively. The ToCs indicates the causal linkages between stakeholder engagement and the attainment of socially desirable outcomes in the research projects. They show how different stakeholder engagement activities and inputs result in socially desirable and acceptable outcomes within the R&I process based on assumptions that are made by the researcher (evaluator) and the people involved in the ICT research projects.

5.2 Evaluating Key Elements for Stakeholder Engagement in Project 1

To evaluate the value of stakeholder engagement in Project 1, data was collected using interviews and a document review (see section 4.9). As a result, 17 sources were used for the analysis of stakeholder engagement in the ICT research project. The sources consisted of seven documents and ten interviews. For anonymity, each source has been given a code as shown in Table 5.1 below.

Table 5.1: Data Collection Sources for Project 1

Source	Code	Type of source	Date of collection	Length of collection
Librarian	SS01	Stakeholder interview	6/05/16	39 minutes
Local Authority representative	SS02	Stakeholder interview	11/05/16 (Skype)	31 minutes
Academic	SS03	Stakeholder interview	06/05/16 (Skype)	34 minutes
Researcher	SS04	Stakeholder interview	04/05/16	40 minutes
End user	SS05	Stakeholder interview	03/05/16	26 minutes
End User	SS06	Stakeholder interview	04/05/16	41 minutes
Researcher	SS07	Stakeholder interview	03/04/16	32 minutes
Researcher	SS08	Stakeholder interview	26/04/16	45 minutes
Local Authority representative	SS09	Stakeholder interview	28/04/16	37 minutes
Local Authority representative	SS10	Stakeholder interview	28/04/16	43 minutes
Web page	SSD1	Document review		n/a
Web page	SSD2	Document review		n/a
Web page	SSD3	Document review		n/a
Blog	SSD4	Document review		n/a
Forum	SSD5	Document review		n/a
Article	SSD6	Document review		n/a
Deliverable	SSD7	Document review		n/a

This section presents the first part of an evaluative analysis of the value of stakeholder engagement in Project 1. The first part provides an understanding of the efficacy of stakeholder engagement process through an evaluation of the five key elements for evaluating stakeholder engagement that are suggested as essential in section 3.3.

5.2.1 Context of the Stakeholder Engagement

Project 1 aimed to research the use of ICT in promoting environmental sustainability. The Project 1 focused on how carbon dioxide emissions from buildings could be monitored and consequently reduced. The project was involved in energy use optimisation through a comprehensive approach to exploiting the potential of ICT. As part of the optimisation, the research employed the use of smart metering to achieve significant energy saving in public buildings. To accomplish this aim, the research project built on existing services to develop a comprehensive ICT system (sometimes referred to as a '*dashboard*') that provides feedback on energy consumption and information for organisational energy management. The system used ICT to offer access to energy consumption data and provide the results of the sophisticated data analysis intuitively and engagingly. The range of public buildings where the ICT system was implemented and operated included city administration buildings, office buildings, museums, university buildings but also schools, nurseries and sports and event centres.

The purpose of Project 1 was '*to enable public authorities to improve their management of energy in the buildings significantly through the use of ICT*' (SS03). This was going to be achieved by reducing the energy consumption of the public sector by a very significant amount to meet overall emission reduction targets. The use of ICT was targeted at three different potential stakeholder categories, building users (and managers), the researchers and local authorities. The information was aimed at these three specific audiences '*to give them a better understanding of the role of ICT in helping to move towards low carbon spaces*' (SSD3).

The implementation of operational services included 11 pilot sites with more than 550 buildings in 8 countries (United Kingdom, France, Germany, Italy, Spain, Netherlands, and Turkey, Serbia) with almost 20,000 professionals and staff users and reaching more than 6,000,000 visitors annually (SSD1). Due to the vastness of the project and resource limitations, this study used purposive sampling (see section 6.7) to select one of the pilot cities in the UK for the case study. The pilot city will be called 'city X'. The project ran for three years from 2012 to 2015 and was funded by European Commission within the CIP ICT Policy Support Programme.

For the Project 1 to conduct research, the research Project 5ngaged multi-disciplinary stakeholders from academia (researchers), local authority and public (end users). The role of the stakeholders in the research project was first, to help other stakeholders understand the role of ICT in behaviour change and investment in energy efficiency to meet the low carbon agenda. Secondly, other stakeholders such as end users, who included estates staff and the students were engaged to be informed about the changing performance of their building(s) over time, allowing them to take action to mitigate wastage according to the feedback that they received from the ICT system. Thirdly, stakeholders such as the local authorities were engaged to see the relative performance of different buildings thus increasing their awareness of energy efficiency issues.

To give a picture of the stakeholders that were involved in Project 1, specifically in city 'X', Table 5.2 below shows the stakeholders who were contacted to take part in the data collection process for this study. The table indicates the role of the stakeholders, their category together with the numbers of invited participants and those participants who accepted to participate in this study.

Table 5.2: Project 1's Stakeholders for Study Participation

Stakeholder role	Stakeholder category	Number invited for interviews	Number accepted
Librarian	University representative	2	1
Researcher	Academia	5	4
End-user	Estates staff	5	2
Energy experts	Local authority representative	6	3

All in all, 18 potential participants were invited but 14 stakeholders responded to the introductory email which was also an invitation for participation. However, out of the 14 potential interviewees that responded, 10 accepted to be interviewed. The other four gave excuses that were related to not having time to spare for the interview.

5.2.2 Identification of Stakeholders

With regards to evaluating the first element for evaluating stakeholder engagement, which is stakeholder identification, two themes appeared to be of significance. These themes focused on the process of stakeholder identification and the range of stakeholders that were identified for engagement in Project 1. Regarding the process of identification, one interviewee mentioned that they were identified and recruited through referral as mentioned in their response that *'it was more like a referral perhaps. They needed somebody to do that job'* (SS06).

On the other hand, with regards to the range of stakeholders, there was evidence that there was a wide range of stakeholders with various roles in the R&I process. This was demonstrated in both the interviews and the document review. For instance, some were engaged to take up roles that were related to software development as mentioned by SS05 that his background was in software development, *'particularly interested in issues of online privacy and privacy'*.

Another stakeholder, SS01, was identified as an end user of the ICT system that was developed in the research. The respondent said that he *'was involved as head of user experience for the library'*.

Similarly, SS05 said that he *'became a user on the forum because [he had] some experience in using the buildings'*. SS05 indicated that he *'became a user after implementation of the ICT system and was engaged in discussions about the information'* it was telling the different stakeholders in the research. In addition to contributing to the forum, SS05 was also identified because of his *'background in software coding'*, and as a result, the stakeholder even contributed a small amount of code for the research.

From the data collected, it was established that the stakeholders that were identified for engagement in Project 1 included academics, researchers, users and local authority representatives (SSD3). These stakeholders were identified to undertake roles that ranged from building users whose role involved using the ICT system to *'adjust their daily routines and behaviour' (SS08)* accordingly and ultimately provide and discuss the data being shown on the system dashboard.

In addition, researchers (academia) were using the information from the other stakeholders to research the impact of the ICT system further and suggest way for improvement. From the local authority's side, the identified stakeholders were Energy experts who used the information provided by the ICT system to improve onbuilding infrastructure.

5.2.3 Nature of Stakeholder engagement

The next key element that was evaluated was the nature of stakeholder engagement. The themes that emerged from the evaluative analysis were categorised into two groups, that is, form of stakeholder engagement and the barriers to stakeholder engagement. Firstly, concerning the form of stakeholder engagement in Project 1, from the interviews, it was established that the stakeholder engagement took a number of forms.

First of all, some stakeholders revealed that their engagement was in the form of dissemination of information. This was evidenced in the response by SS01 who said that they were disseminating information to publicise and promote the agenda (rationale). The respondent stated that he thought *'in all modesty [that they] did a significant amount to help promote the agenda of the project, that is environmental sustainability and ... what was going on'*. SS01 further suggested that they provided a vehicle for the project team to promote the agenda through the dissemination of information. For example, *'they prepared events [...] and encouraged other stakeholders [including staff and students] to come and do exercises'*.

Correspondingly, SS06 said that they *'helped to communicate how important the research project was to those groups that the project was involving, that is the other stakeholders [...] who [were] involved in the consultation process of the project'*. The respondent further mentioned that the communication also included details on the roles of different stakeholders in the project *'regarding the responsibility of the project and also their responsibility concerning reducing energy use and greenhouse gas emissions'*. Apart from publicising and promoting the agenda, SS06 said that they also reported on the findings of the research and *'had to analyse all that data [...] to produce a final report with the outcomes of the behavioural change due to the xxx Project 1ashboard'*.

Another form of engagement was that some stakeholders that were engaged in Project 1 facilitated dialogue among stakeholders. This was mentioned by SS07 that they were *'wanting people to talk to each other about the processes' within the research project and beyond.* Therefore, they were *'engaging with people over a short time series to explain to them what the project was about, getting their consent to participate in it [...] and making sure they knew what the project was doing.* As a part of that, stakeholders were given an opportunity to ask questions and give feedbackon what Project 1 was doing with the information on energy and water data.

Regarding facilitating dialogue, SS08 also pointed to the fact that they *'had consultations with people and articulated to them about how best to conserve energy using the dashboard system'*. They managed to do this *'by literally going around and talking to everybody about how the system works and having regular meetings and helping people on how to understand it and manage their buildings and consumption'*. In connection to the facilitation of dialogue among stakeholders, it was also established that some stakeholders were *'bridging people together and supporting them to set up networks'* (SS03) along the R&I process. As such, they were able to provide feedback and advice which for example, was used to *'flag up inefficiencies'* (SS05). Therefore, the stakeholders were *'not just promoting the fact that dashboard was live [but] also did measuring exercises'* (SS01) for feedback and guidance. Part of this was done through writing *'software that would help demonstrate the data [...] in a way that non-technical users could understand'* (SS02).

Relatedly, some stakeholders said that they *'looked at the data that was coming through, and then directly engaged with other stakeholders to ensure that they were green'* (SS01) in their practices and daily behaviours. Furthermore, two stakeholders (SS02, SS08) mentioned that their engagement was in the form of offering their expertise to the research project. One of them claimed that *'they helped develop the approach and technology that was used in the project across the board'* (SS02), while the other said that *'the expertise that is brought to the project is priceless [therefore they were] brought in to the project because of [their] expertise in energy conservation and ability to analyse the data and give advice based on the data that is collected'* (SS08)

The last form of engagement was leading. This was mentioned by SS02 who said that they were involved in the leadership of the project as evidenced in their response in which the respondent said that they were highly involved in the discussions about where the research project would go and who was appropriate to involve in the project. The respondents *'role in the beginning, as the most senior person [...], was defining how well to take it [the research]'*.

Nevertheless, in spite of the different forms of engagement that came about from the different stakeholders, there were some barriers too. The first barrier that affected the stakeholder engagement was lack of interest in engagement as put forward by SS01 that *'the biggest barrier was [...] perhaps recusancy on the part of some of the stakes to engage with the project'*. The respondent pointed out that some stakeholders declined their invitation to engage in the research project. This was similarly observed by SS07 who mentioned that *'some people didn't really want to engage because they didn't find it useful to them personally or useful to them in their jobs'*. As such they *'had to try and persuade them so that they should participate and sometimes that was successful other times it wasn't. [They] also had to try to persuade people to continue to engage with us over the duration of the project, and again sometimes it was successful and sometimes it wasn't'*.

On the same note, SS08 simply said that there was *'a lot of scepticism [...]. A lot of premises officers were not interested in [the research project] unless if they were really into conservation [otherwise], they had other priorities'*. This was echoed by SS03 who said that when it came to engaging stakeholders they found out that *'people are very busy anyway. People have their day jobs'* so most of the people that were spoken to about the research project or the potential to be involved in the research project *'had other priorities'*. As a follow-on, stakeholders were let down by other stakeholders, for instance, *'some of the stakeholders could not provide relevant and enough data for the research'* (SS06).

Another barrier was connected to people not understanding responsible innovation or outcomes as pointed by SS03 suggested that *'based on the terminology used, people tend to dig their heels in when you tell them about responsibility, and this could be a barrier regarding implementing or contributing towards it'*. The last barrier was down to lack of capacity. For example, SS06 mentioned that technical glitches affected the engagement efforts *'for example, sometimes the project dashboard [the ICT system] was not running very well in some computers because the browsers were very old'*.

5.2.4 Rationale for the Stakeholder Engagement

The other key element that was evaluated was the motive behind the stakeholder engagement in Project 1. From the interviews it was established that stakeholders were engaged in the Project 1 for the following motives. The first motive was consultation. This was something that SS03 mentioned during the interview that *'their role in that project was to bring together some of the building users with the researchers in developing the interface'*. Part of the rationale behind SS03's engagement was to ensure that *'there was a good dialogue between, building users and researchers so that they could come up with an interface that the users could understand and also engage with as well'*.

The consultation was in two ways. In one way, the stakeholders that were engaged recommended new perspectives on how people could deal with the social challenge by *'offering a different approach'* (SS01) because of their involvement in the Green Impact scheme. The other way was to give feedback on the development and implementation process of the ICT system as pointed out by SS05 that *'it [was] very important to understand different people's perspective on what responsible research is, and how the resulting technology can be used'*. The respondent further stressed that *'unless you involve different stakeholders you won't necessarily get those different perspectives'*.

This was echoed by SS08 who said that the rationale for engaging stakeholders in Project 1 was *'Diversity!'* SS08 suggested that *'with many stakeholders engaged, [the stakeholders in the research project] can actually tell people about what is going and what they do.* The respondent further pointed out that the idea of stakeholder engagement in Project 1 was to bring down energy consumption through promoting awareness among a diverse range of stakeholders.

Another rationale that was established from the interviews was that the stakeholders were engaged in Project 1 for control and direction of the R&I process. This control and direction was down to many reasons, one of which was the stakeholders' expertise as suggested by SS08 who emphasised they were brought to the project because of their *'expertise in energy conservation'*. Therefore, with such expertise, the stakeholders were able to *'give advice on the way forward'* (SS02). Relatedly, the stakeholders were engaged in Project 1 to influence innovation towards an approach for reducing energy consumption and reducing greenhouse gas emissions. According to SS02, this was going to be achieved *'through a greater awareness of the issues around energy consumption and performance of buildings'*. As such, some stakeholders were there to provide direction, control and *'lead the research'* (SS03) taking place in the Project 1.

In addition to the motives stated above, the stakeholders were also engaged to encourage mutual learning among different stakeholders. One way of doing this was via a forum. Some stakeholders had *'to join the forum as part of the project and participation in the project to engage users'* (SS05) and share knowledge. For example, they shared knowledge on how the ICT system was working, how to reduce carbon footprints, and how both the system and the carbon footprints can be improved. This was echoed by SS03 who said that *'researchers had an idea of what they wanted to do, but they were not quite sure of what form that would take. So, involving stakeholders [...] to help them develop the sort of interface that would explain energy usage to them, [...] was a really good way of sharing responsibility and knowledge'*.

Still, on mutual learning, some stakeholders were engaged to contribute towards learning and reflection through *'providing a vehicle for the project team to prepare events and encourage other stakeholders and staff to come and do exercises with students'* (SS01). According to the respondent, these exercises and engagement activities were important for reflection and learning because they *'showed so tangibly how much energy was used by spaces'*. Therefore they held *'a mirror to users of their responsibility in using space'* and brought a *'discussion about what individuals can do about the society and conserving energy'*. SS01 further added that the idea of the stakeholder engagement was that *'users [could] think about their contribution or their use of those spaces and the impact it has'*,

The stakeholders were also engaged to promote ownership of the research project and its outcomes. This was achieved by promoting the agenda (section 7.2.3) among different stakes as evidently put by SS01 that they *'did play [their] part as a stakeholder in promoting the agenda in engaging with the public'*. Not only was the promotion of ownership directed to the public, but it was also promoted towards *'those different levels of stakeholders whether they [had] strategic responsibilities, technical involvement with managing the building or they were just based in the building as building users or visiting the building. All these people needed to have slightly different levels of information'* (SS02). Also as part of promoting the agenda, some stakeholders encouraged sharing of responsibilities by getting some *'colleagues who [had] not previously been involved in green impact to be involved in the project as there were aspects of the project that appealed to them in terms of energy monitoring and the way that would work'* (SS01). SS01 said that he took it further to discuss with other stakeholders on how much could be saved if the feedback from the ICT system was followed and invest more in smart energy reducing technologies.

The last rationale for stakeholder engagement in Project 1 that was revealed fromthe interviews was that stakeholders were also engaged for resourcing. This was pointed out by SS03 who said that stakeholder *'networks were set to provide resources'* that were necessary for the research to be effective and successful. These resources included both human and financial resources.

5.2.5 Outcome of Stakeholder Engagement

The final key element that was evaluated was the outcome of the engagement. In Project 1, the first outcome that came out of the stakeholder engagement was the awareness of the potential responsibility issues. This awareness culminated in the users changing their behaviour. This was mentioned by SS01 who said that *'the outcomes [of the engagement] would be users changing their behaviours or perhaps at the very least recognising that they play a part and that they have a wider responsibility'*. The respondent further suggested that *'technologies like what the research project is developing, actually can show people their behaviours and impact on energy consumption, [and] all those things that can hold a mirror up to people and their behaviours'*.

In agreement to what was mentioned by SS01, SS03 talked about how influential he was in bringing awareness and changing the behaviour of stakeholders. SS03 said that since he was *'further up the structure, therefore [could] encourage people further down the structure to change and perhaps think about their responsibility'*. The respondent further said that they *'changed people's conceptions of sustainability of energy use or environmental issues'*. Consequently, due to the engagement of stakeholders in the research project, particularly end users, *'responsibility become embedded within [their] day to day actions'* therefore changing *'their habits in a positive way as a result of understanding their responsibility'*.

Correspondingly, SS07 said that as a result of their engagement in the research project, some people were persuaded *'to change their practices if the energy consumption was a bit high'*. The respondent said that they *'wanted to engage with [people] specifically to get them to reduce their energy and water consumption [...] by providing the right information that motivated them to do something'*. As a result of the promotion of the agenda, SS03 mentioned that they *'got people interested in energy research, started to reduce it [...] and obviously reducing emissions of greenhouse gases [...] which is good to society'*.

Once the stakeholders were aware of the potential responsibility issues, they took ownership of the R&I process and the outcomes that resulted from it. This was reiterated by SS06 who said that *'ownership is quite important'* for stakeholders to accept the results of the R&I process. The respondent further added that *'with consultation [...] people have more ownership of whatever innovation is bringing'*. This related to another outcome of stakeholder engagement that was established from the interviews, that of co-creation.

Regarding co-creation, SS05 mentioned that as a result of different stakeholders bringing in a variety of perspectives there was a *'greater coverage of the spectrum of issues rather than just having for example, one designer'*. As a consequence, different stakeholders came together to share knowledge and perspectives on how the ICT system could be developed. Considering that the stakeholders that were engaged were from different disciplines, therefore had *'their own personal perspectives and probably a disciplinary perspectives'* (SS02), the engagement provided a platform where they could co-create the output and outcomes of the R&I process undertaken in Project 1.

Relatedly, SS02 gave an example that *'a computer scientist might be very interested in the issues with encryption of private data, and potentially metadata gathering and machine learning but may not be so engaged with the responsibility to turn on gas boilers properly'*. So, engaging the computer scientist together with another stakeholder that is so versed about estate management could create an environment where they will combine their interests and come up with one acceptable solution that takes into account their respective interests. This was encapsulated by SS03 who said that *'bridging people together was necessary to come up with solutions'* that were realised by *'all those involved in the research process'*.

Moving on from co-creation as an outcome of stakeholder engagement, from the interviews it also emerged that because of the engagement, there was optimal utilisation of resources. This was suggested by SS01 that with the ICT system acting as a *'mirror'* on how they use energy, the stakeholders that were engaged in the research project changed the way they used the energy in their buildings. Similarly, SS02 mentioned that stakeholders from all ranks and levels got interested in the research project and the dashboard because it promised and promoted efficiencies and therefore cost reduction. This was echoed by SS07 who stated that *'hopefully when people learn from the research they can do it in their homes and save money'* and SS08 who simply said that *'the outcome of my contribution could be cost saving'* among those that she made aware of the system developed by the research project.

The last outcome of stakeholder engagement in Project 1 was to sustain the aims of the research. SS06 indicated that if there were no stakeholders engaged in the research project, its aim and *'impact would just die out as soon as the funding for the project was finished'*. The respondent suggested that stakeholder engagement created a heritage of the aims and results of the research that was carried out in Project 1. SS06 said that *'a lot of people forget about the research and then well it's a waste of money, a waste of resources. If the people are going to use what you offered them or to look through the project, accept that even when the research project finishes they will keep finding it useful. That is very important for the stakeholders. Once they have ownership, they can keep that project going'*.

Also, since the main aim was to find solutions to societal challenges, the engagement supported the attainment of that aim of the ICT research project (see section 5.2.1)by bringing technology and people together to address environmental degradation and lay structure for future use of the research outputs (SS01, SS02, and SSD 3).

5.3 Applying the RRI Lens to Project 1

This section presents the second part of the evaluation for Project 1 which is an evaluative analysis of the stakeholder engagement within the context of RRI. Thus, the second part of the analytical illustration presented in section 4.12.2 was applied for analysis. This involved an application of the RRI lens presented in section 3.5.

5.3.1 Engagement of Stakeholders

From the sources used in the interviews and the document review, the project engaged a range of stakeholders with varying experiences, backgrounds and expertise. The identified stakeholder types were researchers, academics, end users (staff members and students), local authority representatives (energy experts) (SSD1, SSD3). As pointed out by SS03 there were different levels of stakeholders that were engaged in the project. Some *'high-level stakeholders were really involved in the project and then [...] the lower level stakeholders [were] consulted as part of the project' (SS03)*. It was established that the stakeholders engaged were aware that *'for the whole project to work quickly or the project to work perfectly there has to be a link between those different layers of stakeholders'* (SS03).

There was *'diversity'* (SS08) in the stakeholders that were engaged. The stakeholders were engaged to have *'early high-level conversation'* about entering research, and they needed to do (SS02). The stakeholders were engaged because there was a realisation that *'the success of a project is based on engaging people'* and therefore for the project to meet its aims was *'all about engaging people'* (SS02). Therefore *'without that, it would have been a lot more difficult to run [the project] in terms of achieving the big end'* (SS03).

With such a level of engagement, it is evident that Project 1 took on board different viewpoints from those engaged as previously mentioned by SS05 and SS02 in sections 5.2.4 and 5.2.5 above. Therefore, with stakeholders engaged in the R&I process the agenda, and the outcomes of the research was bound to be desirable and acceptable. The acceptability was a result of the extent of the engagement of those stakeholders for whom the research was being done. It was established that the building users were highly engaged in the process through events and the forum where they were given information about the research and the ICT system and at the same time given an opportunity to provide feedback.

5.3.2 Anticipation and Reflection

In Project 1 the stakeholders were engaged to anticipate and reflect on the consequences of high energy consumption and its effect on environmental degradation. As pointed out by SS01 that one of the ways that this was achieved in the research project was by making the *'metering visible for the monitoring of energy usage [therefore] engaging with users [...] to talk about their patterns of behaviour'*. Additionally, there was use of *'automatic metering to establish profiles of consumption', and therefore with the aid of 'the software [...] learn the profiles'* (SS02) which played a major role in encouraging the stakeholders to anticipate and get valuable insights on their behaviours and therefore think of ways to improve (SS08). This shows that there were mechanisms put in place to reflect on the process and see whether it was working towards its intended impact.

Because of such mechanisms and the sort of stakeholders that were engagement in Project 1, it was possible to reflect and realise if something was not working properly and therefore agree on ways of carrying out the process differently. This issomething that SS08 mentioned that *'if there [were] sudden deviations from those profiles [from the dashboard] it was possible to know what things are going wrong'*.

In terms of anticipation, the stakeholders that were engaged had an influence on the inclusion of the right stakeholders and the purpose of the research in terms of potential use and desirability. In support of this observation, SS02 pointed out that during the research, the engaged stakeholders *'were having discussions about where [they] wanted to go, who [they] wanted to involve [...] in the project'* to ensure that the research was successful in addressing the challenge that it was called for. Also, *'researchers had an idea of what they wanted to do, but they were not quite sure of what form that would take'* therefore involving stakeholders in R&I process was a really good way to anticipate and *'reflect on the process and its outcomes'* (SS03) and how they could achieve it. SS03 further mentioned that the stakeholders had to *'understand their responsibility, think that they have a responsibility, and feel that their responsibility has changed as part of the project'*. Ultimately as part of the process, the engagement of different stakeholders ensured in part *'that responsibility become embedded within their day to day actions'* therefore *'changing their habits in a positive way as a way of understanding what their responsibility is'*.

The energy experts and the researchers engaged worked hand in hand, sharing perspectives and expertise to develop an ICT system that produces sustainable outcomes and engaged the end users to ensure social desirability of the technology that was being developed in Project 1.

5.3.3 Openness and Transparency

With regards to openness and transparency, looking at the interviews and the documents that were reviewed, it is evidential that stakeholder engagement significantly contributed towards a transparent and open R&I process within Project 1. To begin with, the research project attempted to communicate the agenda and the methodology that was being developed for use in improving air quality and reducing energy consumption to its stakeholders in promotion events, on the forum and the online (SSD3, SSD4 and SSD5). In the same vein, SS07 mentioned that they engaged with *'people [...] and had to explain to them what the project was about, getting their consent to the participate in it [...] making sure they knew what we are doing, what information was collected and giving them feedback on what we are doing with the information'*.

This shows that there was a balanced and meaningful communication in the research project that was essential for transparency. Also, information was put on a discussion board, or *'forum'* (SS07, SSD5). According to SS07, the forum provided a platform where everyone could see what was posted and they could see what other people were posting and what replies were given to different questions. The evidence of an open and transparent process was further reinforced by SS07 who stated that the *'project [...] tried to make [information] relevant to [stakeholders] and give them information that they would find helpful and if they didn't find it helpful we wantedto understand why so that we could change the information that we provided to them'*. This statement from SS07 indicates that stakeholders were given a chance to scrutinise information and therefore get into direct *'conversations'* (SS03) with other stakeholders who were actively involved in research to improve its effectiveness.

Furthermore, it was revealed that *'there was a good dialogue between, building users and researchers so that they could come up with an interface that the users could understand'* (SS03). This meant that to develop an interface that was acceptable and desirable both stakeholders had to be open about their expectations and in particular, the researchers had to be open about the methodology and techniques used. On this note, SS05 stated that he was *'engaged in discussions about the information [the interface] was telling [the stakeholders] and in the end even contributed a small amount of code for the project'*. The involvement in the discussions further affirms the level of openness and transparency that was taking place within the research project.

According to SS07, as part of being transparent and open, the stakeholder engagement facilitated a medium where people were talking to each other about the R&I process and the data that was being produced during the research process. The respondent further said that as part of his engagement it was *'important to talk to people [...] and to get them to give you feedback on how they provide you with the information and how you then share it with others so that everything is transparent and that they will be no potential issues in the future'*.

To finalise, stakeholder engagement was influential in ensuring that there was openness and transparency in Project 1 through cascading the potential benefits of the ICT system across all stakeholder ranks starting from the sponsors all the way to the end users. According to SS08 *'being open and transparent helped [stakeholders] to see what is happening and compare it'* and it was discovered that *'once you tell people about the benefits of the system [...] there is a good level of buy-in'*.

5.3.4 Responsiveness

The research in Project 1 was directed towards modification of thoughts and behaviours of different stakeholders. As a consequence of engaging diverse stakeholders with different backgrounds, there were different perspectives on the R&I process and its potential to solve the societal challenge of environmental sustainability.

SS05 suggested that *'it was very important to understand different people's perspective on what responsible research is, and also how a technology project could be used'* to deal with societal problems. Thus, this indicates that the stakeholder engagement was valuable in changing behaviours of different stakeholders or at least make them start thinking of ways that they could change their energy consumption and therefore reduce their carbon footprints.

It was also learnt that there was consultation on using the monitoring system that was developed which further showed that there was responsiveness. As suggested by SS01 *'technologies like the one the project was developing, actually can show people their behaviours and impact on energy consumption, [and] can hold a mirror up to people and their behaviours'.* Holding a mirror to people changed the behaviours of those engaged according to the new knowledge and perspectives that emerged using the new ICT system (dashboard).

The stakeholder engagement provided an opportunity for different people to be *'aware of the issues and energy consumption [...] through a new technological movement' (SS02)* and *'got people interested in energy research focused on the reduction of emissions of greenhouse'* (SS03). Out of that interest and awareness, people became responsive.

For instance, on the one hand the end users changed their behaviour based on 'the *data provided by the software'.* On the other hand, the researchers changed some of the research processes based on the feedback from *'forum and discussion board'* that was provided by the research project (SS03). An example was given in the interviews where SS07 mentioned that some stakeholders flagged up issues which enabled the researchers to make changes in response to the issues that were flagged. One of the changes mentioned was that the researchers would *'change the way information is disseminated'* (SS07) to make it easy to understand and therefore more effective.

To sum it up, responsiveness was upheld by listening to the needs and perspectives of the stakeholders that were engaged in the R&I process and then developing the systems based on those needs and perspectives.

5.4 THEORY OF CHANGE FOR PROJECT 1

A deductive theory of change (ToC) (see section 2.10.3.1) for the stakeholder engagement process was developed through the sources of data used in this study, which were documents and the interviews with the stakeholders in Project 1. Although such a retrospective ToC has less value in terms of improving the process, unlike the more common prospective application of ToC approaches outlined in section 2.10.3.1, it still provides a lens to explore and understand the interactions between stakeholder engagement and the attainment of socially desirable and acceptable outcomes in ICT research projects. Consequently, it facilitates learning and reflection that is useful for improving stakeholder engagement in practice in either current or future research projects. Thus, a ToC for Project 1 is set out in Figure 5.1 below. In essence, while Figure 10 simplifies the ToC for Project 1 into a relatively linear structure, the cyclical relationship between inputs and activities specifically highlight the reciprocity between the two. Hence, the inputs from stakeholder engagement (rationale for stakeholder engagement) determines the sort of activities (nature of stakeholder engagement) that the engagement will entail. Correspondingly, the manifestation of the stakeholder engagement activities require the inputs from the stakeholder engagement.

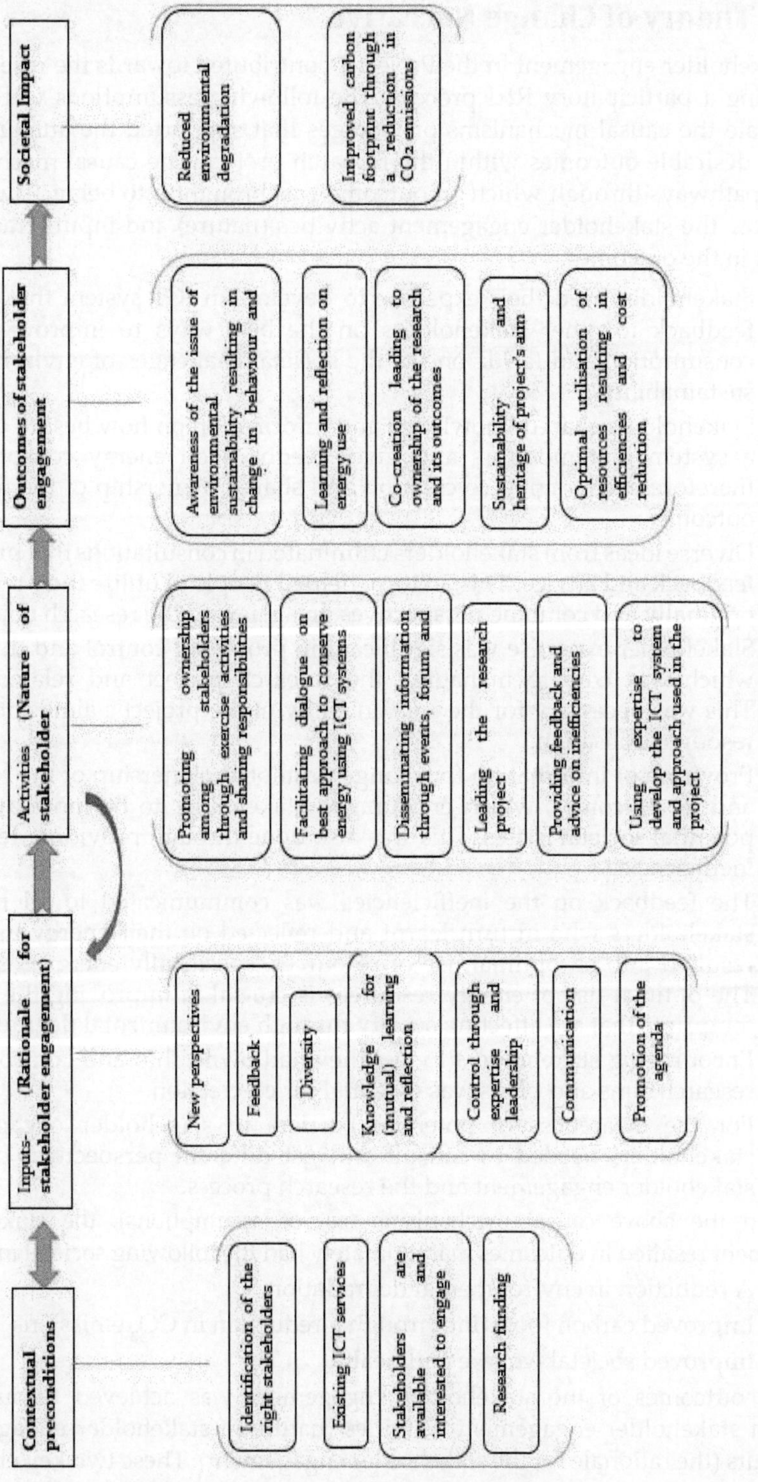

Figure 5.1: A Theory of Change for Project 1

5.4.1 Theory of Change Narrative

The stakeholder engagement in the Project 1 contributed towards the research by facilitating a participatory R&I process. The following assumptions were made to indicate the causal mechanisms or linkages that supported the attainment of socially desirable outcomes within the research project. The causal mechanisms are the pathways through which an outcome was brought into being. Thus, they show how the stakeholder engagement activities (nature) and inputs (rationale) resulted in the outcomes.

i. Stakeholder used their expertise to develop an ICT system that offered feedback to other stakeholders on the best ways to improve energy consumption and tackle one of the societal challenges of environmental sustainability.

ii. Stakeholders shared knowledge and information on how best to develop a system that monitors and gives feedback on energy consumption, therefore encouraging co-creation and shared ownership of the research outcomes.

iii. Diverse ideas from stakeholders culminated in consultations that provided feedback and advice. This, in turn, helped people to utilise their resources optimally and combine perspectives on achieving the research objectives.

iv. Stakeholder expertise was significant in providing control and direction, which was core to managing the research project and related tasks. This was necessary for the sustainability of the project's aims and better resource utilisation.

v. Provision of information for change promoted ownership of the research and its outcomes, which encouraged stakeholder to be more aware of potential societal issues. This was also done through providing feedback inefficiencies.

vi. The feedback on the inefficiencies was communicated to all relevant stakeholders who in turn learnt and reflected on their energy use. This resulted into an optimal use of resources, specifically energy resources. The optimal use of energy resources is crucial in improving the carbon footprints that are affecting society through environmental degradation.

vii. Encouraging stakeholders to feel they had ownership and control of the research aims and plans was essential for co-creation.

viii. For the awareness of potential barriers to stakeholder engagement, stakeholders needed to consult and get different perspectives on both stakeholder engagement and the research process.

From the above causal mechanisms (set of assumptions), the stakeholder engagement resulted in outcomes that ultimately had the following societal impact;

i. A reduction in environmental degradation

ii. Improved carbon footprint through a reduction in CO_2 emissions

iii. Improved societal welfare and health

The outcomes of the stakeholder engagement was achieved through the different stakeholder engagement activities (nature of stakeholder engagement) and inputs (the rationale for the stakeholder engagement). These two key elements were mutual in achieving the societally desired impact that was directed towards the challenge of environmental degradation.

The ToC indicates that despite Project 1 focusing on ICT outputs within its processes, there was a lot of stakeholder input, which made the process socially desirable and therefore implemented responsible innovation within the research project. It shows that stakeholder engagement was crucial in addressing the social challenge through the involvement of different stakeholders who contributed towards, transparency, responsiveness and anticipating through the consultation and dialogue that existed because of the stakeholder engagement.

Further, there were contextual factors that were pre-conditions for the stakeholder engagement to be effective towards achieving the outcomes, particularly concerning responsible outcomes (socially desirable outcomes) and ultimately supporting the research to have a societal impact. The following necessary factors were in place:

i. The existence of the stakeholder engagement depended on the research funding that could provide resources for both the research and engagement activities.
ii. The effectiveness of the stakeholder engagement in the R&I process needed existing ICT services in the buildings where the system was being piloted and implemented so that the stakeholders could interact with the dashboard (ICT system) that was being developed and henceforth researched on.
iii. The effectiveness of the stakeholder engagement depended on the identification and availability of relevant people or stakeholder groups.

In summary, the research project identified the appropriate stakeholders through referrals and existing networks. The identified stakeholders were engaged to co-create an ICT system that would bring awareness of energy efficiency issues and help other stakeholders understand the role of ICT in changing behaviour towards energy consumption. As part of the stakeholder engagement, stakeholders offered their expertise and knowledge in conducting the research. Also, they consulted on the effectiveness of the ICT system that was being developed and piloted in the ICT research project. Thus, they provided advice and feedback that was essential for coming up with a desirable and acceptable dashboard that was easy to interact with. The input (rationale for the engagement) and activities (nature of the engagement) from the stakeholder engagement were crucial in achieving socially desirable and acceptable outcomes. For instance, as result of the stakeholder engagement, there was reflection and learning throughout the research process. This was evident through different stakeholders changing their behaviour and attitude towards energy consumption. The change in behaviour and attitude was a result of the feedback that they received from the ICT system and the awareness through engagement activities. Thus, the stakeholder engagement facilitated learning, awareness, reflection and anticipation by enabling the different stakeholders to bring in different perspectives in the whole R&I process. Subsequently, stakeholders were able to respond to the different perspectives to develop and implement the ICT system for improving the environment that was desirable and acceptable to all those involved. The, the next section presents the evaluation of Project 2.

5.5 Evaluating Key Elements for Stakeholder Engagement in Project 2

10 data collection sources were used for the analysis of stakeholder engagement in the research project. The sources included three interviews and seven documents. For anonymity, each source has been given a code as shown in Table 5.3 below.

Table 5.3: Data Collection Sources for Project 2

Source	Code	Type of source	Date of Collection	Length of collection
Researcher	DL01	Stakeholder interview	11/06/16 (email)	n/a
Local authority representative	DL02	Stakeholder interview	05/05/16	46 minutes
ELT Facilitator	DL03	Stakeholder interview	07/05/16	26 minutes
Webpage	DLD1	Document review	n/a	n/a
Webpage	DLD2	Document review	n/a	n/a
Blog 1	DLD3	Document review	n/a	n/a
Blog 2	DLD4	Document review	n/a	n/a
Deliverable - Activities	DLD5	Document review	n/a	n/a
Deliverable - Report	DLD6	Document review	n/a	n/a
Deliverable - Survey	DLD7	Document review	n/a	n/a

This section presents the first part of an evaluative analysis of stakeholder engagement in Project 2. The first part provides an understanding of the stakeholder engagement process through an evaluation of the five key elements for evaluating stakeholder engagement that are suggested as essential in section 3.3.

5.5.1 Context of the Stakeholder Engagement

The theme of Project 2 was to investigate the use of ICT in transforming the way education is delivered in secondary schools across city X in the UK. The purpose of Project 2 was to ensure that school staff and learners are making the best use of ICT to meet their aspirations for a better and transformative delivery and access to education in secondary schools. The project aimed at '*ensuring that teachers and learners are getting the most from the significant investment in ICT being made*' (DL02) across city X. In addition, the ICT research Project 4nvolved teaching support staff in developing their digital literacy knowledge, skills and practice so that they can use ICT tools and environment efficiently in approaching their work with learners. Project 2 helped schools to ensure that every learner attending a school under the Building Schools for the Future (BSF) Programme benefits '*not only from world-class technology but also from an education that is supported and enhanced by the use of ICT to raise attainment and aspiration, connect communities and openopportunities*' (DLD1).

Project 2 was a collaboration between 'X City Council' and 'Y' University. The project contributed to the strategic aims of X City Council, and to the key BSF ICT priorities towards *'providing the right spaces for innovative teaching and learning, benefitting staff, students and the community'* (DLD3). This involved *'new designs that are centred on flexible teaching and learning spaces, innovative classroom environments, reduced carbon footprint, improved energy efficiency and access to the latest digital and mobile devices'* (DLD2).

Project 2 also contributed to ensuring that the significant investment being made through the BSF Programme on ICT systems, infrastructure and devices is fully realised as *'a catalyst for improving the educational experience and outcomes for young people across the city'* (DL02). The project ran for two years starting from 2012 and ending in 2014 and was funded by the UK government under the BSF Programme (DLD1, DLD3).

For the ICT research project to effectively conduct the research, different stakeholders were engaged in the whole R&I process. The stakeholders that were engaged were from the local authority, secondary schools and academia. The role of the stakeholders in Project 2 was to *'coordinate engagement activities between different stakeholders'* (DLo2) such as teachers and developers of ICT systems and ensuring that the *'implementation of the project was efficient in terms of time and resources'* (DLo1).

To provide a picture of the stakeholders that were engaged in Project 2, Table 5.4 below, shows the details of the stakeholders that were contacted to participate. The table indicates the stakeholders' role, their category as well as the number of the stakeholders that were invited and those that accepted to take part in the interviews.

Table 5.4: Project 2's Stakeholders for Study Participation

Stakeholder role	Stakeholder category	Number invited for interviews	Number accepted
BSF facilitator	Local authority representative	1	1
Researcher	Academia	2	1
ELT facilitator	Academia	1	1
CEN School Teacher	Secondary school representative	2	0
Teacher	Secondary school representative	3	0

Out of the nine stakeholders that were contacted for participation in this study, only three accepted to be interviewed. It was frustrating that all the five teachers that were contacted did not respond to the invitation emails despite sending them multiple follow-on emails to chase them up. This was frustrating because the teachers would have provided some interesting insights considering that they were highly involved in the implementation process. One researcher excused themselves and suggested his colleague as potential participant. The researcher that was suggested accepted to participate only if he could answer the interview questions through email due to his other commitments. Although, this was also frustrating, the offer was better than having nothing at all. Therefore, DL01 emailed the answers to the interview questions.

5.5.2 Identification of Stakeholders

From the interviews and the document analysis, it was established that the research project identified a range of stakeholders which included teachers, students, researchers, local authority representatives, a funder and academics. Based on the three interviews that were conducted and the documents that were reviewed particularly the project blogs (DLD3 and DLD4), stakeholders were identified to be in the project through past encounters as suggested by DL01 that he was identified *'through previous informal work he had done with xxx on national social media e-learning networks and at conferences'*. In addition, all the three stakeholders that were interviewed were identified at the beginning at pre-project phase. Some were identified to be involved in *'developing a proposal for a partnership'* as was the case of DL01 and DL02.

Further, DL02 mentioned that they got into the ICT research project at *'the time the project was being built'* and was involved in *'formulating the strategy from the beginning'*. Despite the key stakeholders being identified earlier in the research process, both DL02 and DL03 mentioned that there were other stakeholders who were identified and recruited along the way which included teachers, head teachers and students. This was further indicated in DLD 4 (p.24) that the apart from the researchers (academia) and the local authority and the funders, there were stakeholders such as a Cover Supervisor, Teaching Assistant, Higher Level Teaching Assistant, Librarians, SEN Specialist Provision and Senior Leaders.

Despite the wide range of the stakeholders identified for engagement in the research project, the stakeholders that were interviewed included a researcher, a BSF facilitator and an Enhancing Learning through Technology (ELT) facilitator at Xxx University.

5.5.3 Nature of Stakeholder Engagement

The second element to be evaluated was the nature of stakeholder engagement. This particularly focused on the form that the stakeholder engagement activities took. Firstly, DL03 said that she was engaged to facilitate dialogue with other stakeholders such as teachers, head teachers and young learners to consult with them on how well ICT could be used to enhance the learning experience in secondary schools. This was mainly during focus groups aimed at understanding the use of ICT in learning environments such as classrooms. The respondent further said that she acted as a bridge between different stakeholders in the research project including *'the city council team, lawyers, HR [human resources] and ICT personnel'*.

Secondly, the nature of the engagement was also in form of expertise. It was learnt from the interviews that some stakeholders offered their expert knowledge in the R&I process as was highlighted by DL01 that *'the research project was suggested to be a Knowledge Exchange Partnership (KEP)'* because they would be sharing expertise.

Thirdly, from the document analysis, it was further established that the stakeholders were there to promote the aims and agenda of the ICT research project. This was picked up from the blogs that were written by some stakeholders (DL02 and DL04) during the research project, and the report on the stakeholder activities that took place during Project 2 (DLD5). The blogs also covered the attainment of some interim outcomes of the research project and disseminated the information throughout the project time.

Fourthly, DL02 suggested that the stakeholder engagement was also in the form of advice and feedback on issues relating to the research that were flagged up. Depending on the stakeholders' background, knowledge and expertise they were able *'to raise questions and raise awareness of these issues'* (DL02). One of the issues raised was to do with gender equality in ICT related programmes during research or implementation. This was mentioned by DL02 who said that she noticed that during her time in the project, there was a feeling that men and boys were better at understanding technology that was being implemented in the secondary schools compared to their female counterparts. The respondent further said that she made other relevant stakeholders aware of her observation and was fighting to ensure that this was addressed.

Lastly, in Project 2, the stakeholder engagement was also in the form of leading the research project. This leadership included *'an on-going consideration of multiple perspectives in the generation and implementation of the project'* (DL01). Further, DL02 said that her engagement also involved *'seeing the contracts'* and *'putting in place and monitoring indicators of successes* for example, ensuring that ICT solutions were delivered on time. In addition, as part of the leadership some stakeholders such as teachers and ICT technicians were *'ensuring that that the schools have the confidence to use the ICT solutions'* (DL03) that were provided.

However, despite the different forms of stakeholder engagement activities presented above, there were some barriers that affected them. The first one was around the mind-set and control of other stakeholders who were engaged in Project 2. This was mentioned by DL02 about *'the power relations among stakeholders and people within IT department which has affected people having access to knowledge and awareness of stakeholder engagement activity and having the infrastructure that will nurture the use of ICT in an inclusive way'*. As a result, *'this caused issues with access to data for all those interested in the project and the outcomes of the project'*.

The respondent suggested that perhaps this *'was due to safeguarding, since schools are very strict when it comes to safeguarding'*.

Another barrier was in relation to gender inequality, as already introduced above. DL02 said there was unequal representation of stakeholders that were engaged in the research project citing that there were not as many females as would have been deemed fair. The respondent further said that there are issues in terms of people that work in technology for example the *'schools ICT departments were just full of white men and lack of women who work in ICT'*. According to DL02, she thought that schools have *'a long way to go in terms of awareness of activities and stakeholder engagement'*.

5.5.4 Rationale for the Stakeholder Engagement

The other element that was evaluated was the rationale for the stakeholder engagement in Project 2 From the interviews that were conducted and the document analysis, several motives for stakeholder engagement in Project 2 were established. The first motive for engaging stakeholders in the research was consultation. This was evidenced by the responses from both DL01 and DL02.

They both agreed that them and other stakeholders were there to provide *'a real opportunity to have a conversation with stakeholders about things that are potentially no talked about at all'* and hear voices of those *'that are marginalised when it comes to research'*. The level of consultation was evident through DLD4 and DLD5 which outlined the different consultative activities that were carried out in the research project. The consultation was aimed at bringing in different perspectives from an array of stakeholders that were involved so that the research process was inclusive and participatory.

Another rationale for stakeholder engagement in Project 2 was the direction and control that they could provide to the research project. For instance, this was something that was mentioned by DL02 that when she *'came on board nothing was going on, therefore [she] had to devise a plan, [...] and rewrite the programme and start over again'*.

An additional rationale for stakeholder engagement in the research project was that it fostered mutual learning among those engaged in the Project 2 as was highlighted earlier by DL02 that the project was suggested to be a KEP where different stakeholder could share their knowledge, therefore, facilitating learning (see section 5.5.3). As a KEP, information and expertise were exchanged between different stakeholders. These various sources of information were ideal for mutual learning among all those involved.

Furthermore, DL03 mentioned that some of the stakeholders were engaged in the research project for reasons that included encouraging *'meaningful and authentic engagement'*, encouraging *'social inclusion'*, for instance encouraging *'voices that are marginalised to be heard'*. The respondent also said that motive behind stakeholder engagement in the research project was to *'potentially to influence the research and innovation'*. He further said that *'responsible research and innovation was not a key criterion or objective for the research project. However, [its] focus was on social inclusion using digital tools'*, and so the stakeholders such as him (researcher) *'were always mindful of our responsibility'*.

Related to social inclusion as a motive for the stakeholder engagement, the last rationale that was established after talking to the stakeholders was that they were engaged in Project 2 to promote ownership of the project's aims and the outcomes. To that effect, DL02 said that she *'supported people in different ways regardless of their background'*, for example from disadvantaged communities, (socially, economically) and genders *'to use ICT and engage with ICT in a meaningful way'*. As such, people felt there were part of the research project and therefore worked along together towards achieving the aims of the research project.

5.5.5 Outcome of Stakeholder Engagement

The last element was evaluated to understand the outcome of the stakeholder engagement in Project 2. From the interviews, one of the outcomes of stakeholder engagement was that the stakeholders were made aware of the issues that were affecting the effective delivery of education in secondary schools and how these could be addressed using ICT as part of education delivery. DL03 suggested that as a result of bringing different stakeholders together, Project 2 managed to come up with a collective effort in implementing ICTs in the secondary schools.

The respondent further said that *'teachers who had good ICT skills together with researchers, managed to teach those who were not as good'*. Through such collective efforts the stakeholder engagement ensured that the aim of improving education was sustained beyond the lifespan of the research project.

5.6 Applying the RRI Lens to Project 2

This section presents the second part of the evaluation which is an evaluative analysis of the stakeholder engagement within the context of RRI.

5.6.1 Engagement of Stakeholders

From the interviews and the document review it was evident that Project 2 engaged a variety of stakeholders in achieving its aims. From the documents that were reviewed, including web blogs for the project, it was learnt that the ICT research project engaged teachers, researchers, local authority representatives and technical people and the secondary school pupils who were the target users of the ICT being implemented in the secondary schools. The identification and engagement of such a wide range of stakeholders is significant for the attainment of socially desirable and acceptable outcomes in the ICT research project. This is important because it supported inclusion in the R&I process and gave a chance for the stakeholders to be heard as mentioned by DL01 that *'although Responsible innovation was not a key criterion or objective for the project, [the] focus was on social inclusion in using digital tools'*.

Therefore in terms of responsible innovation, the ICT research Project did well by engaging the stakeholders who were very instrumental in achieving the acceptable outcomes discussed in section 5.5.5 above. This was supported by DL01 who mentioned that with the engagement of stakeholders in Project 2, there was an *'on-going consideration of multiple perspectives in the generation and implementation of the project from teachers, teaching unions, the city council, the university team and the other project team members'*.

5.6.2 Anticipation and Reflection

With regards to anticipation and reflection, from both interviews and the document review it was established that with the stakeholder engagement, there was valuable insights from the multiple stakeholders involved in the project who contributed a lot toward an on-going consideration of multiple perspectives in the generation and implementation of the ICTs in schools. With such perspectives, the ICT research project was likely to assess unexpected outcomes and reflect on the research and implementation process in order to have successful outcomes for the schools and ultimately the society.

To back this observation, DL02 suggested that the *'stakeholder engagement gave the opportunity to raise questions and also gave the opportunity to raise awareness of different issues'*. The respondent further said that *'It gave the platform to understand how different users are ok and willing to work with technology, how good they are with the new technology, what needs to be done so that technology helps them in a better way'*. All this is part of anticipation and reflection, and as such, it can be argued that the stakeholder engagement supported the attainment of socially acceptable outcomes in that respect.

5.6.3 Openness and Transparency

The stakeholder engagement in the ICT research project did a commendable job in facilitating openness and transparency within the research. For example, DL02 said that the engagement of stakeholders was *'a real opportunity to have a conversation with stakeholders about things that are potentially no talked about at all [...] and about how they might want ICT to be in their schools'*. The respondent further said that the engagement, *'helped in dealing with cynicism within the teachers because of the very difficult position on how they can suggest where they would like the level of ICT to be in their schools [due to being] bogged down by authority'*. This resonates with the social inclusion that was suggested by DL03.

It was also evident that there was some degree of openness in terms of the research work that was undergoing in the Project 2 and the strides it was taking towards achieving its aims through some web blogs (DLD3 and DLD4) and report on activities (DLD5). In addition, DL03 mentioned that there was a lot of consultative events where stakeholders could ask questions about the research and implementation of the ICTs in their secondary schools.

5.6.4 Responsiveness

The stakeholder engagement supported the consideration of how the ICT systems and their implementation in the secondary schools should be shaped. This is fundamentally being responsive to the processes as indicated by DL02 that because of the engagement, stakeholders were able to ask 'why'? With the stakeholder engagement, there was an awareness of the capacity of the people involved, the school environment and the power of authorities in relation to implementing the ICT systems. This was pointed out by DL03 that the stakeholder engagement *'on one level helped to understand the community and on the other the level of technology necessary'*. The respondent further said that the stakeholder engagement *'highlighted that there is a big gap between understanding what technology is and what technology could do and how mainstream technology is now [...]. Therefore, stakeholders coming together brought awareness of the connection to those who did not see it and highlight the issues surrounding the use of technology whether is being on Twitter or using Skype Instagram and Facebook for example'*. This shows that the stakeholder engagement played a significant role in supporting a responsive and reflexive process regarding the social implications of the research and its outcomes.

5.7 Theory of Change for Project 2

A deductive theory of change (ToC) for Project 2 is set out in Figure 5.2 below. In essence, while Figure 11 simplifies the ToC for Project 2 into a relatively linear structure, the cyclical relationship between inputs and activities specifically highlight the reciprocity between the two. Hence, the inputs from stakeholder engagement (rationale for stakeholder engagement) determines the sort of activities (nature of stakeholder engagement) that the engagement will entail. Correspondingly, the manifestation of the stakeholder engagement activities require the inputs from the stakeholder engagement.

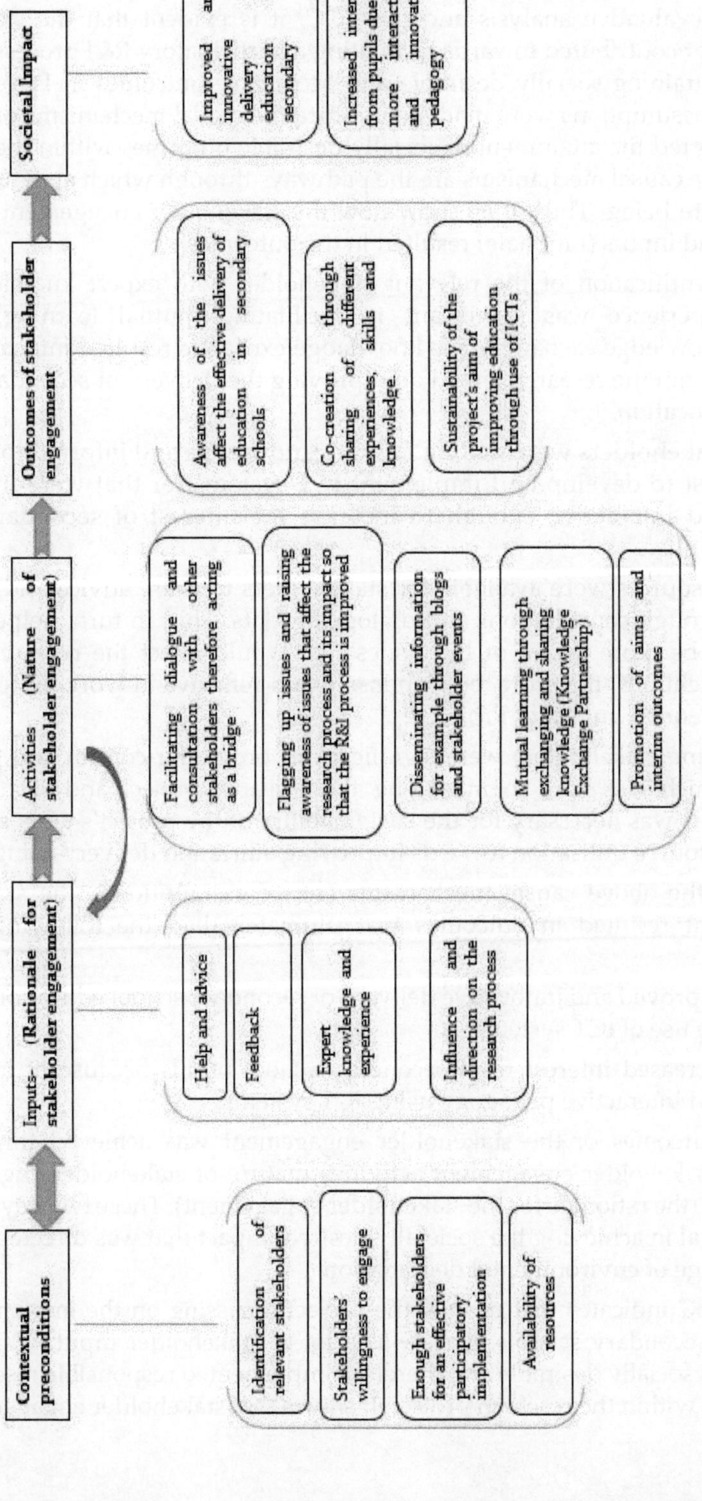

Figure 5.2: Theory of Change for Project 2

5.7.1 Theory of Change Narrative

From the evaluative analysis and the TOC, it is evident that the stakeholder engagement contributed towards facilitating a participatory R&I process that was ideal for attaining socially desirable and acceptable outcomes in Project 2. The following assumptions were made to indicate the causal mechanisms or linkages that supported the attainment of socially desirable outcomes within the research project. The causal mechanisms are the pathways through which an outcome was brought into being. Thus, they show how the stakeholder engagement activities (nature) and inputs (rationale) resulted in the outcomes.

i. Identification of the relevant stakeholder with expert knowledge and experience was significant in facilitating mutual learning through knowledge exchange. The knowledge exchange resulted into co-creation within the research aimed at improving the delivery of secondary school education.

ii. Stakeholders were willing to share knowledge and information on how best to develop and implement ICT systems for that were innovative and interactive enough to increase the interest of secondary school pupils.

iii. Resources were available for stakeholders to share advice and feedback through consultations and dialogue events. This, in turn, helped people to be more aware of the issues that would affect the research and its intentions, therefore, be responsive and reflexive in working toward the intended impact of Project 2.

iv. Some stakeholders were significant in providing control and direction, which was core to managing the research project and related tasks. This was necessary for the sustainability of the project's aims and better resource utilisation towards improving education delivery using ICTs.

From the above causal mechanisms (set of assumptions), the stakeholder engagement resulted in outcomes that ultimately had the following societal impact;

i. Improved and innovative delivery of secondary school education through the use of ICT systems.

ii. Increased interest from secondary school pupils because of innovative and interactive pedagogy using ICT systems.

The outcomes of the stakeholder engagement was achieved through the different stakeholder engagement activities (nature of stakeholder engagement) and inputs (the rationale for the stakeholder engagement). These two key elements were mutual in achieving the societally desired impact that was directed towards the challenge of environmental degradation.

The ToC indicates that despite the project focussing on the implementation of ICT in secondary schools, there was a lot of stakeholder input, which made the process socially desirable and therefore implemented responsible research and innovation within the research project. It shows that stakeholder engagement was crucial in addressing the social challenge through the involvement of different stakeholders who contributed towards, transparency, responsiveness and anticipating through the consultation and dialogue that existed because of the stakeholder engagement.

Further, there were contextual factors that were pre-conditions for the stakeholder engagement to be effective towards achieving the outcomes, particularly concerning responsible outcomes and ultimatelysupporting the research to have a societal impact. The following necessary factors were in place:

i. The effectiveness of the stakeholder engagement depended on the identification and willingness of relevant people to engage in the research process.
ii. The existence of the stakeholder engagement depended on the research funding that could provide resources for both the research and engagement activities.
iii. The effectiveness of the stakeholder engagement in the R&I process needed existing ICT services in the secondary schools where the ICT systems were being piloted and implemented so that the stakeholders could interact with them.

To sum up, Project 2 identified a variety of stakeholders through referrals and existing networks. The identified stakeholders included teachers, researchers and local authority representative who were all engaged in exchanging knowledge and expertise on how ICT systems could be designed and implemented in secondary schools across city X. The identified stakeholders were also involved with providing control and direction of the research towards realising socially desirable and acceptable outcomes such as mutual learning and co-creation.

As part of the stakeholder engagement, stakeholders consulted on the effectivenessof the ICT systems that were being implemented in the secondary to ensure that the outcomes were socially desirable and acceptable. The consultation afforded the stakeholders to reflect, anticipate and be transparent about the research processes and its intended outcomes. Thus, the input (rationale for the engagement) and activities (nature of the engagement) from the stakeholder engagement were crucial in achieving socially desirable and acceptable outcomes. For instance, as result of the stakeholder engagement, there was reflection and learning throughout the research process. This was a result of the KEPs that existed between the different stakeholder groups and through the engagement activities that were being conducted through the research.

Thus, the stakeholder engagement facilitated learning, awareness, reflection and anticipation by enabling the different stakeholders to bring in different perspectives and knowledge in the whole R&I process. Subsequently, stakeholders were able to respond to these different perspectives to design and implement the ICT systems for improving delivery of education in secondary schools. The next section presents the evaluation of Project 3.

5.8 Evaluating Key Elements for Stakeholder Engagement in Project 3

To evaluate stakeholder engagement in Project 3, data was collected using interviews and a document review from eight sources. The sources consisted of five interviews and three document reviews. For anonymity, each source has been given a code as shown in Table 5.5 below.

Table 5.5: Data Collection Sources for Project 3

Source	Code	Type of source	Date of data collection	Length of data collection
Audiologist	3TI01	Stakeholder interview	13/07/17	42 minutes
Project Manager	3TI02	Stakeholder interview	17/07/17	31 minutes
Music Developer	3TI03	Stakeholder interview	28/07/17	40 minutes
App Developer	3TI04	Stakeholder interview	17/07/16	36 minutes
Researcher	3TI05	Stakeholder interview	25/07/17	52 minutes
Website (blogs, articles)	3TID1	Document review	n/a	n/a
Partner webpage	3TID2	Document review	n/a	n/a
Deliverables	3TID3	Document review	n/a	n/a

This section presents the first part of an evaluative analysis of stakeholder engagement in Project 3. The first part provides an understanding of the stakeholder engagement process through an evaluation of the five key elements for evaluating stakeholder engagement that are suggested as essential in section 3.3.

5.8.1 Context of the Stakeholder Engagement

The theme of Project 3 was to bring together relevant stakeholders from traditional gaming industries, academic institutes, a large European hearing aid manufacturer and hearing communities to develop a technology that improves hearing loss. The relevant stakeholders were brought together to produce digital games in the field of hearing aid technologies and hearing loss in children and older adults, addressing social inclusion, generating new markets and creating job opportunities (3TID1, 3TID3, 3TI02). The purpose of the project was to research on how ICT could be used to improve hearing aids with *'a hope of coming up with better and innovative hearing aid (HA) technologies'* (3TI04). Following a realisation that the majority of individuals who use or could use the devices were finding it difficult to exploit and access better and innovative HAs, the research project involved different stakeholders to cometogether and find ways of how the *'technology could be improved with the needs of the end users in mind'* (3TI03).The ICT research project ran for three years starting from 2015 to May 2018 and was funded by the EU under the Horizon 2020 - the Framework Programme for R&I of the European Union (3DTID2).

The research project was of importance to the society because hearing loss and deafness is a societal challenge that can act as a barrier to inclusion and lead to isolation. Consequently, hearing loss can *'result in more risk of depression in older people'* (3DTI1). To deal with the issue, the research project engaged multiple stakeholders to develop and apply scientific methodologies and technologies towards a new set of non-leisure applications which have real benefits for citizens (3DTI2, 3DTI3). The ICT research project achieved this by stimulating and fostering knowledge and technology exchange between stakeholders working in digital gaming, the research community, hearing-aid manufacturers and hearing-impaired communities.

From the Project 3's perspective, to conduct research, multi-disciplinary stakeholders from academia, gaming industry, hearing aid manufacturing and hearing communities (external stakeholders) were engaged in the research process. The role of these stakeholders was to take part in a *'participatory-design process'* (3TID1) that aimed at researching the use of ICT to create a toolkit and a series of applications (digital games) to enable end users to explore and understand how to access and use better as well as innovative HAs.

To indicate the stakeholders that were involved in Project 3, Table 5.6 below shows the stakeholders who were contacted to take part in the data collection process for this study. The table indicates the role of the stakeholders, their category together with the numbers of invited participants and those participants who accepted to participate in this study.

Table 5.6: Details of the stakeholders engaged in the Project 3

Stakeholder role	Stakeholder Category	Number invited for interviews	Number accepted
Audiologist	Hearing community representative	1	1
Project Manager	Hearing aid manufacturer	2	1
Music Developer	Hearing aid manufacturer	1	1
App Developer	Gaming industry	3	1
Researcher	Academia	3	1

Out of the ten stakeholders that were sent emails to participate in this study, six responded. Out of the six that responded, five accepted to be interviewed and one excused themselves due to other commitments. The stakeholders that were interviewed included an audiologist, project manager, music developer, an app developer and a researcher.

5.8.2 Identification of Stakeholders

In evaluating stakeholder identification in Project 3, two themes appeared to be of significance. The themes related to the process of identification and the range of stakeholders that were identified for engagement. Regarding the process of identification, two interviewees, 3TI01 and 3TI04, clearly mentioned that they were identified and recruited through referrals. 3TI01 mentioned that she was referred by her *'head of service to join the project'*. While 3TI04 said he was identified througha referral by *'a professor [that] they had worked together on another project'*.

Regarding the range, the ICT research Project 4dentified a wide range of stakeholders based on the background and different roles that they could play in the research project. This was evident in the document review. It was found that stakeholders were identified from the traditional gaming industry, manufacturing, hearing community and academia. For instance, some of the stakeholders were working with hearing aid community as an audiologist (3TI01), small and medium enterprise (SME) as *'a project manager [...] managing the relationship between ICT professionals and what the proposal needs'* (3TI02) and some were music developers (3TI03) and application developers as was the case for 3TI04. Also, the project identified researchers from academia (3TI05) to be part of the engagement.

5.8.3 Nature of Stakeholder Contribution

The second element that was analysed was the nature of the stakeholder engagement. Similar to the other ICT research projects evaluated above, two thematic categories emerged from the evaluation results for Project 3. The first one was the form of stakeholder engagement that took place. Some respondents mentioned that their engagement was in the form of information dissemination. This was done in different ways such as publicising and promoting the research agenda as alluded by 3TI02 that they intended to make people aware that hearing loss was a social problem. Therefore, they needed *'to improve [...] some hearing loss problems in order to improve social life'*. This involved disseminating research information through reports as suggested by 3TI05.

The other form of engagement from the stakeholders was the facilitation of dialogue among different stakeholders. This involved engaging with people and facilitating consultations on the research process as pointed out by 3TI01 that they engaged with hearing loss patients and consulted with them on their needs and how the technology could be better developed to address those needs. Similarly, 3TI05 said that they consulted with *'the actual end users, people who use hearing aids, [in] designing digital games that will help them to understand the hearing aid technologies [by] talking to them'*.

The respondent went on to say that the engagement was also in the form of offering expertise towards the research. For instance, 3TI01 said that her main interests were bringing clinical work and research work together as a result of her background as a clinical audiologist and expert in hearing aid use and hearing loss. In the same vein, 3TI04 said that with his engineering expertise he was able to offer expert knowledge in *'developing applications [and] effective codes and quality algorithms'* that were necessary for the research output. Relatedly, the stakeholder provided feedback which was either used to flag up issues or improve the process.

This was also supported by 3TI04 who mentioned that as part of their engagement in the project, they were there *'to ensure that systems are working properly'* and flagged when they saw *'an ethical issue'*. The responded further said that they *'put measures to ensure that algorithms [were] doing what they said they were doing'*. One way to achieve that was through a collection of data that was analysed and used to provide feedback. 3TI03 said that they *'interviewed relevant people and got their feedback on situations they find difficult'* which included *'not only users but also experts, and then [...] improve based on their feedback'*. Lastly, the stakeholder engagement was inthe form of leading the research process, specifically *'planning'* (3TI05) and *'project management'* (3TI02).

The second thematic category was on the barriers that impede the engagement activities mentioned above. The first barrier was that *'it was pretty hard to recruit participants as stakeholders for their research'* (3TI03). These stakeholders were needed to provide or contribute to the engagement activities discussed above. The more stakeholders the ICT research projects would have recruited, the deeper would have been the breadth of the different forms of engagement. Relatedly, 3TI01 raised another barrier with regards to the recruitment of stakeholders. The respondent said that *'it [was] difficult to actually get in touch with participants [...] because they are a select group of people and [...] it is difficult to identify people who use hearing aids, especially children.* Again, this affected the scope of the engagement activities the research project could have accessed.

Another barrier was down to different ways of doing things. The stakeholders that were engaged in Project 3 had different ways of doing research and therefore this had an impact on the form the engagement. For example, 3TI02 mentioned that some of the advice or feedback provided was not effective because the focus and the understanding of social aspects by *'developers and other professionals [was] very different.* The respondent said that with former *'there is more emphasis on the technical issues rather than the social issues'*.

Lastly, due to the nature of the technologies that were being developed in the research project and the strong connection with industry, there was a business threat to some of the SMEs. As a result, they were withholding some information and data. It was suggested by 3TI03 and 3TI04 that some of the stakeholders were trying to establish a sustainable business out of it. Therefore they were sceptical of providing information, such as code and advice so that they retain a competitive advantage.

5.8.4 Rationale for the Stakeholder Engagement

The evaluation of Project 3 also was aimed at understanding the rationale behind stakeholder engagement in the ICT research project. The first motive for stakeholder engagement that emerged from the research, was that the stakeholders were engaged because of consultation. It was found that they were either there to facilitate consultation with different other stakeholders or to be consulted with respect to various aspects of the ICT research project. For instance, regarding facilitating consultation, three respondents suggested that they were drafted into the project to facilitate consultative dialogue.

The first one said it was with patients due to her *'education background'* and *'experience with clinical consultation in audiology'* (3TI01). The second respondent said as part of facilitating consultations he *'created a version and got real users [...] and experts to use it [...] and then take their feedback'* for improvement (3TI03). The third respondent said that part of the reason for her engagement in the Project 3 was to facilitate consultation with *'the end users, that is, people who use hearing aids, [by] talking to them as well as game users'* (3TI05)

Apart from facilitating consultation, another motive for the engagement in the ICT research project was to be consulted by other stakeholders as pointed out by 3TI02 that they were engaged to bring different perspectives in the research. 3TI02 said that *'European projects are very good to engage professions with different backgrounds because they bring in different skills [...]. It is not easy, but in this project, for example, I see that the dialogue is possible'*. This was echoed by 3TI05 who stated that *'in particular for this project and particularly for our developers, the developers had never really worked with people with hearing loss before, so they kind of needed the input of like people with hearing loss'*. These responses point towards how that stakeholder engagement was fundamental for the success of the research taking place in Project 3.

The other reasons given were that stakeholder engagement was important in the research project because it supported the discovery of new solutions through the use of diverse knowledge and experience form those engaged (3TI02, 3TI04, 3TID2). Also, that some of the stakeholders engaged provided control and direction of the ICT research project through their expertise. For example, 3TI01 mentioned that her *'years in clinical audiology setting'* and therefore *'an understanding of hearing loss patients' needs'* was important in directing the research towards the intended outcomes. Similarly 3TI02 talked about their *'years of project management'* while 3TI03 *mentioned about the 'years of software development and business management'* as critical for directing the research.

In addition, 3TI04 said that he had the skills and expertise in *'writing and developing quality code and algorithms'* which was also important in directing the research towards its goals. Therefore, as result of their expertise, the stakeholders that were engaged could influence the R&I that was taking place in the Project 3. Also, he mentioned that due the complexity of the ICT research project it was necessary to engage different stakeholders so that they help each other in directing the research process. The respondent further said that the project was complex *'in the sense of the development [...]. It was also complex in terms [...] the business models for the companies and open sharing of [...] a software library for developers'*. Lastly regarding control and direction, the stakeholders were engaged so that they provide reputable advice due to their *'relevant expertise'* (3TI03) and *'experiences'* (3TI01).

Moving on from control and direction, it was also found that another rationale behind stakeholder engagement in Project 3 was mutual learning. Stakeholders were engaged in the research project to share knowledge and expertise. Stakeholders that were engaged had different knowledge sets, and therefore in working together, they were learning from each other's experiences and skill sets. For instance, some knew about software development (3TI03, 3TI04) while others had knowledge of research management and patient engagement in research (3TI01, 3TI02).

The other rationale was that stakeholders were engaged in the ICT research to promote an agenda and support ownership among those with a stake. On the one hand, promoting an agenda was mentioned by 3TI02. The respondent said that through the *'exploitation and dissemination of the results [...] [they wanted to create knowledge about [the] research project and [...] use a lot of tools to improve the awareness about hearing loss'*. On the other hand, the premise to encourage ownership was pointed out by 3TI04. He said that *'after the project, [...] the expectations for the future [are] that the open source library we are producing can be really used and can become one of those libraries that a lot of people use. It is like a resource for researching that is available there'*.

In addition, it emerged that as part of promoting agenda and encouraging ownership, the stakeholders were also engaged to encourage meaningful engagement between stakeholders as exemplified by 3TI02. 3TI02 suggested that stakeholder engagement *'is very important because technology is not only for developers [...], the apps are for people. So for the developer to work in the background, he needs to understand what people's needs are, and the final user has to know what is possible or what is impossible to do with technology'*. The same was mentioned by 3TI05 that some of the stakeholders *'were engaged to engage and talk with the end users,'* so that people who use hearing aids and those designing the digital games *'will have a good understanding of the hearing loss' and* how it could be addressed. Therefore, in the long run, the stakeholder engagement encourages *'social inclusion'* (3TI02) since *'it gives the app developers a chance to engage with people who have been isolated by hearing loss'* and *'get input to understand how it affects them and that can be improved'* (3TI05).

Correspondingly, it was stated by 3TI03 that *'whenever [they] have conversations with users or audiologists, [they are] always listening [...] trying to take their needs into account'*. Therefore, another reason for engagement was that stakeholders were involved in the Project 3 to include marginalised voices as suggested by 3TI05 that their role was *'to be that kind of middle person to go and talk to people with hearing loss and then feed it all back to them'*. The respondent further suggested that probably those with hearing loss could have done that by themselves, but *'they don't have the kind of the resources'*. This relates with the last rationale for stakeholder engagement in Project 3 which was the provision of resources. These resources were either in the form of financial resources for undertaking the research activities and human resource regarding knowledge, skills and expertise.

5.8.5 Outcomes of Stakeholder Engagement

The last element of stakeholder engagement that was evaluated was the outcomes of the engagement. The first outcome that emerged from the analysis is the awareness of the potential responsibility issues related to the research being undertaken. 3TI04 said that due to the engagement of different stakeholder in the research, some would see areas where *'there was a failure issues or the research project was not working properly'* and therefore apply some *'ethical measures'* to address that. In addition, as a result, stakeholders were aware of the challenge of hearing loss and social isolation by working with stakeholders that are directly affected by it and 'understand what people's needs are' (3TI02) to come with appropriate research outputs. Another outcome that is related to awareness was the acknowledgement of the issues that the project was aimed at. 3TI03 said that as part of their engagement they were *'providing information about hearing loss, writing blog posts and [went] to conferences raising awareness about the project and hearing loss in general'*. This further translated into change in behaviour and attitudes that was brought about through *'the dissemination and communication'* taking place among stakeholders.

It was also found that as a consequence of stakeholder engagement, there was a unified understanding of the social challenge and how that can be addressed. This was evident in 3TI02 response who was happy to say that it is characteristic for European research projects to bring about different stakeholders to unify their understanding and skills in addressing societal challenges. This observation was supported by 3TI04 who suggested that some stakeholders from companies (industry) would now understand how hearing loss is a big problem and how music and ICT can be used to mitigate that problem.

Moving on from awareness, the other outcome that emerged was related to sustainability of the research project's aims. Due the different expertise and knowledge brought by the stakeholder engagement, the aims of the Project 3 were tenable. The research project managed to produce outputs that will be used beyond the project's lifespan as suggested by 3TI04 that *'the code library that was developed will still be out there for researchers to use'*. Similarly, 3TI05 mentioned that considering level of engagement and type of stakeholders involved there is a possibility that [the stakeholders] *'might get more funding to carry out more [research] projects that are sort of similar and extend the kind of the engagement with hearing aids use with this population may be even extend to different populations with different needs'*.

The last outcome was that stakeholder engagement resulted into co-creation. From the research, it was found that the engaged stakeholder had resources for the developing all the things that were needed. And, in the end they had the *'freedom to share inputs and results through open source'* (3TI 04). This was resonated by 3TI04 who said that *'due to the complexity of the research it was essential to develop an open software library for developers'* and audiologists who understand patients better than the developers. As a result of this co-creation, another outcome was suggested by 3TI05 that the through engagement of different stakeholders that Project 4mproved people's lives. The respondent pointed there will be *'apps that will actually help people to gain a better [...] quality of the hearing which might then reflect on their quality of life'*.

5.9 Applying the RRI Lens to Project 3

This section presents the second part of the evaluation which is an evaluative analysis of the stakeholder engagement within the context of RRI.

5.9.1 Engagement of Stakeholders

It was established form the data that sources that the project identified and engaged a varied range of stakeholders. These stakeholders had a range of skills and expertise that were necessary to develop technologies that took on board the needs of different users. The process was inclusive as it was understood from the interviews and document analysis that experts and patients (users with hearing loss) were consulted and engaged throughout the process. To support this view one of the responses mentioned that they directly targeted *'audiologists and hearing aid users who are the stakeholders'* (3TI03) to provide feedback and ideas on how best to develop the software and technologies for the hearing aids. This was also echoed by 3TI04 who said that they *'considered other stakeholders not just customers but even more the developers'* to have access to their work and contribute somehow and also, they were *'involved in doing the requirements solicitation as the project partners'*. 3TI05 mentioned that also *'got a lot of children participants'* in the research. These responses show that the research project addressed one feature of RRI in being inclusive and engaging a range of stakeholders in the research that was taking place in Project 3.

5.9.2 Anticipation and Reflection

When it came to anticipation and reflection, through stakeholder engagement the project was able to *'understand what people's needs are'* and there from that understanding both the researchers, developers and final users were able to have a dialogue *'to know what is possible or what is impossible to do with technology'* (3TI02). This then enabled them to anticipate on the benefits or consequences of the technology, for instance if technology could not adequately deal with the problems. Also, taking into consideration the response from 3TI03, there was some anticipation in the research and innovation process taking through the involvement of stakeholders in soliciting requirements which was an indication of anticipation. In addition to requirement gathering 3TI03 pointed to something that alluded to anticipation. The respondent stated that they *'developed algorithms that [would] predict the use'* which meant that *'in the background of [their] mind they anticipated whether something that could be [ethical] or unethical'*. From the feedback that the feedback and knowledge that they got from dialogue, requirements gathering and predictive algorithms, the researcher and developers were able to reflect on the process and learn from the reflection and improve. This was something that is linked to another feature of RRI, that of responsiveness (section 5.9.4).

5.9.3 Openness and Transparency

Looking at the evaluation findings, there was some level of openness and transparency in the R&I process that was taking place in Project 3. For instance, there was ongoing *'dissemination of the results'* (3TI02) and the project created knowledge and tools that shared among different stakeholders to either use or understand the importance of the technologies being developed. This is something that is also established from the response given by 3TI03 who that *'in terms of openness [they] were part of an open research data pilot [...] that was an initiative to be more open with how these processes are taking place'*. Furthermore, the project was not just bringing awareness about the research on the technologies that were aimed at addressing hearing loss, but it was also open in the *'code that [was] being written'* (3TI03) and therefore put in an open source library for anyone to access.

However, despite the evidence of openness and transparency in the project, it was learnt that there was not total openness due to the nature of some of the stakeholders. Those stakeholders who were from small and medium enterprises (SMEs) were not willing to be fully transparent because of their business interests. As a result, they decided to have an *'open source library for non-commercial use and a different strategy for the commercial use'*. Accordingly, this was because some of the stakeholders were *'making a business out of the applications'* (3TI04).

5.9.4 Responsiveness

The stakeholder engagement in Project 3 was paramount in changing the ways hearing loss is understood in society and among those who design and develop hearing aid technologies. For example, some stakeholders such an audiologist with experience and understanding of how patients affected by the loss gave an insight to the more technical stakeholders on how they could responsively design and develop technology that addresses the issues better. This was done through consultation with hearing patients and providing clinical knowledge about the problem. To support this observation, 3TI03 said that *'nobody knows what the real problem in hearing loss is. It's a problem about inclusion about relationship between people, family and friends. So, it's not only a technical problem but it is a social problem'*. So, the goal of the stakeholders that were involved in Project 3 was 'to *improve the relationship between hearing loss problems, and better social life*' through the use of technology.

As pointed out by 3TI03, responsiveness in the research project was achieved through *'a participatory design that involved regular meetings with advisory boards, involving audiologists and the relevant experts'*. This participatory design involved sending *'regular versions of the applications to try and get feedback and implement as many of the changes as we [could]'* (3TI03). Therefore, the stakeholders engaged listened to what the users said and modified the process and the outputs based on what was said so that they innovated responsibly.

5.10 Theory of Change for Project 3

A deductive theory of change (ToC) for Project 3 is set out in Figure 5.3 below.

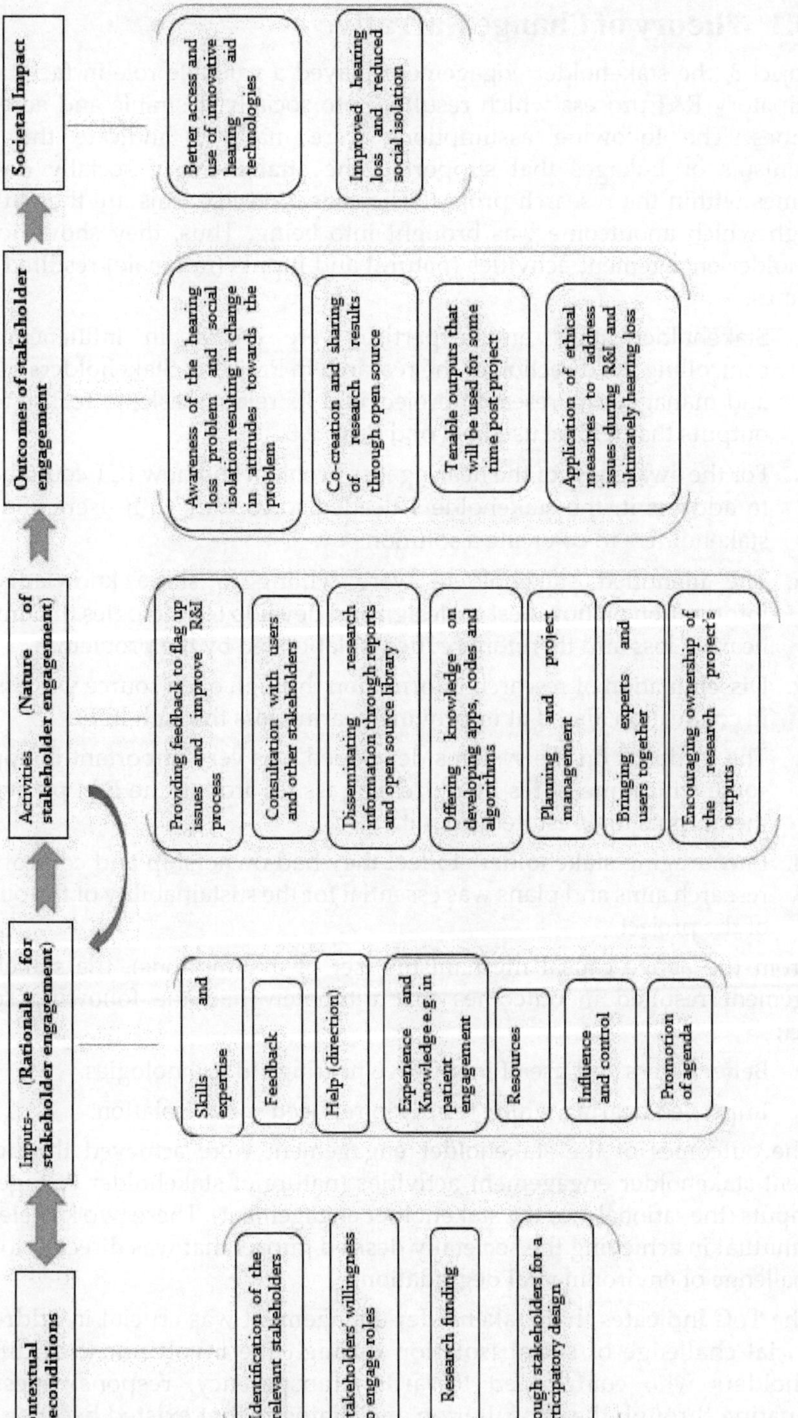

Figure 5.3: A Theory of Change for Project 3

5.10.1 Theory of Change Narrative

In Project 3, the stakeholder engagement played a valuable role in facilitating a participatory R&I process which resulted into socially desirable and acceptable outcomes. The following assumptions were made to indicate the causal mechanisms or linkages that supported the attainment of socially desirable outcomes within the research project. The causal mechanisms are the pathways through which anoutcome was brought into being. Thus, they show how the stakeholder engagement activities (nature) and inputs (rationale) resulted in the outcomes.

i. Stakeholder skills and expertise were crucial in influencing and controlling the direction of the research in Project 3. Stakeholders planned and managed the research project and its related tasks to realise tenable outputs that will be used beyond Project 3.

ii. For the awareness of the hearing loss problem and how ICT could be used to address it, the stakeholders needed to consult with users and other stakeholders to co-create a solution.

iii. The identified stakeholders were willing to share knowledge and information on how best to design and develop technologies that improve hearing loss and therefore reduce isolation led by the problem.

iv. Dissemination of research information through open source was essential in co-creation aimed at improving hearing loss through ICTs.

v. The feedback on the systems developed was very important in applying some ethical measures in addressing issues around the R&I process and the outputs that resulted from it.

vi. Encouraging stakeholders to feel they had ownership and control of the research aims and plans was essential for the sustainability of the outcome of the project.

From the above causal mechanisms (set of assumptions), the stakeholder engagement resulted in outcomes that ultimately had the following societal impact;

i. Better access and use of innovative hearing aid technologies.

ii. Improved hearing which results in reduced social isolation.

The outcomes of the stakeholder engagement were achieved through the different stakeholder engagement activities (nature of stakeholder engagement) and inputs (the rationale for the stakeholder engagement). These two key elements were mutual in achieving the societally desired impact that was directed towards the challenge of environmental degradation.

The ToC indicates that stakeholder engagement was crucial in addressing the social challenge of social isolation through the involvement of different stakeholders who contributed towards, transparency, responsiveness and anticipating through the consultation and dialogue that existed because of the stakeholder engagement.

Further, there were contextual factors that were pre-conditions for the stakeholder engagement to be effective towards achieving the outcomes, particularly concerning responsible innovation and ultimately supporting the research to have a societal impact. The following factors were in place:

i. The existence of the stakeholder engagement depended on the research funding that could provide resources for both the research and engagement activities.

ii. The effectiveness of the stakeholder engagement depended on the identification and willingness of relevant people to be part of the research.

To conclude this section, Project 3 identified stakeholders which included researchers, developers, clinical staff and users. The engaged stakeholders had different roles in the research. For instance, some were engaged to bring awareness of the hearing loss problem and how it increases social isolation. Other stakeholders offered their expertise and knowledge in software design, project management and research. In addition, stakeholders consulted on how the software and technologies that were being developed could be more effective in addressing the societal problem which Project 3 was dealing with.

Thus, they provided advice and feedback that was essential for coming up with desirable and acceptable hearing aid technologies that were innovative and better. With regards to realising socially desirable and acceptable outcomes, the input (rationale for the engagement) and activities (nature of the engagement) from the stakeholder engagement were crucial. For instance, as result of the stakeholder engagement, there was reflection and learning throughout the research process. This was evident through different stakeholders exchanging their skills and expertise via open sourcing and stakeholder engagement activities. As a result, the stakeholder engagement facilitated learning, awareness, reflection and anticipation by enabling the different stakeholders to bring in different ideas, perspectives and experiences in the research process to develop technologies that were desirable and acceptable by society. The next section presents the findings from an evaluation of Project 4.

5.11 Evaluating Key Elements for Stakeholder Engagement in Project 4

This section presents an evaluative analysis of stakeholder engagement in Project 4.

5.11.1 Context of the Stakeholder Engagement

The focus of Project 4 was the use of ICT in developing a dynamic traffic management system across 'city X'. The purpose of the Project 4 was to research and develop an innovative way for optimising the use of the road network while meeting growing demands to sustain high standards of air quality in urban environments. The ICT research Project 4nvolved developing a system concept around an existingoperational traffic control system that was already in use in one of the UK cities. The system was augmented with traffic flow and air quality information and near real-time data from space and in situ measurements (ITD1).

The operational priorities for Project 4 were to mitigate traffic congestion, improve delivery from public transportation networks and improve air quality through the use of ICT. In addition to improving existing management in these areas, the project provided evidence to support regulatory reporting and enable a valuable assessment of current and future policy (ITD1, ITD4 and ITD5).

The project ran from 2012 to 2014 and was funded by European Space Agency (ESA). The priorities for the project were driven by local, national and European level policy in the areas of air quality, local transport and climate. The target market for the resulting system was anticipated to be local authorities of medium to large towns. The system that was produced by Project 4 was based on machine learning, and it consisted of two components: traffic and pollution optimisation and pollution forecast. The system used current and historical traffic data and pollution levels associated with the traffic data.

From the research project's perspective, multi-disciplinary stakeholders were engaged in the research process. The stakeholders engaged in the ICT research project were from industry, academia and local authority. The stakeholders played a distinct role in designing the research and setting the context for the research project in three ways.

Firstly, stakeholders such as researchers were engaged in the research project to bring in their '*expert knowledge in ICT to design and develop a methodology*' (IT01) that could be used for improving traffic flow with an intention to improve air quality. Secondly, stakeholders from the industry were engaged in the research project to '*provide resources*' (IT02) for the research and innovation (R&I) process. Thirdly, stakeholders such as local authorities were engaged in the research project to collaborate and provide relevant information about the city and traffic management systems which was crucial to the success of the research project (ITD6).

To give a picture of the stakeholders that were involved in Project 4, Table 5.7 shows the stakeholders who were contacted to take part in the data collection process for this study. The table indicates the role of the stakeholders, their category together with the numbers of invited participants and those participants who accepted to participate in this study.

Table 5.7: Project 4's Stakeholders for Study Participation

Stakeholder role	Stakeholder category	Number invited for interviews	Number accepted
Planning Engineer	Local authority	2	0
Researcher	Academia	4	2
Project sponsor	Industry	1	0
Project manager	Industry	1	0

Out of the eight stakeholders that were contacted for interviews, only two stakeholders accepted to be interviewed. In order to chase the stakeholders up, they were sent follow up emails, but they never replied. In addition, two stakeholders from the industry were contacted over the telephone. One gave an excuse straight away saying that they were too busyfor an interview, while the other said that they would think about it and reply via email, only to later turn the invitation down.

5.11.2 Identification of Stakeholders

One of the elements that was evaluated was the identification of the stakeholders that were engaged in Project 4. Two overarching themes came up from both the interviews and the document review while evaluating this element. The first theme that emerged related to the process of stakeholder identification and the other related to the range of stakeholders identified. Regarding the process of stakeholder engagement, the focus was on the two areas.

Firstly, it was on the stage at which the stakeholders were identified and secondly on how they were identified for engagement in the ICT research project. Some stakeholders were identified at the pre-project phase, which was the *'developing stage, and they looked at the proposal, [and] helped shape the proposal before it was submitted'* (IT02). Correspondingly, IT01 mentioned that stakeholders were identified at the beginning of the project to work together in both the conception and the development of the research project. The respondent said that they *'worked together with people involved in the industry, in XXX University and put the proposal together to EMDA' (IT01).*

The stakeholders were identified because of their past relationships and the networks that they built within ICT research. For example, IT02 said that *'xxx told me about the role when it came out and actually before it came out, and once it came out, I was called in'*. This shows that when it comes to identifying stakeholders for engagement in ICT research projects past networks play a crucial role. This could be the case to ensure that the identified stakeholders are appropriate for the engagement and the rationale behind it.

Another view that was noticeable in the evaluation of the identification of stakeholders was the range of stakeholders that were engaged in Project 4. As part of the R&I that was taking place in the project, Project 4 identified a number of stakeholders mainly from academia, industry and local authority (ITD1, ITD2 and ITD4). These stakeholders had different roles. From an academic perspective, the roles ranged from a *'post-doc research fellow'*, whose responsibility was to *'implement a demonstrator to prove the feasibility of xxx project'* (IT02) all the way to a principal investigator (IT02) who was *'the main contact at the Xxx University for the Project'*. While from an industry perspective the stakeholders identified included project managers and sponsors (ITD5). Furthermore, from the local authority perspective, the identified stakeholders included engineering professionals who had knowledge of the road networks across the city (ITD6).

5.11.3 Nature of Stakeholder Engagement

To understand the nature of stakeholder engagement in Project 4, two areas of focus emerged. One area of focus was mainly on the form of stakeholder engagement, that is, the engagement activities and the other was on the barriers to stakeholder engagement. With regards to the former, the interviews revealed that the stakeholder engagement in the project took a number of forms. To start with, the engagement involved the dissemination of information and provision of feedback and advice on the R&I process.

In particular, one of the stakeholders said that they provided information for change. They said that the information they provided could be used by the public to change their perspective on being responsible. The respondent suggested that the information *'will enable people to look into it when choosing a house for example'* and decide based on of the quality of air in a particular area. In addition, they said that the *'information provided will help the public to towards improving their carbon footprint'* and in so doing, create a *'positive direct impact to health and therefore a social impact'* (IT02).

In terms of providing feedback and advice, IT01 said that they helped in coming up with better and innovative solutions for solving the societal challenges of air pollution and traffic congestion. Thus, following the feedback and advice that was given by those engaged in the research project, Project 4 was able to *'come up [with] something that will make a difference in the world'*.

The other form of engagement that was mentioned in the interviews was that the stakeholders offered expertise to the research project. This was mentioned by both the two stakeholders that were interviewed. IT01 said that *'I designed [...] the overall system that would be able to do such a thing as integrating traffic and air quality together'*. Similarly, IT02 stressed that their form of engagement was predominantly the expertise that they brought to the project by expressing that they were *'involved in the project because [...] for such a project to make a difference, [they] had to use state of the art technology'*. The respondent further claimed that the 'computational *intelligence techniques that [they] work with on a regular basis could bring a significant impact in this project'*. IT02 further confirmed that he was *'an expert in the area of artificial neural networks worked with simulation and optimisation'*.

From the responses given above, the use of the state of the art technology and the techniques mentioned requires a certain level of expertise that not every stakeholder can possess. Therefore, offering that unique expertise was crucial for the ICT research project to meet the aims mentioned in section 5.11.1 above.

Further, another form of stakeholder engagement that is related to the one above was also realised from the interviews. This involved the stakeholders offering a unique perspective on the R&I process. The unique perspective was on both the inputs and the potential impact of those inputs on R&I. This was indicated by IT01 who mentioned that he *'certainly brought a unique perspective of how you could design and implement a system [...] due to [their] background and expertise in the field, a system that nobody else designed beforehand or published about beforehand'*.

The last form of engagement was leading the research project. This was something mentioned by IT02. The respondent indicated that as part of the engagement in Project 4, they provided project management *'mainly coordinating, making sure that research [is being] carried out according to the plan [...].*

However, despite all these forms of engagement, the interviews highlighted some barriers encountered by the stakeholders during their engagement in Project 4. These barriers notably included lack of interest from people as pointed out by both interviewees. IT01 said that other types of stakeholders were only interested in engaging in the ICT research project if it meant that it would result in a cut in costs or if there was a policy behind it that required it, otherwise people were not interested. The interviewee stressed that this was *'the biggest obstacle or barrier'*. The other barrier was prioritising. This was revealed by IT02 that the project *'had to run an extension for two years'* due to the company that was part of the project *'running through some economic problems'*, therefore deciding that *'the research project was no longer a priority of theirs'* (IT02). Because of that, the industry stakeholder was no longer engaging as was expected. IT02 expressed that *'sometimes it could be challenging trying to make a point across and trying to liaise with other people especially when engagement is not their priority'*.

IT01 suggested another barrier connected to prioritising. This barrier was specifically in relation to implementing or supporting responsible innovation in the research project. The respondent alleged that people were afraid of change and therefore they did not want to engage in activities that bring change. IT01 compare responsible innovation to change and said that stakeholders *'certainly know now that responsible innovation requires people to look outside of the box or to accept change and that is probably the biggest problem when it comes to projects in terms of engagement in innovation'*. The respondent gave an example of one of the stakeholder groups that was *'certainly open to the project, very engaging, supportive and positive about the research, but then at the same time there were always worried about their way of doing things if they change necessarily'*. This was a barrier in terms of contributing towards socially desirable outcomes as part of responsible innovation. Responsible innovation requires stakeholders to be responsive and therefore change in the way they conduct R&I, of which the respondent saw *'that as being a re-occurring problem when it comes to the reason for why do responsible innovation'*.

Lastly, another barrier was recognised as a lack of capacity to engage with other stakeholders. The lack of capacity was a result of reduced or absence of resources for activities directed at engagement and perhaps the research due to unforeseen resource constraints such as the one mentioned above by IT02 about the industry stakeholder that ran into *'economic problems'*. The interviewee suggested that on top of economic constraints, the engagement was also less effective because some stakeholders provided inadequate resources such as data and time due to lack of interest and having other priorities. For instance, concerning inadequate data, the respondent mentioned that *'there were some stakeholders who were gathering the data. They would sometimes promise that they will do data collection, but sometimes the data provided was not very valuable as we thought it would be. Therefore, this had an impact on the modelling that we developed'*.

In a way, this had an impact on the influence that was expected from having stakeholder engagement in the ICT research project.

5.11.4 Rationale for the Stakeholder Engagement

The other element that was evaluated is the rationale for the engagement. Evaluating this element provided an understanding of the motivation to engage different stakeholders in Project 4. From the interviews, four themes emerged under this broad category. The first one was that stakeholders were engaged in Project 4 for consultation. The central aim for consulting with the stakeholders was to offer new solutions to the challenges that are faced by the society. This was mentioned by both IT01 and IT02 that they *'were in charge of delivering the computational intelligence side of things working with the computation of traffic lights'* to develop a new solution to the air quality issues that were resulting from traffic pollution.

The interviewees also pointed out that they were drafted into the ICT research project to diversify ideas on how the research could achieve its aim. This was indicated by IT01 who mentioned that there was a need for *'a whole hierarchy [...] in the project'* with *'different PIs from different entities that are part of the project'* who could sit together and find ways of executing the research effectively.

Another rationale behind engaging the stakeholders in Project 4 was that they could control and direct the research due to the expertise that they could bring with them to the project. IT01 pointed out that *'what was needed [...] was somebody who can design a system that can be implemented'*. In the same light, IT02 said that he was *'expert in the area of artificial neural networks [and] works with simulation and optimisation' therefore he could design and implement an effective methodology for the research project.* With such capabilities, the two stakeholders were adept at directing, influencing and controlling the R&I process towards achieving its aim of improving the environment. The stakeholders were also drafted into the research project to give advice and make *'some decisions as to how best to solve the problem'* (IT02). As part of controlling and directing the research project, IT02 was engaged in the research to coordinate tasks and make sure that the research *'was carried out according to the plan'*.

From the interviews, it was also established that the stakeholders were engaged in the project to share knowledge as part of mutual learning as suggested by IT01. The respondent stated that he was *'working together with xxx and deciding what best techniques can [be] applied and how to best go about it'*. Likewise, IT02 mentioned that they *'had to combine [their] knowledge with the knowledge of people from the Xxx University and also the knowledge from xxx (industry stakeholder) to come and make something that will make a difference in the world'*. The respondent further said that there was *'a combination of ideas on how ICT could be used to correlate air quality with other problems, [...] such as health problems of asthma or health problems'*. As a consequence, the system that was designed and implemented *'was a result of the interaction of different people with roles in the project.'*

Lastly, under the rationale for stakeholder engagement, it was revealed that the stakeholders were also engaged to promote ownership of the ICT research project and its outcomes among different stakeholders and provide recommendations to that effect. This was something that was pointed out by IT02 who mentioned that the *'sort of system that was designed would enable people to look into air pollution and to some degree put a bit of pressure to the city council and other members of the public on issues that affect a particular area'*.

5.11.5 Outcomes of the Stakeholder engagement

The last element was evaluated to understand the outcome of the stakeholder engagement in Project 4. From the interviews, one of the outcomes of stakeholder engagement was that different stakeholders provided an awareness of potential societal issues and how these could be addressed. Therefore, solutions were developed to address the different issues that affected, on one hand, the R&I process and on the other hand, society as a whole. This was pointed out by IT01 who said that having *'more stakeholders [...] from wherever helped the project to shape not only the research but also see additional barriers'* that were not vivid to them until they engaged other stakeholders in the research project. The engagement of the stakeholders brought about the awareness of the challenges. Therefore, the stakeholders were able to find ways to *'possibly take them down and so prepare the road for bringing the research to the market effectively'* (IT02).

Another outcome was that stakeholder engagement promoted a better use of resources. As a result of the better use, there was a reduction in the carbon footprint, which was something that was geared towards making *'a difference in the world'* (IT02). This then led to the sustainability of the project's aims as mentioned by IT02. The respondent suspected that *'from a social perspective'*, the sort of techniques that were shared as part of the engagement, *'would allow the city council to decide what the best strategy in charting the management of the traffic'*, and therefore contribute towards the achievement of the aims of Project 4.

The last outcome of the stakeholder engagement in Project 4 was co-creation. This was highlighted by both IT01 and IT02 who stressed that they had to combine their knowledge and expertise to improve people's welfare. They said that they did this by coming up with a methodology that was a result of combined perspectives on the different objectives. As stated in ITD6, the different stakeholders managed to co-create an ICT system that could potentially change lives by reducing air quality and at the same time reducing traffic congestion.

5.12 APPLYING THE RRI LENS TO PROJECT 4

This section presents an application of the RRI lens to Project 3 in order to understand the value of the stakeholder engagement in the context of socially desirable outcomes.

5.12.1 Engagement of Stakeholders

Despite the poor response of stakeholders for interviews, that is two out of apotential eight, the documents reviewed (ITD2, ITD6) indicated that there were at least four stakeholder types that were identified and engaged in Project 4. The engaged stakeholders were from academia, local authority and industry. The range of stakeholders was important because it brought different viewpoints on thedeveloping and producing a system that *'that will make a difference in the world'* (IT02). This inclusion of a variety of stakeholders is in line with responsible innovation. The inclusion ensured that the research and its agenda was acceptable by societal actors who were engaged in the R&I process and also had a stake in the outcomes from it. Therefore, the ICT research project satisfied this key feature of RRI by engaging different stakeholders for a number of reasons (see section 5.11.4) who undertook different activities (see section 5.11.3) that resulted in the outcomes outlined in section 5.11.5 above in a socially desirable way. The right identification of stakeholders for engagement was ideal for anticipating the outcomes of and reflecting on the R&I process that was taking place in Project 4.

5.12.2 Anticipation and Reflection

In preparing the proposal and identifying which stakeholders to engage and what roles they will play in the R&I process, the stakeholders were given the opportunity to prepare and reflect on the outcome of the research project. This was evident through a consideration of different perspectives and then developing an appropriate system that would deliver a positive outcome. This was demonstrated by the response from IT01 who suggested that they brought their *'unique perspective of how you could implement [...] and design such a system into the project'*. The unique perspective related to doing things differently in the R&I process and reflecting on the process of R&I.

The reflection aided the anticipation concerning possible impacts of the research by having the right stakeholders included in the research. This was something that was supported by IT02 who said that *'you never know what could have happened otherwise if they [stakeholders] were not involved in the process'*. Therefore, from the responses, it can be understood that some of the stakeholders in Project 4 contributed by reflecting on the process and anticipating outcomes that would result from the stakeholder engagement in the research project.

Anticipation and reflection in Project 4 was also achieved by bringing together different perspectives on how the issue of air quality could be tackled as IT01 mentioned that *'those engaged in the research had certainly brought in their perspectives of how such a system could be implemented'*. Correspondingly, the stakeholders were required to think outside the box as suggested by IT01 who said that *'responsible innovation requires people to look outside of the box or to accept change'*. Thinking outside the box required a deeper level of anticipation and reflection on the impact of the ICT research project that was not vivid and obvious to those engaged until they worked together.

Subsequently, due to the expertise of the stakeholders engaged in the research project, all stakeholders were able to collectively *'explore and optimise traffic flow to perform better in air quality even when they had unforeseeable circumstances'* with the help of computational intelligence techniques. This was somehow a result of reflecting on the methodology used in the research and ensuring that it was acceptable and appropriate in anticipating the future uses and impact of the ICT system through *'air quality modelling to gain knowledge of the social impact'* (IT02).

5.12.3 Openness and Transparency

Regarding openness and transparency, not much was explicitly said that showed that there was openness and transparency in the research project except IT02 mentioning that, in some cases they were expected to share knowledge and advice in coming up with the ICT system. To apply this feature of RRI for evaluative analysis, the assumption could be that the combination of knowledge and expertise from different stakeholders meant that there was some dialogue and communication on how technology could be used to solve the problem and improve social welfare. For that reason, it could be said that there was some level of openness and transparency among those engaged through the sharing of different perspectives and insights about the issue that the research project was aimed at addressing and the best way to tackle it.

5.12.4 Responsiveness

The stakeholders were engaged in Project 4 for the reasons discussed in section 5.11.4 above. One of the motives behind the stakeholder engagement was to combine their knowledge so that they could respond to the issue that was being addressed by the research project and change behaviours. In so doing, they could find ways of removing the barriers that affected the alignment of their actions and the intended outcomes. It was pointed out by IT02 that *'they had more stakeholders from other local authorities, companies, who helped to shape the research and also see additional barriers' therefore making the research flexible in dealing with those barriers.* In addition, in responding to the societal challenges in the R&I process, some of the stakeholders contributed in deciding which other stakeholders mattered in the ICT research project and what sort of data, software and techniques were required to achieve the goals of the research.

For instance, it was established from the interviews that one of the stakeholders (IT01) was there to ensure that the *'actual infrastructure needed'* to effectively deal with the societal problem was in place. In the same vein, IT02 gave a suggestion that indicated that the stakeholder engagement encouraged responsiveness in the research. The respondent said that the stakeholders responded to the *'social aspect'* of *'air quality and how that benefits people through using computational intelligence to measure and improve the air quality and related traffic'*. From the suggestion, it could be assumed that the system and methodology employed by the stakeholders were intended to be responsive in achieving desirable impact such as a reduction in carbon footprints. Stakeholders engaged in Project 4 were able to respond to different perspectives and views of others in order to shape ICT systems according to a public good, which was better health.

5.13 Theory of Change for Project 4

A deductive theory of change for the stakeholder engagement process was developed through the sources of data used in this study, which were the reviewed documents and the interviews with the stakeholders in Project 4 and is shown in Figure 5.4 below.

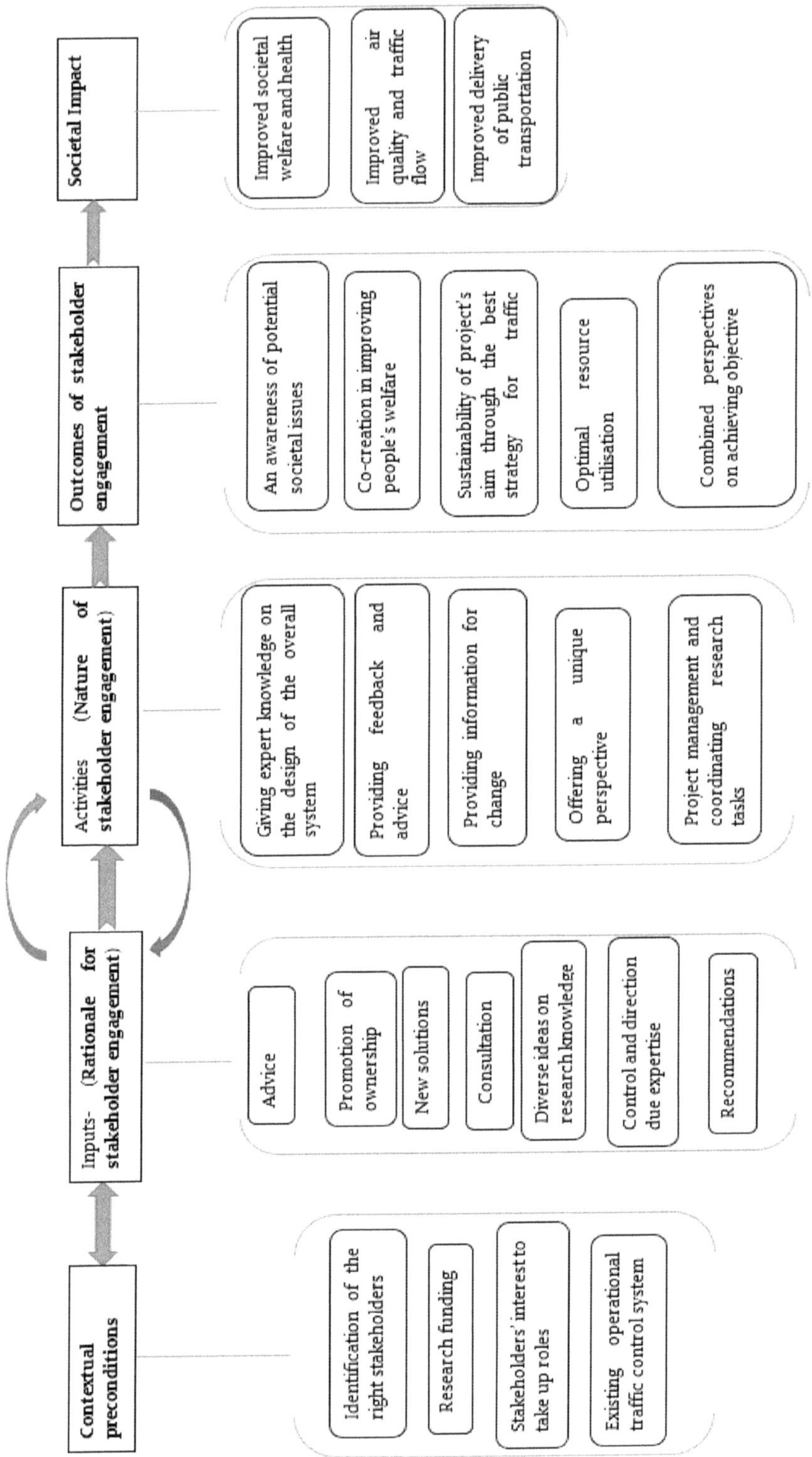

Figure 5.4: A Theory of Change for Project 4

5.13.1 Theory of Change Narrative

The stakeholder engagement in the Project 4 contributed towards the research by facilitating an inclusive R&I process. The following assumptions were made to indicate the causal mechanisms or linkages that supported the attainment of socially desirable outcomes within the ICT research project. The causal mechanisms are the pathways through which an outcome was brought into being. Thus, they show how the stakeholder engagement activities (nature) and inputs (rationale) resulted in the outcomes.

i. Giving expert knowledge on the design of the overall system offered the advice and recommendations on how the research could be carried out which resulted in co-creating new solutions in improving society's welfare.

ii. Diverse ideas from stakeholders culminated in consultations that provided feedback and advice. This, in turn, helped people to utilise their resources optimally and combine perspectives on achieving the research objectives.

iii. Stakeholder expertise was significant in providing control and direction, which was core to managing the ICT research project and related tasks. This was necessary for the sustainability of the project's aims and better resource utilisation.

iv. Provision of information for change promoted ownership of the research and its outcomes, which encouraged stakeholder to be more aware of potential societal issues.

v. Encouraging stakeholders to feel they had ownership and control of the research aims and plans was essential for co-creation.

vi. For the awareness of potential barriers to stakeholder engagement, stakeholders needed to consult and get different perspectives on both stakeholder engagement and the research process.

From the above causal mechanisms (set of assumptions), the stakeholder engagement resulted in outcomes that ultimately had the following societal impact;

i. Improved delivery of public transportation.

ii. Improved air quality and traffic flow.

iii. Improved societal welfare and health.

This outcome of the stakeholder engagement was achieved through the different stakeholder engagement activities (nature of stakeholder engagement) and inputs (the rationale for the stakeholder engagement). These two key elements were mutual in achieving the societally desired impact that was directed towards the challenge of environmental degradation.

The ToC indicates that despite Project 4 focusing on ICT within its processes, there was a lot of stakeholder input, which made the process socially desirable and therefore implemented responsible innovation within the ICT research project. It shows that stakeholder engagement was crucial in addressing the social challenge through the involvement of different stakeholders who contributed towards, transparency, responsiveness and anticipating through the consultation and dialogue that existed because of the stakeholder engagement.

Further, there were contextual factors that were pre-conditions for the stakeholder engagement to be effective towards achieving the outcomes, particularly concerning attainment of socially desirable outcomes and ultimately supporting the research to have a societal impact. The following necessary factors were in place:

i. The existence of the stakeholder engagement depended on the research funding that could provide resources for both the research and engagement activities.

ii. An existing operational traffic control system on which the stakeholders could come together and work on to develop a specific approach to tackling traffic flow and air quality.

iii. The success of the stakeholder engagement was dependent on availability of time on the stakeholders' part and their interest to take up roles.

iv. The effectiveness of the stakeholder engagement depended on the identification and availability of relevant people or stakeholder groups in particular experts.

In summary, the finding in this section indicates that as part of the stakeholder engagement, stakeholders offered their expertise and knowledge in conducting the research. In addition, they consulted on the best techniques for tackling the problem and directed the whole R&I process. The input (rationale for the engagement) and activities (nature of the engagement) from the stakeholder engagement were crucial in achieving socially desirable and acceptable outcomes. For instance, as result of the stakeholder engagement, there was co-creation in the ICT research project. This was evident by different stakeholders sharing ideas and expertise in the development of the system that was used to control traffic flow in the city 'X'. In addition, the stakeholder engagement facilitated learning, awareness, reflection and anticipation by enabling the different stakeholders to bring in different perspectives on developing a methodology for designing and implementing the ICT system. The methodology focussed on mitigating the issue of air pollution through simulation and the use of computational intelligence. Subsequently, stakeholders were able to respond to the different perspectives to shape the ICT systems in a socially desirable and acceptable manner.

5.14 Conclusion

This chapter presented findings from evaluative analysis of four ICT research projects, which included Projects 1, 2, 3 and 4 respectively. The projects engaged different stakeholders who contributed in a variety of ways towards the attainment of socially desirable outcomes within their particular projects. Using a Theory of Change, their value towards socially desirable outcomes became clear through linking their various activities and motivations for their engagement in the projects to specific socially acceptable outcomes. Despite being identified for roles that were not explicitly connected to achieving socially desirable outcomes, using RRI as a lens provided a basis for connecting the different elements that are involved in the stakeholder engagement process with the attainment of such outcomes. The findings of the evaluative analysis conducted in this chapter will be fed to into a cross-case analysis in chapter 6.

CHAPTER

6

A Cross-Case Analysis

6.1 INTRODUCTION

This chapter puts together the findings and analysis of the four chapters that individually covered the four cases that were used in this research. In so doing, the chapter constructs an answer to the overall research question introduced in chapter 1 (see section 1.5). Hence, the chapter answers the question: ***'How can the efficacy of stakeholder engagement in Information Communication Technology (ICT) research projects be evaluated?*** In answering this research question, three sub-research questions are addressed. These include;

i. What is the role of stakeholder engagement in ICT research projects?

ii. How can Responsible Research and Innovation (RRI) support the evaluation of stakeholder engagement in ICT research projects?

iii. What elements are key for evaluating the efficacy of stakeholder engagement in ICT research projects?

Conforming to the evaluation and analysing of the cases in chapter 5, this chapter is based on the analytical illustration that was introduced in section 4.12. Thus, to start with, the key elements for evaluating stakeholder engagement are discussed with reference to an application of the (Responsible Research and Innovation) RRI lens which was discussed in section 3.5. The chapter starts by outlining the themes that materialised across all four case research projects and how these relate to the attainment of socially desirable outcomes in ICT research projects. Thus, using the concept of RRI as a lens in evaluating stakeholder engagement in ICT research projects is useful for understanding its efficacy towards the attainment of the socially desirable outcomes. Following this, insights are drawn from the cross-case analysis and discussed relative to the literature on RRI, evaluation and stakeholder engagement. Thus the cross-case analysis goes beyond the individual cases in chapter 5 and extends the main insights to answer the research questions.

6.2 How the Conceptual Model Facilitates the Evaluation

The conceptual evaluation model proposed and used in this research ties together different parts of stakeholder engagement in ICT research projects. The process of stakeholder engagement in research projects involves many aspects that range from the context of the engagement, the motive of the engagement all the way to the outcomes of the engagement. The conceptual evaluation model facilitates a segmental approach in understanding the different elements of stakeholder engagement with a goal to get a full picture at the end of the process. Thus the conceptual evaluation model, draw attention to the key areas to focus on when evaluating stakeholder engagement in ICT research projects. Looking through the literature, there are no set models for evaluating stakeholder engagement as also suggested by Smith (2015). This means that when it comes practical fieldwork, there is not much for practitioners to base the evaluation strategy or use a guide for an effective and straightforward evaluation. For example, Mark *et al.*, (2006) point out to the lack of approaches or a combination of approaches that could be used in evaluation especially in social sciences and qualitative evaluations (Billings, 2016; Smith, 2015). Considering such suggestions relating to approaches of qualitative nature, the conceptual evaluation model suggested in chapter 3 and operationalised in chapter 5 works towards addressing that gap. The conceptual evaluation model has two main constituents.

The first constituent makes a case for evaluating the main elements of the stakeholder engagement process when understanding its value towards particular outcomes. These are determined based on stakeholder theory and RRI. These two are deemed as guiding bodies of knowledge that could be used to understand why stakeholders are engaged in ICT research projects. These are discussed in more detail in section 6.3 (with reference to insights from stakeholder theory) and section 6.4 (with reference to insights from RRI).

The second constituent of the model benefitted from the capability of the Theory of Change (ToC) in connecting the value of an evaluand, which in this case is the stakeholder engagement, in achieving specific outcomes. The ToC supports making assumptions that are used to link the inputs of stakeholder engagement, that is, the activities and motives, to their outcomes. This further discussed in section 6.5 below.

6.3 Key Elements for Evaluating Stakeholder Engagement

This section discusses the analysis of the key elements for evaluating stakeholder engagement in ICT research projects. These elements were realised from the theoretical and empirical insights to provide the analytical framework for this research and are operationalised in the conceptual evaluation model (see sections 3.6 and 4.12). For instance, one theoretical insight came from Mayne (2012), who suggested that one way of effectively evaluating stakeholder engagement is through a Theory of change (ToC). The ToC was used in understanding the intended outcomes, activities expected to achieve those outcomes and the contextual factors that influenced the activities. These insights were then enriched by the empirical insights from the different stakeholder participants in all four case research projects. The participants gave useful insights on each of the different elements suggested in the literature such as those suggested by Penfield *et al.*, (2014), Scriven and Coryn, (2008) and Connell and Kubisch (1998). Thus, this section first discusses 17 cross-cutting themes that emerged from the four cases. From these themes, four main common insights are derived. The main insights derived will answer the research questions in section 6.7.

To pull the cross-cutting themes together, a spreadsheet was used to analyse and mark the different themes that were emerging in each case research project as shown in Appendices 6-1 to 6-5. From the analysis, those themes that were repeatedly emerging across all the four cases were pulled out and are discussed below.

6.3.1 Contextual Factors

In all the four case projects contextual factors were very important for stakeholder engagement to be effective towards the attainment of socially desirable outcomes in the ICT research projects. This concurs with the suggestion by Connell and Kubisch (1998) that contextual factors are likely to influence the effectiveness of stakeholder engagement activities and outcomes that result from those activities. As such, contextual factors are an important element to evaluate. Gaining an understanding of the contextual dimensions of stakeholder engagement was valuable because information collected about the setting was necessary in understanding the boundaries and margins in which the engagement was taking place (Stufflebeam and Shinkfield, 2007). The stakeholder engagement activities were taking place within a context of action, which was the ICT research projects. Therefore, as suggested by Stufflebeam and Shinkfield's (2007), it was essential to understand the different aspects for the context of action in which the stakeholder engagement was taking place.

Evaluating the contextual factors involved a Case-based approach (CBA) (as suggested by Stufflebeam and Coryn (2014)) and a Theory based-approach (TBA) (as suggested by Weiss (1997). It was necessary to use both a CBA and TBA in gaining a contextual understanding of the stakeholder engagement. This was necessary because the lessons that were learnt from the four cases could be extrapolated to future evaluation activities and stakeholder engagement efforts. Therefore, what was learnt in the four cases could be used to identify, prioritise, and then assess the key stakeholder engagement activities and contextual factors that are likely to influence a valuable engagement (Mayne, 2012; 2016; Connell and Kubisch, 1998) towards the attainment of socially desirable outcomes in ICT research projects. Principally, two main areas of focus under contextual dimensions emerged in all four ICT research projects and are discussed below.

6.3.1.1 Resources as an enabling factor

In all the four cases, it was recognised that resources were a fundamental enabling factor that was necessary for the stakeholder engagement to be effective. The availability of research resources was paramount in ensuring that the stakeholder engagement and its associated activities were effectively organised to carry out the scope of work that achieved beneficial change (Turner and Müller, 2003). For the stakeholder engagement to be of value, some organisations provided the necessary resources for the stakeholders to come together and work towards specific aims. These resources were either financial, human or material.

For example, in Project 1, for the stakeholders to have a fruitful engagement, there was a provision of research funding and an existing ICT infrastructure to support the research on the ICT system that was being developed. In all four projects, the funding was accessed through research funding institutions and industry partners. In the case of the infrastructure, this was mainly important in three projects, Project 1, 2 and 3 due to the nature of their research. Also, for valuable stakeholder engagement, there was also a requirement for human resources in all four cases. For example, human resources were essential for the coordination of engagement activities, which was crucial in ensuring that the process was efficient and effective towards achieving positive goals (Bryson, 2004; Bryson *et al.*, 2013).

6.3.1.2 Uptake of expected roles

The second theme that was important regarding the contextual dimension of stakeholder engagement was the uptake of expected roles by stakeholders that were engaged in the ICT research projects. It was important to understand the issues that affect the uptake of roles as part of the stakeholder engagement because such an understanding has a potential to improve the way stakeholder engagement is approached in ICT research. However, despite the expectation by the project sponsors and principal researchers to involve stakeholders that would assume different roles, the engagement did not go accordingly. It was learnt from all cases that two main issues affected the uptake of the different roles. These issues were the appropriateness and willingness of the stakeholders to take up the different roles as part of their engagement.

Core to these issues was a lack of interest by some identified stakeholders. Stakeholders that were expected to be highly engaged in the ICT research projects were prioritising other commitments. Also, since most of them had limited resources, they did not support most of the engagement activities as they could have otherwise done. These issues which were given by the stakeholders in the cases, were comparable to those suggested by Bunn *et al.*, (2002) and Reed *et al.*, (2009). Therefore, to improve stakeholder engagement, perhaps it is necessary to make the engagement process more interesting and provide ample resources to support the stakeholder engagement process.

In order to make the engagement interestting, there should be clear incentives to the stakeholders that are engaged in the research projects. These incentives could be material, for instance, financial and non-material. An example could be giving stakeholders that are not actively involved with the research activities a say on the way forward and alternatives. As a result, this could yield positive uptake of roles. Such positive examples of role uptake may include increased attendance of stakeholder engagement activities, providing timely feedback or constructive comments on progress and research projects' deliverables.

6.3.2 Identification of Stakeholders

The identification of stakeholders is essential for the effectiveness of the stakeholder engagement process because it helps the ICT research projects to achieve their aims by scoping which stakeholders will support the attainment of different outcomes (Bryson *et al.*, 2013; Durham *et al.*, 2014; Leventon *et al.*, 2016). In all the four ICT research projects, the identification of stakeholders for engagement was similar. The identification of relevant stakeholders for engagement was mainly based on two broad thematic categories, the process of identification and timing of the identification.

6.3.2.1 Process of identification

With regards to the process, in all the four cases stakeholders were identified based on existing networks. Stakeholders were mostly identified because there was someone who knew them either because of a past encounter in the research world or was known to have some experience or expertise that was relevant to the aims of the ICT research projects (Leventon *et al.*, 2016). Regarding existing networks, in Project 1 stakeholders were identified through referrals while in Project 2 they were identified through past encounters in research work or similar (the instrumental perspective as suggested by Bailur (2006)). This was a trend in all the cases were the identified stakeholders, especially those who were directly linked to conducting the research, had been involved in previous research or worked together in other endeavours other than research.

On the other hand, experience or expertise was crucial in identifying the stakeholders to take up roles (as mentioned by Bryson *et al.*, 2013). These roles were wide enough to include those who were actively involved in research in all the four cases and those who were there to represent the public interests (Durham *et al.*, 2014) for example, researchers and end users. This was the case in Project 2 with teachers and head teachers representing the public interest and similarly in Project 1, with estate users and students representing the same. Regarding the attainment of socially desirable outcomes, the stakeholder engagement was not explicitly connected to responsible innovation as an end. The engaged stakeholders were identified to take up roles that were directly linked to the outputs and processes of the R&I taking place in the research projects. However, although this was the case, the stakeholders implicitly influenced the attainment of desirable outcomes. To indicate the linkages, ToCs were constructed to indicate the links between the activities that the stakeholders were undertaking (rationale and nature of their engagement) and the desirable outcomes that resulted from it (see sections 6.3.3; 6.3.4 and 6.3.5).

6.3.2.2 Timing of identification

In all the four ICT research projects, stakeholders were identified *ex-ante* (Reed and Curzon, 2015, p. 24) that is, the stakeholder identification took place in advance. However, it also emerged that in some of them there was an *ad-hoc* identification of stakeholders that is, the identification took place as the research process progressed. In Project 4, the stakeholders were only identified *ex-ante,* and none were identified during the research. Perhaps this was due to the nature of the research that was being undertaken in the research project. The research in Project 4 only needed to have the stakeholders identified at the beginning and be engaged throughout the whole R&I process until the final output and outcomes were achieved. This was contrary to Project 1, 2 and 3 where the identification was happening iteratively at all stages of the research a process as recommended by Reed and Curzon (2015). For example, Project 3 kept identifying *ad hoc* stakeholders as the ICT system (dashboard) was being developed in order to have feedback and bring awareness of the agenda that was being promoted by the ICT research project.

6.3.2.3 The range of identified stakeholders

In all the four case research projects there was a wide range of stakeholders that were identified. From the data collected it could be seen that there were stakeholders who were identified because of their expert knowledge such as scientists, researchers and project managers (as was the case of the Project 3's 3TI02 who was a project manager for one of the SMEs' that were involved in the project). Apart from expert knowledge, some stakeholders were identified because of their experiences. These stakeholders were engaged in the research projects to share their lived experiences, values and expectations in developing or implementing desirable ICTs (Chatfield *et al.,* 2017; Rip, 2014; Stahl *et al.,* 2016). For example, Project 4 engaged teachers who were not experts in ICT but were capable of bringing rich knowledge that was necessary for effective implementation of ICTs in secondary school education. The identification of a wide range of stakeholders was ideal for matching the users' expectations and the usability of the ICT systems that were being developed or implemented in the ICT research projects (Olphert and Damodaran, 2007b).

6.3.3 Nature of Stakeholder Engagement

In evaluating the nature of stakeholder engagement, the focus was on the activities which the stakeholders were undertaking in their respective research projects. It was important to evaluate whether the activities were relevant for attaining the socially desirable outcomes in the ICT research projects or not (see Kubisch and Connell, 1998 and Rogers, 2016 on ToC). Five different types of stakeholder activities describing the nature of stakeholder engagement emerged from the analysis and are discussed below. Also, the five different types of stakeholder engagement activities are the common ones that appeared in the literature related to research projects.

6.3.3.1 Dissemination of Information

In all the four cases the stakeholder engagement provided a platform where the different stakeholders could disseminate information among those engaged in the

ICT research projects. For instance, the information that was disseminated was about the intended outcomes of R&I process or the activities that were taking place as part of the research. In the case of the former, an example was given in Project 1, where as part of the stakeholder engagement stakeholders were given the information about the intended innovative solutions for solving the societal challenge of air pollution and traffic congestion. While for the latter, an example was shown in Project 2 in which information was disseminated as part of knowledge exchange among the stakeholders that were engaged in the ICT research project.

In all the ICT research projects, the dissemination of information among the stakeholders was crucial in the R&I because it afforded them with a sound and extensive knowledge base about the needs, goals and expectations of other stakeholders. This was very important in achieving outputs and outcomes which could be acceptable and desirable for the society.

6.3.3.2 Facilitation of dialogue and consultation

In all the four cases, stakeholder engagement was a good platform for facilitating dialogue and consultation on different aspects that were related to the research processes, for example, the choice of effective methodologies. This was highlighted as one of the stakeholder engagement activities that were taking place in all four ICT research projects. For example in Project 1, Project 3 and Project 2, the respondents that were interviewed clearly said that as part of the stakeholder engagement, there was a lot of consultation with those who would be the end users of the ICT systems that were either being developed (as in the case of Project 1 and Project 3) or being implemented (as in the of Project 2).

Facilitating dialogue and consultative actions such as blogs and events were supportive towards achieving the different outcomes for the ICT research projects (as in the case of Project 4). These outcomes were both related to the specific objectives of the research projects (see chapters 7 to 10) and to attainment of socially desirable outcomes (as discussed by Bauer *et al.*, 2016; Zwart *et al.*, 2014; Jirotka *et al.*, 2017 and Stahl *et al.* 2016). Regarding the attainment of socially desirable outcomes, the consultations and dialogue were an inclusive process of establishing different ways of creating possible future scenarios which could help minimise possible future negative outcomes of the research by providing viable alternatives (Guston and Sarewitz, 2002).

6.3.3.3 Offering expertise

When it came to offering expertise as a stakeholder engagement activity, in all four cases, stakeholders had some form of expertise that they provided towards the research process and ultimately towards the intended outputs and outcomes of the ICT research projects. For example, in Project 4, Project 1 and Project 3 some of the stakeholders were engaged to provide their technical expertise in developing ICT systems that were expected to address the societal challenges which these ICT research projects were focusing on, respectively. With respect to the attainment of socially desirable outcomes, engaging stakeholders that offer expertise is an anticipative approach that ensures that the planned research methodology and its outcome is acceptable (Jirotka *et al.*, 2017). The different expertise that is offered as part of stakeholder engagement is vital in co-creation and responsiveness of ICT research projects to social impacts.

6.3.3.4 Providing feedback and advice

Another stakeholder engagement activity that was overarching in all the four cases was the provision of feedback and advice (as suggested by Bryson *et al.*, 2013). The stakeholders engaged in the ICT research projects provided feedback on the ICT systems that there were being developed. For example, in Project 1 and Project 2 there were fora where the stakeholders could discuss the research and its outputs, and in so doing provide feedback that was used to improve the R&I processes and in the long run the final results.

As mentioned by Bryson *et al.* (2013), stakeholders provide feedback about alternatives and decisions on how certain processes should be carried out, for instance, to mitigate societal harm. The focus on such feedback is on the procedures that R&I follows in the ICT research projects.

For example, as part of the engagement in the ICT research projects, researchers engaged in dialogue with other stakeholders to reveal the diverse objectives, aspirations, needs, and characteristics of different members of the society with an aim to define and validate requirements for the research outputs. This was indicative of reflection and inclusiveness in the ICT research projects that is crucial for attaining socially desirable and desirable outcomes (Blok *et al.* 2015).

6.3.3.5 Promoting ownership

In all the four cases, the stakeholder engagement was also in the form of promoting ownership of the agendas that the ICT research projects were working towards. Through the engagement of different stakeholders, people understood the need for the research and appreciated and took ownership of either the research process or the results that came from it. For instance, as part of the stakeholder engagement in Project 3, information for change was provided to different stakeholders in the ICT research project. The provided information was used by the stakeholders to change their perspective on hearing loss as a societal problem and went deeper into discussions of how the issue could be addressed using technology, and also how they could contribute toward that solution.

Similarly, in Project 2, some of the stakeholders that were engaged promoted the research agenda and the outcomes that were being realised. They were promoting them in blogs and stakeholder engagement events in secondary schools so that different stakeholders could be aware of the use of ICT in education. As a result of such promotion, other stakeholders such as teachers were encouraged to be part of the efforts that the ICT research project was working on. In terms of achieving socially desirable goals, this was significant because it encouraged mutual learning and knowledge exchange between stakeholders. As such, through that, there was some reflexivity and responsiveness due to the awareness that they got which resulted in an outcome which was desirable for many (Simon, 2017). The promotion of the agenda brought in some awareness and reflection which resulted in the stakeholders being responsive to the aims and causes of the ICT research projects to address the societal challenge.

6.3.4 Rationale for Stakeholder Engagement

In all the four cases the rationale or motive for stakeholder engagement was similar. One thing that was noticeable was that the rationale for the engagement varied according to the stage of the research process and the objectives that the research projects were trying to achieve at a respective stage (Bryson *et al.*, 2013). From the analysis of the four cases, it was realised that the main rationale for stakeholder engagement is to bring together different stakeholders to embed anticipation and reflection into practice within the R&I processes to stimulate new ways of addressing societal challenges and therefore achieve socially desirable outcomes (Chatfield *et al.*, 2017; Rose *et al.*, 2015; Stahl *et al.*, 2016). In the four cases, the rationale for stakeholder engagement included the following.

6.3.4.1 Consultation

Consultation was one of the main rationales for stakeholder engagement in all the ICT research projects (as suggested by Bryson *et al.*, 2013 and Durham *et al.*, 2014). Different stakeholders were brought together to consult on how the projects could address the societal challenge that each ICT research project was focussing on respectively. Corresponding to Bryson *et al.* (2013), stakeholders were engaged so that they could provide feedback on the different aspects of the ICT research projects. Also, there was consultation to raise awareness of the potential responsibility issues and how they affect society (Boulos, 2014).

As an example, in Project 1 building users and researchers were engaged in consultative interactions throughout the whole R&I process to develop an ICT interface that was easy to use and understand. The consultation was either conducted during promotional activities at stakeholder engagement events or through the project's dedicated online forum. Similarly, in Project 2, the rationale behind stakeholder engagement was to have consultations with an aim to bring in different perspectives from the stakeholders whohad different experiences and backgrounds.

Regarding the socially desirable outcomes, the consultation was very supportive towards realising them in all the four ICT research projects because it facilitated inclusiveness in the research processes. Because of such inclusiveness, the participating stakeholders were able to deliberate on different aspects of the R&I processes to ensure that the outcomes were desirable and acceptable for all (Blok *et al.*, 2015). With the deliberation, the stakeholders were then able to be anticipative and responsive in working towards the respective aims of the ICT research projects. The consultation afforded the anticipation of moral concerns about the research's intended outputs including issues with potential harm. It also helped in embedding them in the design and sustainability of the research processes (van den Hoven, 2013) that were taking place in the projects. Thus, the consultation supported the ICT research projects to achieve outcomes that were particularly desirable and acceptable for the society (see section 6.3.5).

6.3.4.2 Control and direction

Regarding control and direction, in all four ICT research projects, part of the stakeholder engagement was in the form of leadership. Some of the stakeholders were engaged to control and direct the research projects towards the attainment of their aims in a desirable way. The control and direction were dependent on the expertise, experience and background of the stakeholders. For example, in Projects 2 and 3, for some of the stakeholders, their engagement predominantly was in the form of directing the research efforts towards managing the implementation of a methodology and coordination of different tasks. As a result of such coordination, there was a lot of co-creation and inclusion of different perspectives from those who were engaged in the project. The stakeholders that were engaged to direct and control were the ones who had high interest and high influence on the research projects. As mentioned by Bryson (2004), based on the requirements of the research in each ICT research project, those stakeholders that were engaged and had high influence but also high interest were the ones that supplied the most pertinent relevant resources, information to direct the project effectively.

6.3.4.3 Mutual learning

The other rationale for stakeholder engagement was that stakeholders should learn from each other. Learning among the stakeholders was common in all four cases. From the findings, it was established that different stakeholders were engaged, on the one hand, to share their expertise and knowledge, and on the other, to learn things that they were not aware of, or had limited knowledge about before the engagement (see Leventon *et al.*, 2016 and Owen *et al.*, 2015). For example, in Project 4 the rationale for stakeholder engagement was that different stakeholders from industry, academia and local authority combined their knowledge to come up with a solution for improving air quality using ICT.

Similarly, in Projects 1, 2 and 4, the motive behind stakeholder engagement was to bring in stakeholders other than the experts to learn and get information on the issues that were affecting the society such as seclusion because of hearing loss, reduced education performance in secondary and high carbon dioxide (CO_2) emissions in buildings. These stakeholders learnt a lot through the dialogue (as mentioned by Blok, 2014) that was taking place in the ICT research projects through fora, blogs and stakeholder engagement events. By being part of the dialogue, they provided feedback, knowledge and shared experiences with those who had the expertise to learn and implement the research successfully (Owen *et al.*, 2013a). In relation to achieving socially desirable outcomes, mutual learning helped those engaged to pre-empt societal concerns and provide innovative suggestions to the dilemmas of R&I in ICT. With regards to RRI, mutual learning is of significance in ICT research projects because it encourages an exchange of views that may result in reflection and positive change in behaviour. This was the case in most of the case research projects where stakeholders' perceptions of the processes evolved throughout the project through learning. For example, in Project 1, stakeholders changed their behaviours after learning more about their energy consumption through the ICT system (the dashboard) and the online stakeholder forum.

6.3.4.4 Resourcing

Although resourcing was not explicitly mentioned as a rationale in the interviews, it was clear from the document analysis that in all the four ICT research projects, one of the main reasons for stakeholder engagement was the provision of resources that were necessary for the implementation of the research (as suggested by Durham *et al.*, 2014). The resources were in three forms. Firstly, the resources were in the form of materials, aswas the case particularly in Projects 1, 2, and 3. In these case projects, there was a need for existence of ICT infrastructures to support the research. Secondly, the motive for stakeholder engagement in all the four cases was the human resource it brought to ICT research projects. For example, in all the cases, stakeholders had the right skills, expertise, knowledge and experiences that were essential for different aspects of the research process. Thirdly, some stakeholders such as the local authority and industry were engaged in the ICT projects because of the financial resources that they could bring into the research. In relation to the attainment of socially desirable outcomes in the ICT research projects, each type of resources was relevant and crucial. For instance, the materials provided were crucial for providing the capacity to adapt and respond to changing circumstances (Stilgoe *et al.*, 2013) within the research environments in which all the ICT research projects were being implemented. The human resources provided were significant in anticipating, reflecting and being transparent during the research process while the financial resources were necessary to support the engagement of different stakeholders and ultimately the successful implementation of the research processes that were being undertaken in all the cases.

6.3.5 The Outcomes

As suggested by Weiss (1998), evaluation is about assessing the outcome of a certain activity or activities. One way of achieving that is by using a theory-based approach (such as a ToC) to identify the linkages (the rationale) between the activities (nature) of stakeholder engagement and the outcomes (in this case the socially desirable outcomes). From the key elements discussed in the last four sub-sections 6.3.1 to 6.3.4, the focus was on the activities and linkages. In this section, the last element to evaluate as suggested by Weiss (1998) and Mayne (2012) is the outcome of the stakeholder engagement.

In all the four cases there were some overarching socially desirable outcomes of stakeholder engagement in the ICT research projects. The outcomes included stakeholders being more aware of the responsibility issues related to the respective ICT research projects, optimal use of resources as a result of the awareness, sustainability of the aims of each of the ICT project and co-creation through engagement and mutual learning.

6.3.5.1 Awareness of responsibility issues

In all the four ICT research projects, the stakeholders were engaged in dialogue through consultations which provided them with information. The information provided made them become more aware of the societal challenges that the individual ICT research projects were aiming to address and the responsibility issues that were related to the causes of the research. As a result of the awareness, the stakeholders were able to change their behaviours and attitudes towards the respective challenges that each ICT research project was dealing with. For example, in Project 1, the interaction with a dashboard (ICT system) that was developed in the project, stakeholders were able to see patterns of their behaviours on energy consumption. Once they received the feedback from the ICT systems, the stakeholders were then discussing the results and ways of changing their behaviours through an online forum and during consultative engagement events. In relation to attaining socially desirable and desirable outcomes, the awareness made the stakeholders responsive to the issues that were being flagged up by the ICT systems and also during deliberation. Boulus (2014) and Bifulco *et al.* (2016) recommended deliberations within research as an effective way of flushing out issues that affect research and its outcomes. Awareness of responsibility issues is very important in building the capacity of stakeholders to adapt and respond to changing circumstances and also encourages responsible innovation in ICT research projects.

6.3.5.2 Sustainability of project aims

The stakeholder that were engaged in all the four cases brought with them a variety of skills, capabilities and knowledge. Among some of the inputs from the stakeholders that were engaged in the ICT research projects, were leadership, knowledge and management of the research process. One of the things that resulted from such contributions from certain stakeholders was a better utilisation of resources and knowledge that was shared during the engagement processes. As an example, in Projects 1 and 3, stakeholders' expertise and knowledge were central to providing control and direction. Controlling and directing the research process was necessary for the sustainability of the project's aims and better resource utilisation during and beyond the research through a change in behaviour and attitudes. The fact that the sustainability of the ICT research projects aims was one of the outcomes shows that the results or rather outputs of the ICT research projects were accepted by the stakeholders. Engaging the stakeholders in the four ICT research projects, meant that what the stakeholders co-created and learnt through their engagement had a chance to continue beyond the lifespan of the respective ICT research projects. For example, in Projects 1, 2 and 4, there was a change of behaviour and attitudes that lasted beyond the years of the ICT research projects. Stakeholders (and the public) became more aware of their energy consumption; the ICTs implemented in secondary schools has a long-term impact on the society and the same with improvement in air quality as a result of the traffic optimisation. In addition, to change in behaviour, the ICT systems that were developed (as is the case of Projects 1, 2 and 3) and those that were implemented all the four projects were likely to be accepted by the stakeholders because of their involvement in the R&I processes. With such involvement, there was a buy-in across the stakeholders.

6.3.5.3 Co-creation

The last overarching outcome in all the four cases was co-creation. The stakeholder engagement process in all four of them allowed the projects to bring in different stakeholders, harness their capabilities, knowledge and potential in creating solutions to the societal challenges that each project was aiming to address. For example in Projects 1 and 4, computer experts worked together with a sample of users in developing the ICT systems that they were developing so that they could come up with desirable technologies that meet the needs of the society (Stahl, 2013) and (Pavie and Carthy, 2014). One way to ensure that the outcomes of ICT research are socially desirable is through co-creation. The reason behind this is that with co-creation, stakeholders bringtogether their knowledge, experiences, values and perspectives to come up solutions that tend to be accepted by the society (Geoghegan-Quinn, 2012; Phillipson *et al.*, 2012c; Schenke *et al.*, 2016). To sum it up, Table 6.1 below put the similarities and difference between the cases which were realised during the cross-cases analysis.

Table 6.1: Similarities and Difference between the Cases

Theme	Definition of Theme	Similarities	Differences
Contextual dimensions			
1. Resources as enabling factors	These are sources of support that facilitate the research project.	Financial and human resources were paramount in all four ICT research projects	Infrastructure was not mentioned as a resource in one project (i.e. Project 3) due to the nature of research being undertaken
2. Uptake of expected roles	This is the extent to which the stakeholders are willing to take roles as part of their engagement.	In all four cases, stakeholders were not willing to effectively take up roles due to lack of interest and resources limitations	In some projects, roles were clearly defined compared to others. For example, the roles were clear in Projects 1 and 4
Identification of stakeholders			
3. Process of identification	A series of actions or steps taken to identify stakeholders for engagement.	Stakeholder identification was based on networks and expertise	
4. Timing of identification	A particular point or period when stakeholder identification takes place.	All ICT research projects had ex-ante stakeholder identification	While all had ex-ante stakeholder identification, Project 3 had ad-hoc stakeholder identification
5. Range of identified stakeholders	The scope of the stakeholders identified and their knowledge or abilities	A wide range of stakeholders identified for engagement	The expertise, experiences and skills of the identified stakeholders were different
Nature of stakeholder engagement			
6. Dissemination of information	The act of spreading information widely.	Directed at the communicating the outcomes of the all ICT research projects.	Media used to disseminate information was different.
7. Facilitation of dialogue and consultation	Making dialogue and consultation possible	Same purpose across all the ICT research projects.	

Theme	Definition of Theme	Similarities	Differences
8. Offering expertise	Provision of expert skill or knowledge in a particular field	Expertise was crucial in all ICT research projects	Varying degrees of expert knowledge depending on the aim of the ICT research projects
9. Providing feedback and advice	Offering information for improvement	Feedback and advice was crucial in all ICT research projects	
10. Promoting ownership	Encouraging stakeholders to feel that they own the research and its outcomes.	Stakeholders were involved in promoting agendas for their research	The level and intensity of promotion. In some ICT research projects, this involved face-to-face meetings while in other it was over online media
Rationale for Stakeholder Engagement			
11. Consultation	The process of discussing issues around the research in order to get advice or opinion about it.	The goals were similar. Consultation in all four ICT research projects provided feedback on process and alternatives	
12. Control and direction	The power to influence or direct the research process, stakeholders' behaviour or the course of the research process.	In all four cases stakeholder engagement facilitated effective coordination and implementation of the research.	The skills to direct the research were based on the aims of the ICT research projects since they were either developing or implementing different ICTs.
13. Mutual learning	The process whereby stakeholders learn from each other during the research process.	Present in all ICT research projects. This was supported by ongoing dialogue	
14. Resourcing	Act of providing resources necessary for the research process.	Necessary in all four cases	The type of resource needed. Not all needed an existing ICT infrastructure
The outcomes			
15. Awareness of responsibility issues	Concern about, perception and well-informed interest in issues that will impact the society.	This was an outcome in all ICT research projects. Stakeholders were made aware of the issues that related to the societal	The issues were different depending on the aim of each research.

Theme	Definition of Theme	Similarities	Differences
		challenges that each project was dealing with.	
16. Sustainability of project aims	The ability to be maintained the aims and intentions of the research at a certain level post project.	Evident in all four cases	
17. Co-creation	A way of bringing different parties together, in order to jointly produce a mutually valued outcome.	Evident in all four cases	

6.4 RRI as a Mirror for Effective Stakeholder Engagement

When it comes to effective stakeholder engagement, the proof is the outcomes that result from it. Considering that RRI is about socially desirable outcomes of research (Chatfield *et al.*, 2017; Rip, 2014; Stahl *et al.*, 2016), it provides a fit for purpose mirror to gauge the value of stakeholder engagement towards achieving such outcomes. This is something that has been suggested by several RRI proponents (Owen *et al.*, 2013; Stahl, 2012; Sutcliffe, 2011; Wilford *et al.*, 2016). For example, RRI is important for ICT research because it reduces the risk of developing technologies that have irreversible consequences especially as the technologies become more complex, pervasive and difficult to understand (Sutcliffe, 2011). Also, RRI is important in ICT research to prevent adverse impacts on society such as loss of privacy and autonomy, among users (Stahl, 2013a). From the findings, RRI was used to analyse if how the stakeholders contribute to the reflective and anticipatory processes with the research and innovation processes that were taking place in the four cases. Under RRI the stakeholders were expected to engage in a dialogue and deliberate on how to improve the research and implementation processes in order to cultivate socially desirable outcomes from the individual research projects. Therefore, reflecting on both the case study and suggestions from the literature, it can be argued that the concept RRI has the potentially provided an important tool for evaluating and analysing the efficacy of stakeholder engagement towards the attainment of responsible outcomes of ICT research projects.

6.5 A Collective Theory of Change

Following the findings in chapter 5, a general or collective theory of change of stakeholder engagement is constructed. The collective ToC resonates with the literature on the rationale behind stakeholder engagement in an ICT research project.

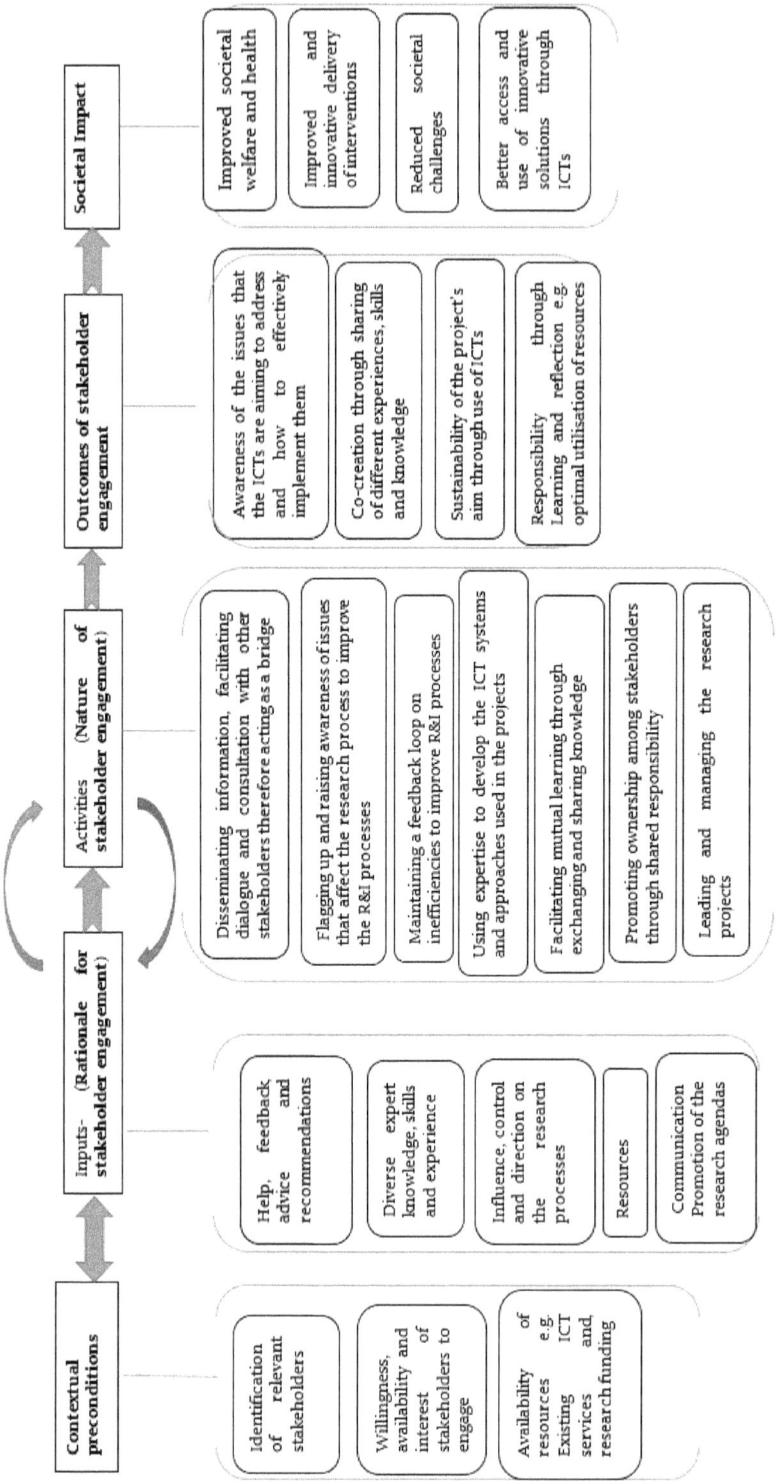

Figure 6.1: Collective Theory of Change for the ICT Research Projects

Figure 6.1 shows the main findings from the evaluation of the four cases through a collective Theory of change. From the Theory of change, it can be seen that for effective stakeholder engagement to take place there are contextual factors or rather enabling factors that support the engagement of stakeholders in ICT research projects (Mayne, 2012). Thus, for the stakeholders to contribute towards desirable outcomes of the research and innovation process, there is a need for effective identification. This entails identifying the stakeholders who will have roles that are vital for the ICT research project to achieve specific goals (Durham *et al.* 2014). Despite the identification, stakeholders have to be interested and show a willingness to engage otherwise the identification will result in ineffective engagement (Haddaway *et al.*, 2017). On top of the stakeholders' willingness, there is a need for resources that will enable and support the engagement activities that are necessary to achieve particular outcomes including socially desirable ones.

The activities that are necessary to achieve socially desirable outcomes are based on the motives behind the stakeholder engagement. These motives or rationale for stakeholder engagement are depicted by the inputs that the stakeholders provide to the ICT research projects (Bryson *et al.*, 2013; Carney *et al.*, 2009; Phillipson *et al.*, 2012a; Schenke *et al.*, 2016). These include control, feedback, expert advice and recommendations on the research and innovation process. Based on the rationale of the stakeholder engagement, the stakeholders carry out different activities that work towards achieving a range of intended and sometime non-intended outcomes from the research and innovation process (Bauer *et al.*, 2016; Shelley-Egan *et al.*, 2017; Stahl *et al.*, 2013; Stilgoe *et al.*, 2013; Sykes and Macnaghten, 2013). For instance, the activities may include disseminating information, facilitating dialogue and consultation with other stakeholders, therefore, acting as a bridge and providing diverse expert knowledge and experience.

Using the Theory of change, assumptions are made on the linkages between such activities and the desirable outcomes that result from them (Rogers, 2014; Taplin *et al.*, 2013). In the case of the four cases, the Theory of change in Figure 14 above, shows that as the result of the different stakeholder engagement activities there were some desirable goals that came about. For example, through facilitating mutual learning by exchanging and sharing knowledge, there was co-creation. This resonates with the RRI discourse which advocates that stakeholder engagement can support co-creation in the research and innovation (Sutcliffe, 2011; Von Schomberg, 2013). The co-creation helps in collectively highlighting some of the issues that may impact the research and innovation process as well as the society. Other socially desirable outcomes that result from stakeholder engagement such as responsibility through learning and reflection and awareness of the societal issues that the ICTs were aiming to address also corresponds with the reasons for having stakeholder engagement in ICT research as suggested by Jirotka *et al.* (2017).

Therefore using evaluation approaches such the theory-based approach, helps to understand the value of stakeholder engagement towards the intended and non-intended socially desirable outcomes of the research and innovation process that is taking in research projects, including ICT research projects. Also, the evaluation has the potential to be used as a guide for effective stakeholder identification and design of stakeholder activities that will have links to particular outcomes as suggested by Chelimsky (2006) and Mark *et al.* (2006).

6.6 Main Insights

Based on the discussion of the cross-case analysis in this chapter, key insights which are relevant to the research questions are pulled together. These are discussed below.

6.6.1 Key Insight 1: The role of stakeholder engagement in ICT research projects is more instrumental than normative

Although stakeholders were identified and expected to take up roles that could be influential towards the attainment of socially desirable outcomes, they do not always engage effectively as expected by those who identified the different stakeholders for engagement in the ICT research projects. The effectiveness of stakeholder engagement towards the attainment of socially desirable and acceptable outcomes is subject to the interests and agendas of the stakeholders engaged (Bryson *et al.*, 2013; Jepsen and Eskerod, 2009; Rahman *et al.*, 2015). If these are not aligned to achieving certain outcomes, then the value of the stakeholder engagement in terms of achieving those outcomes, in the case of this research socially desirable and acceptable outcomes, is very minimal. The cross-case analysis indicates that most of the stakeholders were engaged in the ICT research projects based on existing networks. As such, they were considered appropriate in achieving the ICT research projects' aims and objectives which were directed to tangible outputs (see section 2.5.1) rather than normative outcomes that are inherent in the aim of the engagement.

In all the four cases, stakeholder engagement was based on their networks, past encounters and knowledge about how the respective stakeholders could support attainment of the research projects' aims (this is something that has also been mentioned by Bailur, 2006). If the stakeholder engagement were for normative purposes, the identification and engagement of the stakeholders would have been around values and moral guidelines for conducting research and promoting fairness in the R&I processes rather using it as a tool to attain outputs and outcomes (instrumental). Also, if the role of stakeholder engagement in the ICT research projects was normative, the stakeholders would have clearly understood that part of their engagement was to deliberate and promote responsible innovation from the start. However, this was not the case as established during the interviews.

6.6.2 Key Insight 2: The role of stakeholder engagement in the attainment of socially desirable outcomes is implicit, not explicit

Related to the above key insight (6.3.1), the identification of stakeholders to contribute to the attainment of socially desirable and acceptable outcomes in ICT research projects is not explicit. Despite the literature discussing the contribution of stakeholders towards the attainment of socially desirable and acceptable outcomes in ICT research (Chatfield *et al.*, 2017; Eden *et al.*, 2013; Jirotka *et al.*, 2017; Stahl *et al.*, 2016, 2014, 2013; von Schomberg *et al.*, 2011) not many stakeholders understand the direct connection of their involvement in ICT research projects and the attainment of socially desirable and acceptable outcomes unless they are familiar with the notion or concept of responsible innovation. Stakeholders are identified to engage in ICT research projects for other reasons as pointed out in sections 2.6 and 6.2.4). However, using evaluation theory, particularly ToC, assumptions could be made to express the linkages between the activities and outcomes of those activities in relation to responsible outcomes of the stakeholder engagement in ICT research as suggested by Weiss (1997) and Rogers (2014). From the case study, it is seen that when stakeholders are engaged, it is not obvious to them that they will be contributing to the attainment of socially desirable and acceptable outcomes in the ICT research projects. However, through the use of ToC (theory-based approach to evaluation) their role in attaining the outcomes become clear when the different motives and activities are linked to the outcomes.

6.6.3 Key Insight 3: RRI could be used as a tool to understand the relationship between stakeholder engagement in ICT research projects and attainment of socially desirable and acceptable outcomes

From both the literature and the cross-case analysis, the indication is that there is a link between the intention for stakeholder engagement in ICT research projects and the attainment of socially desirable and acceptable outcomes. Since RRI is focused on socially desirable outcomes of research (Chatfield *et al.*, 2017; Stilgoe *et al.*, 2013; Wilford *et al.*, 2016), using it as a lens, can help in understanding how stakeholder engagement influence the attainment of the socially desirable outcomes even when the roles of the stakeholders engaged in the research are not explicitly defined to contribute towards responsible outcomes.

Although, the motives for stakeholder engagement that are given in the literature (see section 2.6) and the case analysis (see section 6.2.4) does not bluntly suggest the attainment of socially desirable outcomes, therefore responsible innovation, considering the features of RRI given by most of the RRI accounts (see section 2.6) reveals that most of the motives given have some inferences of responsible innovation. In most of the outcomes indicated in the different ToCs for each ICT project, there are connotations of socially desirable outcomes which can be fairly linked to the stakeholder engagement activities using RRI as a lens. For instance, the awareness could be linked to transparency within the ICT research projects, learning and sharing knowledge linked to reflection, optimal use of resources linked to responsiveness and bringing multiple perspectives as symbolic of anticipation.

Thus, evaluating the efficacy of stakeholder engagement within the context of RRI supports learning, reflexivity and responsiveness to societal issues when attaining ICT research outcomes. Evaluating stakeholder engagement in the context of RRI encourages practising a more responsible R&I since it provides feedback and facilitates reflection by the stakeholders that are engaged in the ICT research projects. The feedback from the evaluation has the potential to aid the assessment of whether the processes within ICT research projects are inclusive, anticipative, reflective, open, transparent, responsive and adaptive to change which then leads to socially desirable and desirable outcomes (see sections 2.5 and 4.5).

Also, evaluating stakeholder engagement in the context of RRI aids mutual learning among the stakeholders of the ICT research projects (see section 4.2). The knowledge gained from such an evaluation can then be used to improve stakeholder engagementthat is focussed on responsible outcomes in present and future ICT research projects.

6.6.4 Key Insight 4: The efficacy of stakeholder engagement in attaining socially desirable outcomes can be well understood by breaking down the process

Since stakeholder engagement is a holistic process that is often existent during the whole lifecycle of the ICT research projects, the theoretical and empirical observations suggest some key elements that should be considered to understand its value in the attainment of socially desirable and acceptable outcomes. Using the three different evaluation approaches in evaluation (see sections 4.4 and 5.4) gave a better way of focusing on each of the elements.

The three evaluation approaches of case-based approach (CA), Theory-based approach (TBA) and participatory approach (PA), individually focused on specific elements of stakeholder engagement depending on their suitability. In so doing the evaluation was methodological and effective. A CA was used in the case study to understand the contextual information of the stakeholder engagement including the aim of the ICT research project and therefore help us understand the role of the stakeholders engaged. In addition to understanding the context, the rationale for engagement was also important to understand. It was important to understand the reasons for identifying different stakeholders in the ICT research projects and what they will bring to the table. Understanding the reasons for the stakeholder engagement helped to assess their contribution to the different outcomes for the ICT research projects.

A TBA was instrumental in understanding the nature of the stakeholder engagement, the different stakeholder engagement activities together with their barriers. The TBA was also useful to understand the outcomes of the stakeholder engagement. In terms of PA, the evaluation of the stakeholder engagement involved participation of stakeholders from the four cases.

From the discussion above, the stakeholder engagement was broken down into five key elements of which each was assessed using an appropriate evaluation approach or a combination of approaches depending on what was specifically required to be understood.

6.6.5 Key Insight 5: Lack of Effective Stakeholder Engagement

Despite stakeholder engagement being vital in attaining desirable outcomes for an ICT research project (Haddaway *et al.*, 2017; Eskerod *et al.*, 2015) there is still a lack of commitment from stakeholders to effectively engage. This was evident throughout the case study, and it corresponds to what the literature suggests with regards to stakeholder apathy when it comes to effective engagement (Ayuso *et al.*, 2011; Jepsen and Eskerod, 2009). For example, in the four cases, it was learnt that it was difficult to get a good level of stakeholder engagement due to several reasons. The reasons that surfaced included lack of interest, stakeholders prioritising other commitments, lack of capacity and having e negative mindset.

All these reasons or rather barriers to effective stakeholder engagement are not unfamiliar. The findings from this research confirm that despite the barriers being known, they are still occurring. This perhaps calls for more research on how these barriers could be mitigated and find ways to support effective stakeholder engagement processes in ICT research projects. This is very important particularly when it comes to achieving socially desirable outcomes as suggested in RRI discourses (for example Bauer *et al.*, 2016; Jirotka *et al.*, 2017 and European Commission, 2017). Arguably, one of the efforts to towards encouraging the fruition of effective stakeholder engagement is through evaluation. Evaluation provides a mechanism to learn and reflect on how stakeholder engagement should be implemented in ICT research projects (Forsythe *et al.*, 2016). For instance, evaluation instrumental in gauging which stakeholder groups are necessary towards achieving specific outcomes. Also, evaluation helps to understand the value of the stakeholder engagement towards the aims of the ICT research projects and therefore promote the involvement of stakeholders in future research. This is done by showing the linkages between the activities and motivations of the stakeholder engagement and the outcomes that relate to them.

6.7 Addressing the Research Question

This section draws together themes and key insights discussed above to answer the main and sub-research questions outlined below;

How can the efficacy of stakeholder engagement in ICT research projects be evaluated?

i. *What is the role of stakeholder engagement in ICT research projects?*

ii. *How can RRI support the evaluation of stakeholder engagement in ICT research projects?*

iii. *What elements are key for evaluating that efficacy of stakeholder engagement in ICT research projects?*

Thus, each sub-research questions is addressed in a separate subsection. The subsection re-introduces the sub-research questions and discusses a key insight and findings that address the research questions. Towards the end, the main research question is addressed by drawing all the key insights together.

6.7.1 Sub-Research Question i: What is the role of stakeholder engagement in ICT research projects?

This sub-research question was aimed at understanding the role of stakeholder engagement in ICT research projects. The role of stakeholder engagement in research projects including ICT research has been widely covered in the literature as discussed in sections 1.3; 2.5; 2.6 and 3.3.4. Rose *et al.* (2015) and Chatfield *et al.* (2017) have suggested that the role of stakeholder engagement within research is to facilitate anticipation and reflection in the research and innovation process. Rose *et al.* (2015) further mentioned that the role of stakeholder engagement is to stimulate new ways of raising awareness of responsibility issues and societal challenges in R&I. Others (Haddaway *et al.*, 2017; Schenke *et al.*, 2016; Williams *et al.*, 2014) have suggested that the role of stakeholder engagement is to legitimise the research, to pool resources, to promote buy-in and bring together different perspectives to the research and innovation process.

However, as pointed out in the first key insight in section 6.6.1 above, it was established that although some of the literature suggests that stakeholder engagement has a normative role in ICT research, from the case study analysis, it emerged that stakeholder engagement in ICT research projects is more instrumental than what the reviewed literature suggests. From the case study, the role of stakeholder engagement was mainly directed to achieving the research objectives of the ICT research projects which were more directed towards the tangible outputs rather than normative outcomes relating to the conception of responsibility, moral values and obligations within the research processes (key insight1).

Despite the role of the stakeholder engagement being more instrumental than normative, the normative position of the engagement in the ICT research projects is in eliminable and therefore intrinsic, at least in a minimal form. From the cross-case analysis, it was indicated that the role of stakeholder engagement in ICT research projects was mainly to facilitate consultation on process rather than intended outcomes. Further, the role was to provide specific expertise that was directly related to the objectives and final outputs (tangible) of the ICT research. Furthermore, the role of stakeholder engagement was also to provide feedback on the processes and outputs that the ICT research projects were developing and implementing.

Despite these being the main roles, from the evaluation, using a TBA (particularly ToC), assumptions were made that during the stakeholder activities, such as consultations, there were some actions and views that were based on moral objectives, therefore, they lead to the attainment of outcomes that were positive for society (key insight 2).

6.7.2 Sub-Research Question ii: How can RRI support the evaluation of stakeholder engagement in ICT research projects?

The second sub research question was about understanding the importance of RRI in evaluating stakeholder engagement in ICT research projects. The literature on RRI (see chapter 3) provides some reasons why RRI in important not only in research projects but also ICT research projects. For example, Owen *et al.*, (2013) suggest that one important of RRI in research projects is that it provides a way to address responsibility issues collectively. While Stahl *et al.*, (2016) and Rip (2014) suggests that RRI provides tools that can be used to inform the attainment of socially desirable and acceptable outcomes in the R&I process that take place in ICT research.

As suggested by the key insight 3 in section 6.6.3, RRI is important in ICT research projects because it provides a basis on which responsible practice in ICT research projects could be assessed. RRI provides a yardstick for gauging how stakeholder engagement in ICT research projects influences socially desirable and desirable outcomes. To bridge the gap between theory practices, the cross-case analysis used the theoretical insights from RRI discourse and the cases to indicate the significance of RRI as a lens for evaluating the efficacy of stakeholder engagement in ICT research projects.

6.7.3 Sub research-Question iii: What elements are key for evaluating the eficacy of stakeholder engagement in ICT research projects?

The third and last sub-research question asked about elements that are key for evaluating that efficacy of stakeholder engagement in the attainment of socially desirable and desirable outcomes in ICT research projects. In addressing this question, the answer was given in chapter 3 of this book which presented a conceptual model for evaluating stakeholder engagement in ICT research projects. The conceptual evaluation model was developed from the theoretical insights (from RRI and evaluation theory) and the empirical insights (from the case studyanalysis). The model consists of different elements of stakeholder engagement that can be used to understand stakeholder engagement in-depth by using a combination of three different evaluation approaches including case-based, participatory based and theory-based approaches (see sections 2.10.3 and 3.4).

The literature on stakeholder engagement was also very instrumental in answering the sub-research question. The existing literature on stakeholder engagement suggested that to effectively understand that the efficacy of stakeholder engagement in any research project, the whole process starting from identification (Bryson, 2004; Leventon *et al.*, 2016; Pouloudi and Whitley, 1997), the motives behind the stakeholder engagement (Bryson *et al.*, 2013; Schenke *et al.*, 2016; Williams *et al.*, 2014) all the way to the outcomes of the engagement (Bauer *et al.*, 2016; Blok *et al.*, 2015; Phillipson *et al.*, 2012a) should be evaluated. This was commensurate with the different evaluating approaches which were appropriate in evaluating these different components of the stakeholder engagement process, respectively.

As a result, the evaluation in the four cases was directed on the following five elements of stakeholder engagement;

i. The context in which the stakeholder engagement is taking place.

ii. The identification of stakeholders to engage.
iii. The nature of stakeholder engagement activities taking place.
iv. The rationale for engaging the stakeholders.
v. The outcomes from the engagement.

6.7.4 Main Research Question

Pulling all the key insights, findings and the literature reviewed in this study, the main research question of this research is addressed. The main research question is on *howcan the efficacy of stakeholder engagement towards the attainment of socially desirable outcomes in ICT research projects be evaluated?* As discussed throughout this book, one discourse that advocates for the attainment of socially desirable and desirable outcomes in ICT research is RRI. Therefore, to contextualise the evaluation, the concept of RRI was used as a lens that provided an analytical tool for the evaluation. The evaluation therefore involved an analysis of the five key elements identified in sub-research question (iii) based on the key features of RRI. These RRI features included engagement of stakeholders, anticipation and reflection, openness and transparency, along with responsiveness (Owen *et al.*, 2013b; Shelley-Egan *et al.*, 2017; Stilgoe *et al.*, 2013).

Thus, to evaluate and understand the efficacy of stakeholder engagement in the attainment of socially desirable and desirable outcomes in ICT research projects, many things should be considered. Firstly, the role of the stakeholder engagement needs to be understood (key insight 1 and 2). While evaluating the roles of the stakeholders, the context of the stakeholder engagement should also be evaluated since this gives the contextual knowledge that is necessary to understand the rationale behind the stakeholder engagement. Correspondingly, the rationale behind the stakeholder engagement can be well understood if the nature of activities that the stakeholders are expected to undertake are clear. Once the context, nature and rationale for the stakeholder engagement are well understood, the outcomes that could result can be analysed and assessed.

In terms of the approaches for understanding these different elements of stakeholder engagement, both the literature and cases studies revealed that on the one hand, participatory and case-based approaches are ideal for understanding the context, roles and identification of the stakeholders for engagement (see sections 3.2 and 3.4). On the other hand, to effectively understand the rationale, nature and outcome of the stakeholder engagement participatory and theory-based approaches are well suited because theyembrace different assumptions in expressing the cause and effects of stakeholder engagement with regards to attaining socially desirable and desirable outcomes in ICT research projects. The use of assumptions is helpful when trying to understand something that is not explicit and is multifaceted such as the value of stakeholder engagement towards the attainment of socially desirable and acceptable outcomes in ICT research projects. This was the case in all four cases where their aims and goals were to develop and produce (tangible) outputs rather than abstract outcomes like responsible innovation.

6.8 Conclusion

This chapter has presented a critical discussion of the case study findings and the existing literature. The chapter has put together the findings through a cross-case analysis of the four case ICT research projects that were used in this research. In doing so, the chapter provided answers to the sub-research questions and ultimately the main research question. As part of answering the research question, a broader discussion of the case study findings has been achieved by applying existing literature. By comparing with the theoretical and empirical insights, a generalised demonstration of the conceptual model for evaluating the efficacy of stakeholder engagement towards socially desirable and desirable outcomes was given. From the demonstration and cross-case analysis, key insights have been pulled to answer the research questions. The next chapter will provide a conclusion of this book and therefore the research.

CHAPTER 7

Conclusion

7.1 OVERVIEW OF THE RESEARCH

This research has aimed to contribute to our understanding of the efficacy of towards the attainment of socially desirable outcomes in Information Communication Technology (ICT) research projects. As such, the study has contributed to the discourse of Responsible Research and Innovation (RRI) and stakeholder engagement evaluation. To this end, using theoretical and empirical insights, the study has proposed a conceptual evaluation model for a qualitative evaluation of the efficacy of stakeholder engagement in ICT research projects with respect to the attainment of socially desirable and acceptable outcomes. The book covered a case study involving four cases in which the conceptual evaluation model was operationalised for validation.

As a recap, the four cases included four ICT research projects namely Projects 1, 2, 3 and 4. The first case was Project 1, and it was about the use ICT to support environmental sustainability through energy optimisation. The second case was Project 2 which was aiming to improve the use of ICT in transforming education provision in secondary schools. The third case was Project 3 which focused on the use of ICT to improve hearing aid technologies. The last case was Project 4 and was aimed at the use of ICT in developing a dynamic traffic management system to improve air quality.

To conclude the book, this chapter starts by briefly reviewing each chapter's contribution to the study. It then discusses the study contribution in section 7.2. This is then followed by a discussion of the limitations and suggestions for further research in section 7.3.

This book started with chapter 1 to introduce the study and set out the general idea of stakeholder engagement in ICT research projects. The chapter argued why ICT research projects were of importance to this study. In chapter 2, a review of the literature on stakeholder engagement, RRI, and evaluation of stakeholder engagement was presented to inform the development of a conceptual evaluation model that was presented in chapter 3. This was then followed by chapter 4 which detailed the research design that was used to answer the research questions. The conceptual evaluation model presented in chapter 3 provided an analytical framework that was used in chapter 5 to analyse and present the findings from the four cases that were used in this research. The findings from the four cases were then pulled together in a cross-case analysis in chapter 6. The cross-case analysis highlighted the main insights that addressed the research questions.

7.2 Study Contribution

The major contribution of this study has been the understanding of the efficacy of stakeholder engagement towards the attainment of socially desirable outcomes in ICT research projects using a conceptual evaluation model that was developed using the theoretical and empirical insights from the case study. Evaluating the efficacy of stakeholder engagement towards the attainment of socially desirable outcomes in ICT research projects using an interpretive evaluation model is novel, and the literature review did not identify any literature on the topic. Within ICT research, there is a concentration on quantitative evaluation models that focus on the technical side of the research projects compared to qualitative evaluation of the importance of stakeholder engagement towards socially positive outcomes of the research.

Thus, to contribute to knowledge and practice, this study developed a conceptual evaluation model that uses theoretical insights from RRI and evaluation theory. It also uses empirical insights from a case study to evaluate stakeholder engagement in ICT research projects. The conceptual evaluation model suggests a novel way of evaluating stakeholder engagement in ICT research projects through the use of RRI as an evaluative lens while being guided by evaluation theory (the approaches in section 2.10.3).

The conceptual evaluation model proposed and used in this study is useful for these two reasons; firstly, it allows analysing stakeholder engagement in ICT research projects by analysing how stakeholders play and understand their role in collective responsibility to reach socially desirable and desirable outcomes of R&I processes. Secondly, it supports an in-depth analysis of stakeholder engagement by allowing the participants to talk about their conceptions, perceptions, experiences, and assumptions in relation to achieving socially desirable outcomes in their respective ICT research projects.

Since empirical insights from the four cases and theoretical insights from the literature were used to develop and validate the conceptual evaluation model. Therefore it can be argued that the contribution of this study has theoretical, methodological and practical implications. These will be discussed in the following subsections.

7.2.1 Theoretical Contribution

The study has made a theoretical contribution towards closing the gap between evaluation theory and practice by improving the use of evaluation theory in practice (Smith, 2015). In so doing, the study has provided a better understanding of the value of stakeholder engagement towards socially desirable outcomes in ICT research. The study has made a contribution to evaluation theory by applying an RRI lens to understand the efficacy of stakeholder engagement towards socially desirable outcomes in ICT research. This is something that has not been previously done.

During the research, it was found that currently there is a well-developed coverage of stakeholder engagement and evaluation theory with regards to other aspects of ICT research projects other than the attainment of socially desirable outcomes. Also, there is a more extensive study of stakeholder engagement in other disciplines such as business management and project management compared to ICT. Therefore this study provided an opportunity where evaluation theory could be further developed in other domains such as ICT research particularly with a focus on the role of stakeholder engagement in responsible innovation.

Using a combination of Theory-based approach (TBA), Case-based approach (CA) and Participatory approach (PA), and the study unveiled five key elements of stakeholder engagement (see section 3.3) to focus on when evaluating its value in ICT research projects. Further, the study used a Theory of Change (ToC), which is part of a TBA, to come up with assumptions on the causal links between the different stakeholder engagement activities and the socially desirable outcomes in the four cases (see sections 5.4; 5.7; 5.10 and 5.13).

7.2.2 Methodological Contribution

This book has also made a methodological contribution by developing and testing a new conceptual evaluation model that can be used to evaluate and analyse the efficacy of stakeholder engagement in the attainment of socially desirable and acceptable outcomes in ICT research project.

The study offers a novel analytical and methodological approach in evaluating the efficacy of stakeholder engagement towards responsible outcomes in ICT research projects. The approach involves a combination of three evaluation approaches (TBA, CA and PA) and an application of the RRI lens to understand the value of stakeholder engagement in ICT research projects. Therefore, using the interpretive evaluation model in this study provides a methodological contribution that can shape the future of stakeholder engagement in ICT research with respect to social impacts through an iterative consideration of reflexivity, transparency, and anticipation throughout the research process.

7.2.3 Practical Contribution

The book further made a practical contribution through the development of the conceptual evaluation model from both theoretical and empirical insights from the study. The insights from the evaluative analysis of the four cases have the potential to help different stakeholders of ICT research understand the expectations about their role in the attainment of socially desirable outcomes in ICT research and what sort of activities could translate into those outcomes. This implies that for effective stakeholder engagement towards the attainment of socially desirable outcomes, emphasis should be placed on the importance of understanding how different stakeholders will contribute towards activities that translate into responsible outcomes of ICT research. For researchers and funders, the conceptual evaluation model proposed in this study may also be used to guide stakeholder engagement efforts with respect to responsible innovation (that is, achievement of socially desirable outcomes) and how that could be evaluated and improved. When implementing RRI in ICT research projects, the evaluation model could serve as a guide for the detailing the appropriate identification of stakeholders, provision of the necessary contextual resources and facilitation of the right activities that will culminate into intended socially desirable outcomes and impact.

Also, the successful use of ToC as part of TBA combined with CBA and PA to examine specific causal mechanisms, not only provides some [tentative] evidence of the efficacy of stakeholder engagement in the attainment of socially desirable outcomes in ICT research projects, but also supplies a practical approach to improving evaluation in the field. Thus there is a prospect that practitioners could use the evaluation model used in this research to identify and assess the value of those that are identified in the projects towards achieving various outcomes of their engagement other than socially desirable ones.

7.3 Limitations and Further Research

There are five limitations to this study that have implications for further research work. Despite this study making some contributions to knowledge and practice, it has some limitations. Some of these limitations are related to the research methodology, the literature reviewed and access to cases. These are outlined below;

i. As expounded in this book, the research attempts to illustrate an evaluation of stakeholder engagement in ICT research projects. However, the four cases represent research projects unique to ICT research that is conducted with the involvement of academia in the research process. This may make lessons learned not transferable to other ICT research projects operating in different contexts such as industry or private sector. For instance, the importance and relevance of the key elements identified for evaluating stakeholder engagement in ICT research projects are contextual depending on R&I practices of a particular ICT research project and its goals. Therefore, they may not be relevant to focus on evaluating stakeholder engagement in ICT research projects in other contexts. Thus, further research could focus on understanding the efficacy of stakeholder engagement in ICT research projects that are conducted in other contexts such as the private sector.

ii. The coding of the data and theme identification was identified by one person, and the analysis was later discussed with the supervisors and a colleague. Although this process allowed for consistency in the data analysis method employed, it failed to provide different perspectives from other people as it could have been the case in collaborative research with multiple coders. For further research and to promote the credibility of the developed evaluation model, such method should involve multiple researchers in the coding of data which involves a discussion with other researchers or the participants themselves.

iii. The use of ToC as part of expressing the causality of stakeholder engagement and the socially desirable outcomes would be more robust if it were inductive rather deductive. The study used a deductive ToC, but for further research, it would be interesting to have an inductive ToC where the stakeholders and the evaluator/researcher are involved from the very beginning of the ICT research projects all the way to the end. This means that there could be a continuous and iterative involvement of stakeholders in constructing the ToC and a continuous re-examination of the ToC to ensure effective use of ToC.

iv. The concept of RRI or RI is not widely known outside academic research, and therefore it was difficult to get the participants to understand their role with respect to its implementation and in some cases even understanding what the whole concept of RRI is about. Some stakeholder participants thought that the concept of RRI is a very wide term and difficult to think whether it is about personal responsibility or organisational responsibility towards research and innovation. It is therefore recommended to further research to what extent having an understanding or knowledge about RI or RRI influence how stakeholders that are engaged in ICT research projects perceive their contribution towards the attainment of socially desirable outcomes in ICT research. Also, how prior knowledge of RI or RRI influences their attitude towards contributing towards the attainment of socially desirable outcomes.

v. As the study focussed on four cases of ICT research projects, with affiliations to DMU, it did not cover many types of stakeholders and ICT research projects. This meant that views of a wide range of stakeholders were not considered. Forfurther research, another valuable area of future research would be to consider the views and perspectives of other stakeholder types in ICT research projects other than researchers, professionals and local authorities. It would be helpful to have abuy-in from those stakeholders who are not directly involved in the research process as it was the case with most of the stakeholders that participated in this study. Maybe a different method of such as a focus group rather than interviews could be more effective in engaging the layer of stakeholders that is missing. One issue that was encountered was the barriers to accessing stakeholder participants from the researcher's side and the interest of stakeholders to engage with research from the projects' side. Further research on how these barriers could be mitigated and reduced to improve stakeholder engagement in ICT research would be very interesting.

Besides the general limitations of the study, two further issues were encountered during the evaluative analysis.

i. Despite the RRI lens providing a basis for evaluating the cases, in terms of socially desirable goals, it posed a restriction on the analysis. This, in turn, limited the scope of the descriptions.

ii. Due to the lack of knowledge or ambiguity of responsible innovation or responsibility on the part of the stakeholder participants, the interpretation of the data collected gave problems at times when a piece of data could be associated with multiple features of RRI.

In future, the analytical model could be further developed with terminology that is clearer and less ambiguous for the subjects of the evaluation to allow a straightforward analysis, particularly when building themes that are relevant to the key features of the RRI lens incorporated in the evaluation model.

In conclusion, this research has provided contributions to the evidence base regarding the efficacy of stakeholder engagement towards the attainment of socially desirable outcomes in ICT research projects and also to theory around RRI, stakeholder engagement, and evaluation, all of which feeds through into implications for practice. Each of these contributions can be taken further within and beyond the current ICT research agenda. It is desired that this book will generate such research interest and thus serve as a useful step for improving our understanding of the importance of stakeholder engagement in ICT research with regards to responsible innovation and therefore contribute further to theory, research and practice.

References

Aflalo, E., 2014. The Invisible Barrier to Integrating Computer Technology in Education. J. Educ. Learn. 3. https://doi.org/10.5539/jel.v3n2p120

Andre, K., Simonsson, L., Swartling, A.., Linner, B., 2012. Method Development for Identifying and Analysing Stakeholders in Climate Change Adaptation Processes. J. Environ. Policy Plan. 14, 243–261.

Andreassen, H.K., Kjekshus, L.E., Tjora, A., 2015. Survival of the project: A case study of ICT innovation in health care. Soc. Sci. Med. 132, 62–69. https://doi.org/10.1016/j.socscimed.2015.03.016

Asghar, J., 2013. Critical Paradigm: A preamble for novice researchers. Life Sci. J. 10, 3121–3127.

Bailur, S., 2006. Using stakeholder theory to analyze telecenter projects. Inf. Technol.Int. Dev. 3, pp–61.

Bal, M., Bryde, D., Fearon, D., Ochieng, E., 2013. Stakeholder Engagement: Achieving Sustainability in the Construction Sector. Sustainability 5, 695–710. https://doi.org/10.3390/su5020695

Baskerville, R., Myers, M.D., 2004. Special Issue on action research in Informaton Systems: Making IS research relevant to practice foreword. Manag. Inf. Syst. Q. 28, 2.

Bauer, A., Bogner, A., Fuchs, D., Kosow, H., Dreyer, M., 2016. Societal engagement under the terms of RRI.

Becker, J., Niehaves, B., 2007. Epistemological perspectives on IS research: a framework for analysing and systematizing epistemological assumptions. Inf. Syst. J. 17, 197–214.

Bifulco, F., Tregua, M., Amitrano, C.C., D'Auria, A., 2016. ICT and sustainability in smart cities management. Int. J. Public Sect. Manag. 29, 132–147. https://doi.org/10.1108/IJPSM-07-2015-0132

Billings, M.L., 2016. The World of Evaluation: Challenges Faced by Student Evaluators. J. Multidiscip. Eval. 13, 24–28.

Blaikie, N., 2010. Wiley: Designing Social Research, 2nd ed. Wiley, Cambridge. Blaikie, N., 2007. Approaches to Social Enquiry: Advancing Knowledge, 3rd ed. Polity,Cambridge.

Blok, V., 2014. Look who's talking: responsible innovation, the paradox of dialogue and the voice of the other in communication and negotiation processes. J. Responsible Innov. 1, 171–190. https://doi.org/10.1080/23299460.2014.924239

Blok, V., Hoffmans, L., Wubben, E.F.M., 2015. Stakeholder engagement for responsible innovation in the private sector: critical issues and management practices. J. Chain Netw. Sci. 15, 147–164. https://doi.org/10.3920/JCNS2015.x003

Boulos, M.N.K., Al-Shorbaji, N.M., 2014. On the Internet of Things, smart cities and the WHO Healthy Cities. Int. J. Health Geogr. 13, 1.

Brunner, I., Guzman, A., 1989. Participatory evaluation: A tool to assess projects and empower people. New Dir. Eval. 1989, 9–18.

Bryman, A., 2004. Social research methods, 2nd ed. Oxford University Press, Oxford.

Bryson, J.M., 2004. What to do when Stakeholders matter: Stakeholder Identification and Analysis Techniques. Public Manag. Rev. 6, 21–53. https://doi.org/10.1080/14719030410001675722

Bryson, J.M., Quick, K.S., Slotterback, C.S., Crosby, B.C., 2013. Designing public participation processes. Public Adm. Rev. 73, 23–34.

Buckner, E., Kim, P., 2014. Integrating technology and pedagogy for inquiry-based learning: The Stanford Mobile Inquiry-based Learning Environment (SMILE). PROSPECTS 44, 99–118. https://doi.org/10.1007/s11125-013-9269-7

Bunn, M.D., Savage, G.T., Holloway, B.B., 2002. Stakeholder analysis for multi-sector innovations. J. Bus. Ind. Mark. 17, 181–203. https://doi.org/10.1108/08858620210419808

Burgess, J., Chilvers, J., 2006. Upping the ante: a conceptual framework for designing and evaluating participatory technology assessments. Sci. Public Policy 33, 713– 728.

Burget, M., Bardone, E., Pedaste, M., 2017. Definitions and Conceptual Dimensions of Responsible Research and Innovation: A Literature Review. Sci. Eng. Ethics 23, 1–19. https://doi.org/10.1007/s11948-016-9782-1

Camara e Silva, L., Costa, A.P.C., 2012. Quality evaluation of information technology project-A multicriteria approach, in: Systems, Man, and Cybernetics (SMC), 2012 IEEE International Conference On. IEEE, pp. 611–616.

Campbell, N., Schiffer, E., Buxbaum, A., McLean, E., Perry, C., Sullivan, T.M., 2014. Taking knowledge for health the extra mile: participatory evaluation of a mobile phone intervention for community health workers in Malawi. Glob. Health Sci. Pract. 2, 23–34.

Carney, S., Whitmarsh, L., Nicholson-Cole, S.A., Shackley, S., 2009. A dynamic typology of stakeholder engagement within climate change research. Tyndall Cent. Clim. Change Res. Work. Pap. 128.

Carretero, S., 2015. Mapping of effective technology-based services for independent living for older people at home: deliverable 1. Publications Office, Luxembourg.

Cassell, C., Symon, G. (Eds.), 2004. Essential guide to qualitative methods in organizational research. SAGE Publications, London ; Thousand Oaks.

Characterizing cross-professional collaboration in research and development projects in secondary education. Teach. Teach. 1–17. https://doi.org/10.1080/13540602.2016.1158465

Charmaz, K., 2011. Grounded theory methods in social justice research., in: The Sage Handbook of Qualitative Research. SAGE, Thousand Oaks, CA, pp. 359–380.

Chatfield, K., Iatridis, K., Stahl, B., Paspallis, N., 2017. Innovating Responsibly in ICT for Ageing: Drivers, Obstacles and Implementation. Sustainability 9, 971. https://doi.org/10.3390/su9060971

Chelimsky, E., 2006. The Purposes of Evaluation in Democratic Society, in: Ian Shaw, Jennifer Greene, Melvin Mark (Eds.), The Sage Handbook of Evaluation. SAGE Publications, London, pp. 33–55.

Chen, Y.-R.R., Schulz, P.J., 2016. The Effect of Information Communication Technology Interventions on Reducing Social Isolation in the Elderly: A Systematic Review. J. Med. Internet Res. 18, e18. https://doi.org/10.2196/jmir.4596

Christophorou, C., Kleanthous, S., Georgiadis, D., Cereghetti, D.M., Andreou, P., Wings, C., Christodoulou, E., Samaras, G., 2016. ICT services for active ageing and independent living: identification and assessment. Healthc. Technol. Lett. 3, 159–164. https://doi.org/10.1049/htl.2016.0031

Clarkson, P.C., Toomey, R., 2001. Information and Communication Technology and Whole School Reform. Australian Catholic University, Melbourne.

Collins, 2016. Theory -Definition, [WWW Document]. Collins Dict. URL http://www.collinsdictionary.com/dictionary/english/theory (accessed 9.7.16).

Cooke-Davies, T., 2002. The "real" success factors on projects. Int. J. Proj. Manag. 20, 185–190.

Coryn, C.L.S., Noakes, L.A., Westine, C.D., Schröter, D.C., 2011. A Systematic Review of Theory-Driven Evaluation Practice From 1990 to 2009. Am. J. Eval. 32, 199–226. https://doi.org/10.1177/1098214010389321

Cousins, J.B., Earl, L.M., 1992. The case for participatory evaluation. Educ. Eval. Policy Anal. 14, 397–418.

Cousins, J.B., Whitmore, E., 1998. Framing participatory evaluation. New Dir. Eval.1998, 5–23.

Cousins, J.B., Whitmore, E., Shulha, L., 2013. Arguments for a Common Set of Principles for Collaborative Inquiry in Evaluation. Am. J. Eval. 34, 7–22. https://doi.org/10.1177/1098214012464037

Coyne, I., 1997. Sampling in qualitative research. Purposeful and theoretical sampling; merging or clear boundaries? J. Adv. Nurs. 26, 623–630. https://doi.org/10.1046/j.1365-2648.1997.t01-25-00999.x

Creswell, J., Plano Clark, V., 2011. Designing and Conducting Mixed Methods Research. Thousand Oaks, CA.

Creswell, J.W., 2012. Designing a Qualitative Study Qualitative inquiry and research design: Choosing among 5 Approaches, 3rd ed. SAGE, Thousand Oaks,CA.

Cullen, J., Sullivan, F., Junge, K., 2007. Evaluating Science and Society Initiatives: A Framework for Evaluation. Tavistock Institute.

De Meyer, A., Loch, C.H., Pich, M.T., 2002. Managing project uncertainty: from variation to chaos. MIT Sloan Manag. Rev. 43, 60. de Vente, J., Reed, M.S., Stringer, L.C., Valente, S., Newig, J., 2016. How does the context and design of participatory decision making processes affect their outcomes? Evidence from sustainable land management in global drylands. Ecol. Soc. 21. https://doi.org/10.5751/ES-08053-210224

De Witte, K., Rogge, N., 2014. Does ICT matter for effectiveness and efficiency in mathematics education? Comput. Educ. 75, 173–184. https://doi.org/10.1016/j.compedu.2014.02.012

Demiris, G., Oliver, D.P., Dickey, G., Skubic, M., Rantz, M., 2008. Findings from a participatory evaluation of a smart home application for older adults. Technol. Health Care 16, 111–118.

Denscombe, M., 2010. The good research guide: for small scale research projects., 4th ed. McGraw-Hill Open University Press, Maidenhead.

Donaldson, S., 2006. Roles of Theory in Contemplary Evaluation Practice: Developing Practical Knowledge, in: Shaw, I., Greene, J., Mark, M.M. (Eds.), The Sage Handbook of Evaluation. SAGE Publications, London, pp. 56–75.

Donaldson, S., Lipsey, M., 2006. Roles of Theory in Contemporary Evaluation Practice: Developing Practical Knoweledge, in: Shaw, I., Greene, J., Melvin, M. (Eds.), The Sage Handbook of Evaluation. SAGE Publications Ltd, London, pp. 56–75.

Donaldson, T., 1999. Making stakehoder theory whole. Acad. Manag. Acad. Manag.Rev. 22, 237– 241.

Donaldson, T., Preston, L.E., 1995. The stakeholder theory of the corporation: Concepts, evidence, and implications. Acad. Manage. Rev. 20, 65–95.

Durham, E., Baker, H., Smith, M., Moore, E., Morgan, V., 2014. The BiodivERsA Stakeholder Engagement Handbook. BiodivERsA, Paris.

Eden, G., Jirotka, M., Stahl, B., 2013. Responsible Research and Innovation: Critical reflection into the potential social consequences of ICT, in: Research Challenges in Information Science (RCIS), 2013 IEEE Seventh International Conference On. IEEE, pp. 1–12.

Eke, D.O., Stahl, B.C., Fidler, C., Fairweather, Nb., Rogerson, S., 2015. Understanding the relevance of ethics reviews of ICT research in UK computing departments using dialectical hermeneutics. J. Inf. Commun. Ethics Soc. 13.

Elliot, S., Webster, J., 2017. Editorial: Special issue on empirical research on information systems addressing the challenges of environmental sustainability: an imperative for urgent action. Inf. Syst. J. 27, 367–378. https://doi.org/10.1111/isj.12150

Entekhabi, M., Arabshahi, G.A., 2012. Classification of innovation projects. Indian J. Innov. Dev. 1, 612–625.

Eskerod, P., Huemann, M., Ringhofer, C., 2015. Stakeholder Inclusiveness: Enriching Project Management with General Stakeholder Theory: Stakeholder Inclusiveness. Proj. Manag. J. 46, 42– 53. https://doi.org/10.1002/pmj.21546

Esmail, L., Moore, E., Rein, A., 2015. Evaluating patient and stakeholder engagement in research: moving from theory to practice. J. Comp. Eff. Res. 4, 133–145. https://doi.org/10.2217/cer.14.79

European Commission, 2013. Work programme for the ICT theme of the FP7 Specific Programme.

European Commission, 2017. Public Engagement in Responsible Research and Innovation - Horizon 2020 - European Commission [WWW Document]. Horiz. 2020. URL /programmes/horizon2020/en/h2020-section/public-engagement-responsible-research-and-innovation (accessed 6.16.17).

European Commission, Directorate-General for Research and Innovation, 2014. Responsible research and innovation: Europe's ability to respond to societal challenges. Publications Office, Luxembourg.

Fagan, A., n.d. Adorno, Theodor [WWW Document]. Internet Encycl. Philos. URL http://www.iep.utm.edu/adorno/ (accessed 2.7.15).

Faulkner, W., Lie, M., 2007. Gender in the information society: Strategies of inclusion. Gend. Technol. Dev. 11, 157–177.

Feilzer, M., 2010. Doing Mixed Methods Research Pragmatically: Implications for the Rediscovery of Pragmatism as a Research Paradigm. J. Mix. Methods Res. 4, 6– 16. https://doi.org/10.1177/1558689809349691

Fereday, J., Muir-Cochrane, E., 2006. Demonstrating rigor using thematic analysis: A hybrid approach of inductive and deductive coding and theme development. Int.J. Qual. Methods 5, 80– 92.

Filippov, S., Mooi, H., 2010. Innovation project management: A research agenda. J. Innov. Sustain. RISUS ISSN 2179-3565 1.

Forsythe, L.P., Ellis, L.E., Edmundson, L., Sabharwal, R., Rein, A., Konopka, K., Frank, L., 2016. Patient and Stakeholder Engagement in the PCORI Pilot Projects: Description and Lessons Learned. J. Gen. Intern. Med. 31, 13–21. https://doi.org/10.1007/s11606-015-3450-z

Freeman, R.E., 1984. Strategic Management: A Stakeholder Approach. Pitman, Boston M.A.

Gatautis, R., 2015. The impact of ICT on public and private sectors in Lithuania. 59(4). Eng. Econ., Information and communication technologies and the knowledge economy 59.

Geoghegan-Quinn, M., 2012. Responsible Research and Innovation [WWW Document]. Sci. Soc. Website. URL https://ec.europa.eu/research/swafs/pdf/pub_public_engagement/responsible-research-and-innovation-leaflet_en.pdf (accessed 4.24.16).

Gilbert, D.U., Rasche, A., 2008. Opportunities and Problems of Standardized Ethics Initiatives – a Stakeholder Theory Perspective. J. Bus. Ethics 82, 755–773. https://doi.org/10.1007/s10551-007-9591-1

Given, L.M., 2008. The Sage Encyclopedia of Qualitative Research Methods: A-L ; Vol.2, M-Z Index. SAGE.

Gomm, R., Hammersley, M., Foster, P., 2000. Case Study and Generalization, in: Case Study Method: Key Issues, Key Texts. SAGE, London.

Gonzalez-Zapata, F., Heeks, R., 2015. The multiple meanings of open government data: Understanding different stakeholders and their perspectives. Gov. Inf. Q. 32, 441–452. https://doi.org/10.1016/j.giq.2015.09.001

Grbich, C., 2012. Qualitative data analysis: An introduction. SAGE.

Greene, J., 2006. Evaluation,Democracy, and Social Change, in: Shaw, I., Greene, J., Melvin, M. (Eds.), The Sage Handbook of Evaluation. SAGE Publications, London.

Groenewald, T., 2004. A phenomenological research design illustrated.

Guba, E.G., Lincoln, Y.S., others, 1994. Competing paradigms in qualitative research. Handb. Qual. Res. 2.

Habermas, J., Cronin, C., De Greiff, P., 1998. The inclusion of the other: studies in political theory, Studies in contemporary German social thought. MIT PRess, Cambridge, Mass.

Haddaway, N.R., Kohl, C., Rebelo da Silva, N., Schiemann, J., Sp?k, A., Stewart, R., Sweet, J.B., Wilhelm, R., 2017. A framework for stakeholder engagement during systematic reviews and maps in environmental management. Environ. Evid. 6. https://doi.org/10.1186/s13750-017-0089-8

Haluza, D., Jungwirth, D., 2018. ICT and the future of healthcare: Aspects of pervasive health monitoring. Inform. Health Soc. Care 43, 1–11. https://doi.org/10.1080/17538157.2016.1255215

Hartley, J., 2004. Case study research., in: Cassell, C., Symon, G. (Eds.), Essential Guide to Qualitative Methods in Organizational Research. SAGE Publications, London, pp. 323–333.

Hasnas, J., 2013. Whither Stakeholder Theory? A Guide for the Perplexed Revisited. J. Bus. Ethics 112, 47–57. https://doi.org/10.1007/s10551-012-1231-8

Hellström, T., 2003. Systemic innovation and risk: technology assessment and the challenge of responsible innovation. Technol. Soc. 25, 369–384. https://doi.org/10.1016/S0160-791X(03)00041-1

Hilty, L.M., Aebischer, B. (Eds.), 2015. ICT Innovations for Sustainability, Advances in Intelligent Systems and Computing. Springer International Publishing, Cham. https://doi.org/10.1007/978-3-319-09228-7

Ihm, J., Hsieh, Y.P., 2015. The implications of information and communication technology use for the social well-being of older adults. Inf. Commun. Soc. 18, 1123–1138. https://doi.org/10.1080/1369118X.2015.1019912

J. Kaler, 2003. Differentiating stakeholder theories. ,. J. Bus. Ethics 46, 71–83.

Jepsen, A.L., Eskerod, P., 2009. Stakeholder analysis in projects: Challenges in using current guidelines in the real world. Int. J. Proj. Manag. 27, 335–343. https://doi.org/10.1016/j.ijproman.2008.04.002

Jirotka, M., Grimpe, B., Stahl, B., Eden, G., Hartswood, M., 2017. Responsible research and innovation in the digital age. Commun. ACM 60, 62–68.

Kamilaris, A., Ngan, D.T.H., Pantazaras, A., Kalluri, B., Kondepudi, S., Wai, T.K., 2014. Good practices in the use of ICT equipment for electricity savings at a university campus, in: Green Computing Conference (IGCC), 2014 International. IEEE, pp. 1–11.

Kanematsu, H., Barry, D.M., 2016. Why Is ICT Important for STEM?, in: Kanematsu, H., M. Barry, D. (Eds.), STEM and ICT Education in Intelligent Environments. Springer International Publishing, Cham, pp. 37–40. https://doi.org/10.1007/978-3-319-19234-5_6

Kelliher, F., 2011. Interpretivism and the pursuit of research legitimisation: an integrated approach to single case design. Lead. Issues Bus. Res. Methods 1, 45.

Khan, Z., Ludlow, D., Rix, J., 2013. Applying the criteria indicators and metrics evaluation method on ICT research: The HUMBOLDT project. Res. Eval. 22, 30–40. https://doi.org/10.1093/reseval/rvs037

Klein, J.T., 2008. Evaluation of Interdisciplinary and Transdisciplinary Research. Am. J. Prev. Med. 35, S116–S123. https://doi.org/10.1016/j.amepre.2008.05.010

Kotvojs, F., Shrimpton, B., others, 2007. Contribution analysis: a new approach to evaluation in international development. Eval. J. Australas. 7, 27.

Kreijns, K., Van Acker, F., Vermeulen, M., van Buuren, H., 2013. What stimulates teachers to integrate ICT in their pedagogical practices? The use of digital learning materials in education. Comput. Hum. Behav. 29, 217–225. https://doi.org/10.1016/j.chb.2012.08.008

Kumar, R.R., Stauvermann, P.J., Samitas, A., 2016. The effects of ICT? on output per worker: A study of the Chinese economy. Telecommun. Policy 40, 102–115. https://doi.org/10.1016/j.telpol.2015.06.004

Kvasny, L., Richardson, H., 2006. Critical research in information systems: looking forward, looking back. Inf. Technol. People 19, 196–202. https://doi.org/10.1108/09593840610689813

Laczniak, G.R., Murphy, P.E., 2012. Stakeholder theory and marketing: Moving from a firm-centric to a societal perspective. J. Public Policy Mark. 31, 284–292.

Laing, K., Todd, L., 2015. Theory-based Methodology: Using theories of change in educational development, research and evaluation.

Lakkala, M., Ilomaki, L., 2015. A case study of developing ICT-supported pedagogy through a?collegial practice transfer process. Comput. Educ. 90, 1–12. https://doi.org/10.1016/j.compedu.2015.09.001

Leedy, P.D., Ormrod, J.E., 2010. Practical Research: Planning and Design, 9th ed. Merril.

Leeuw, F.L., 2012. Linking theory-based evaluation and contribution analysis: Three problems and a few solutions. Evaluation 18, 348–363.

Leventon, J., Fleskens, L., Claringbould, H., Schwilch, G., Hessel, R., 2016. An applied methodology for stakeholder identification in transdisciplinary research. Sustain. Sci. 11, 763– 775. https://doi.org/10.1007/s11625-016-0385-1

Lewin, K., 1946. Action research and minority problems. J. Soc. Issues 2, 34–46.

Lozano, J.M., 2005. Towards the relational corporation: from managing stakeholder relationships to building stakeholder relationships (waiting for Copernicus). Corp. Gov. Int. J. Bus. Soc. 5, 60– 77. https://doi.org/10.1108/14720700510562668

Maia, M.J., Woll, S., Velloso, G., 2015. Responsible Research and Innovation–Perspectives and Challenges.

Mark, M., Greene, J., Shaw, I., 2006. The Evaluation of Policies, Programs, and Practices, in: The Sage Handbook of Evaluation. London, pp. 1–30.

Markie, P., 2015. Rationalism vs. Empiricism.

Martikainen, S., Korpela, M., Luukkonen, I., Vainikainen, V., 2015. Where does the interaction break down? The stakeholder map of health IT systems development and use in Finland. Finn. J. EHealth EWelfare 7, 192–209.

Mayne, J., 2012. Making causal claims. ILAC Brief 26.

Mayne, J., 2015. Useful Theory of Change Models. Can. J. Program Eval. 30, 119–142. https://doi.org/10.3138/cjpe.230

Mazur, A.K., Pisarski, A., 2015. Major project managers' internal and external stakeholder relationships: The development and validation of measurement scales. Int. J. Proj. Manag. 33, 1680–1691. https://doi.org/10.1016/j.ijproman.2015.07.008

McCabe, S., Sharples, M., Foster, C., 2012. Stakeholder engagement in the design of scenarios of technology-enhanced tourism services. Tour. Manag. Perspect. 4, 36–44. https://doi.org/10.1016/j.tmp.2012.04.007

Mingers, J., 2001. Combining IS research methods: towards a pluralist methodology.Inf. Syst. Res. 12, 240–259.

Mioduser, D., 2015. The Pedagogical Ecology of Technology Education: An Agenda for Future Research and Development, in: The Future of Technology Education, Contemporary Issues in Technology Education. Springer, Singapore, pp. 77–98. https://doi.org/10.1007/978-981-287-170-1_5

Murugesan, S., Laplante, P.A., 2011. IT for a Greener Planet [Guest editors' introduction]. IT Prof. 13, 16–18.

Myers, M.D., Klein, H.K., 2011. A Set of Principles for Conducting Critical Research in Information Systems. Mis Q. 35, 17–36.

Nakrošis, V., 2014. Theory-based evaluation of capacity-building interventions. Evaluation 20, 134–150.

Nash, J., Plugge, L., Eurelings, A., 2000. Defining and evaluating CSCL Projects. Unpubl. Pap. Stanf. CA Stanf. Univ.Northcote, M.T., 2012. Selecting criteria to evaluate qualitative research.

O'Sullivan, R.G., 2012. Collaborative Evaluation within a framework of stakeholder-oriented evaluation approaches. Eval. Program Plann. 35, 518–522. https://doi.org/10.1016/j.evalprogplan.2011.12.005

Oates, B.J., 2006. Researching Information Systems and Computing. SAGE, London.

Olphert, W., Damodaran, L., 2007a. Citizen Participation and engagement in the Design of e-Government Services: The Missing Link in Effective ICT Design and Delivery. J. Assoc. Inf. Syst. 8, 491–507.

Olphert, W., Damodaran, L., 2007b. Citizen participation and engagement in the design of e-government services: The missing link in effective ICT design and delivery. J. Assoc. Inf. Syst. 8, 491.

Ondego, B., Moturi, C., 2016. Evaluation of the Implementation of the e-Citizen in Kenya. Evaluation 10.

Orlikowski, W.J., Baroudi, J.J., 1991. Studying information technology in organizations: Research approaches and assumptions. Inf. Syst. Res. 2, 1–28.

Owen, R., Bessant, J.R., Heintz, M. (Eds.), 2013. Responsible innovation: managing the responsible emergence of science and innovation in society. John Wiley & Sons Inc, Chichester, West Sussex.

Owen, R., Bessant, J.R., Heintz, M. (Eds.), 2013a. Responsible innovation: managing the responsible emergence of science and innovation in society. John Wiley & Sons Inc, Chichester, West Sussex.

Owen, R., Stilgoe, J., Macnaghten, P., Gorman, M., Fisher, E., Guston, D., 2013b. A framework for responsible innovation. Responsible Innov. Manag. Responsible Emergence Sci. Innov. Soc. 27–50.

Papazafeiropoulou, A., Pouloudi, A., 2003. Applying the normative aspect of stakeholder analysis to electronic commerce diffusion: Stakeholder consideration for the elimination of the digital divide, in: System Sciences, 2003. Proceedings of the 36th Annual Hawaii International Conference On. IEEE, pp. 6–pp.

Parrott, J.S., Findley, P., Rosenthal, M., Rothpletz-Pugila, P., 2016. Developing a Recursive Evaluation Plan of a Complex Interprofessional Healthcare Education Initiative. J. Res. Interprofessional Pract. Educ. 6.

Patton, M.Q., 2002. Qualitative research and evaluation methods, 3rd ed. Thousand Oaks, CA.

Pavie, X., Carthy, D., 2013. An integration of responsible innovation in the financial sector through design thinking. Peržiūrėta.

Pavie, X., Carthy, D., 2014. Addressing the Wicked Problem of Responsible Innovation through Design Thinking. Available SSRN 2441935.

Pellizzoni, L., 2004. Responsibility and Environmental Governance. Environ. Polit. 13, 541–565. https://doi.org/10.1080/0964401042000229034

Penfield, T., Baker, M.J., Scoble, R., Wykes, M.C., 2014. Assessment, evaluations, and definitions of research impact: A review. Res. Eval. 23, 21–32. https://doi.org/10.1093/reseval/rvt021

Perera, C., Zavlasky, A., Christen, P., 2014. Sensing as a service model for smart cities supported by Internet of Things. Trans. Emerg. Telecommun. Technol. 25, 81– 93.

Phillipson, J., Lowe, P., Proctor, A., Ruto, E., 2012a. Stakeholder engagement and knowledge exchange in environmental research. J. Environ. Manage. 95, 56–65. https://doi.org/10.1016/j.jenvman.2011.10.005

Phillipson, J., Lowe, P., Proctor, A., Ruto, E., 2012b. Stakeholder engagement and knowledge exchange in environmental research. J. Environ. Manage. 95, 56–65. https://doi.org/10.1016/j.jenvman.2011.10.005

Phillipson, J., Lowe, P., Proctor, A., Ruto, E., 2012c. Stakeholder engagement and knowledge exchange in environmental research. J. Environ. Manage. 95, 56–65. https://doi.org/10.1016/j.jenvman.2011.10.005

Ponelis, S.R., 2015. Using interpretive qualitative case studies for exploratory research in doctoral studies: A case of Information Systems research in small and medium enterprises. Int. J. Dr. Stud. 10, 535–550.

Pouloudi, A., 1999. Aspects of the stakeholder concept and their implications for information systems development, in: Systems Sciences, 1999. HICSS-32. Proceedings of the 32nd Annual Hawaii International Conference On. IEEE, pp. 17–pp.

Pouloudi, A., Whitley, E.A., 1997. Stakeholder identification in inter-organizational systems: gaining insights for drug use management systems. Eur. J. Inf. Syst. 6, 1–14.

Pouloudi, A., Whitley, E.A., 2000. Representing human and non-human stakeholders: on speaking with authority, in: Organizational and Social Perspectives on Information Technology. Springer, pp. 339–354.

Pouloudi, N., Currie, W., Whitley, E.A., 2016. Entangled stakeholder roles and perceptions in health information systems: a longitudinal study of the UK NHS N3 network. J. Assoc. Inf. Syst. 17, 107–161.

Pouw, N., Dietz, T., Bélemvire, A., de Groot, D., Millar, D., Obeng, F., Rijneveld, W., Van der Geest, K., Vlaminck, Z., Zaal, F., 2017. Participatory Assessment of Development Interventions: Lessons Learned From a New Evaluation Methodology in Ghana and Burkina Faso. Am. J. Eval. 38, 47–59. https://doi.org/10.1177/1098214016641210

Rahman, M.M., Moonira, M.M., Zuhora, F.T., 2015. A Systematic Methodology and Guidelines for Software Project Manager to Identify Key Stakeholders. IJRCCT 4, 509–517.

Reed, M.S., Curzon, R., 2015. Stakeholder mapping for the governance of biosecurity: a literature review. J. Integr. Environ. Sci. 12, 15–38. https://doi.org/10.1080/1943815X.2014.975723

Reed, M.S., Graves, A., Dandy, N., Posthumus, H., Hubacek, K., Morris, J., Prell, C., Quinn, C.H., Stringer, L.C., 2009. Who's in and why? A typology of stakeholder analysis methods for natural resource management. J. Environ. Manage. 90, 1933–1949. https://doi.org/10.1016/j.jenvman.2009.01.001

Reed, R., 2015. Program evaluation as community-engaged research: Challenges and solutions. Gatew. Int. J. Community Res. Engagem. 8, 118–38.

Responsible Innov. Manag. Responsible Emergence Sci. Innov. Soc. 85–107.

Rip, A., 2014. The past and future of RRI. Life Sci. Soc. Policy 10, 1–15. Rogers, P., 2014. Theory of change. Methodol. Briefs Impact Eval.

Rogers, P.J., Funnell, S.C., 2011. Purposeful Program Theory: Effective Use of Theories of Change and Logic Models. Jossey-Bass, San Francisco.

Rowe, G., Frewer, L.J., 2000. Public Participation Methods: A Framework for Evaluation. Sci. Technol. Hum. Values 25, 3–29. https://doi.org/10.1177/016224390002500101

Rowley, T.J., 1997. Moving beyond dyadic ties: A network theory of stakeholder influences. Acad. Manag. Acad. Manag. Rev. 22, 887–910.

RRING Project, 2018. Responsible Research and Innovation Networking Globally (RRING) project summary [WWW Document]. URL http://www.rring.eu/summary/ (accessed 6.14.14).

Russell, J., Greenhalgh, T., Kushner, S. (Eds.), 2015. Case Study Evaluation: Past, Present and Future Challenges, in: Advances in Program Evaluation. Emerald Group Publishing Limited, p. i. https://doi.org/10.1108/S1474-786320140000015020

Sánchez, M.A., 2015. Integrating sustainability issues into project management. J. Clean. Prod. 96, 319–330. https://doi.org/10.1016/j.jclepro.2013.12.087

Sandelowski, M., 2000. Focus on research methods combining qualitative and quantitative sampling, data collection, and analysis techniques. Res. Nurs. Health 23, 246–255.

Schaffers, H., Komninos, N., Pallot, M., Trousse, B., Nilsson, M., Oliveira, A., 2011. Smart cities and the future internet: Towards cooperation frameworks for open innovation, in: The Future Internet Assembly. Springer, pp. 431–446.

Schenke, W., van Driel, J.H., Geijsel, F.P., Sligte, H.W., Volman, M.L.L., 2016.

Schwandt, T., 2015. Evaluation Foundations Revisited: Cultivating a Life of the Mind for Practice. Stanford University Press.

Schwandt, T.A., 2000. Meta-Analysis and Everyday Life: The Good, the Bad, and the Ugly. Am. J. Eval. 21, 213–219. https://doi.org/10.1177/109821400002100209

Scotland, J., 2012. Exploring the Philosophical Underpinnings of Research: Relating Ontology and Epistemology to the Methodology and Methods of the Scientific, Interpretive, and Critical Research Paradigms. Engl. Lang. Teach. 5.

Scott, P., 2016. Mixed Methods: A Paradigm for Holistic Evaluation of Health IT. Evid.-Based Health Inform. Promot. Saf. Effic. Sci. Methods Ethical Policy 222, 102.

Scriven, M., 1991. Evaluation Thesaurus, 4th ed. SAGE, Newbury Park,CA. Scriven, M., Coryn, C.L.S., 2008. The logic of research evaluation. New Dir. Eval. 2008, 89–105. https://doi.org/10.1002/ev.263

Scriven, M., 2007. The logic of evaluation.

Shadish Jr., W.R., Cook, T.D., Leviton, L.C., 1991. Foundations of program evaluation: Theories of practice. Sage Publications, Inc, Thousand Oaks, CA, US.

Shelley-Egan, C., Hanssen, A.B., Landeweerd, L., Hofmann, B., 2017. Responsible Research and Innovation in the context of human cognitive enhancement: some essential features. J. Responsible Innov. 1–21. https://doi.org/10.1080/23299460.2017.1319034

Silverman, D., 2013. Doing qualitative research: A practical handbook. SAGE Publications Ltd, London.

Simon, J., 2017. Value-Sensitive Design and Responsible Research and Innovation. Ethics Technol. Methods Approaches 219.

Smith, C., P., 2000. Content Analysis and Narrative Analysis, in: Reis, H.T., Judd, C.M. (Eds.), Handbook of Research Methods in Social and Personality Psychology.Cambridge University Press, Cambridge.

Smith, J.K., 1983. Quantitative versus Qualitative Research: An attempt to clarify the issue.

Smith, N.L., 2015. Using Action Design Research to Research and Develop Evaluation Practice: Using Action Design Research to Research and Develop Evaluation Practice. New Dir. Eval. 2015, 57–72. https://doi.org/10.1002/ev.20157

Soeftestad, L.T., Sein, M.K., 2003. ICT and Development: East is East and West is West and the Twain may yet Meet. Digit. Chall. Inf. Technol. Dev. Context 63–82.

Solli-Saether, H., Karlsen, J.T., van Oorschot, K., 2015. Strategic and Cultural Misalignment: Knowledge Sharing Barriers in Project Networks. Proj. Manag. J. 46, 49–60. https://doi.org/10.1002/pmj.21501

Soma, K., Vatn, A., 2014. Representing the common goods – Stakeholders vs. citizens. Land Use Policy 41, 325–333. https://doi.org/10.1016/j.landusepol.2014.06.015

Stahl, B.C., 2007. Positivism or Non-Positivism—Tertium Non Datur, in: Ontologies.Springer, pp. 115–142.

Stahl, B.C., 2008. The ethical nature of critical research in information systems. Inf.Syst. J. 18, 137–163. https://doi.org/10.1111/j.1365-2575.2007.00283.x

Stahl, B.C., 2012. Responsible research and innovation in information systems. Eur. J. Inf. Syst. 21, 207–211.

Stahl, B.C., 2013a. Responsible research and innovation: The role of privacy in an emerging framework. Sci. Public Policy 40, 708–716. https://doi.org/10.1093/scipol/sct067

Stahl, B.C., 2013b. Interpretive accounts and fairy tales: a critical polemic against the empiricist bias in interpretive IS research. Eur. J. Inf. Syst. 23, 1–11. https://doi.org/10.1057/ejis.2012.58

Stahl, B.C., Eden, G., Jirotka, M., 2013. Responsible research and innovation in information and communication technology: Identifying and engaging with the ethical implications of ICTs. Responsible Innov. 199–218.

Stahl, B.C., Eden, G., Jirotka, M., Coeckelbergh, M., 2014. From computer ethics to responsible research and innovation in ICT. Inf. Manage. 51, 810–818. https://doi.org/10.1016/j.im.2014.01.001

Stahl, B.C., Timmermans, J., Flick, C., 2016. Ethics of Emerging Information and Communication Technologies: On the implementation of responsible research and innovation. Sci. Public Policy scw069. https://doi.org/10.1093/scipol/scw069

Stern, E., Stame, N., Mayne, J., Forss, K., Davies, R., Befani, B., 2012. Broadening the range of designs and methods for impact evaluations. (No. 38). Department for International Development, London.

Stilgoe, J., Owen, R., Macnaghten, P., 2013. Developing a framework for responsible innovation. Res. Policy 42, 1568–1580. https://doi.org/10.1016/j.respol.2013.05.008

Stosic, B., Milutinovic, R., 2014. Innovation Projects Classification Issues. Econ. Soc.Dev. Book Proc. Varazdin Dev. Entrep. Agency VADEA 96–104.

Stufflebeam, D., 2001. Evaluation models. New Dir. Eval. 2001, 7–98.

Stufflebeam, D.L., 2003. Stufflebeam D.L. (2003) The CIPP Model for Evaluation., in: Kellaghan, T., D.L. (Eds.), International Handbook of Educational Evaluation, Kluwer International Handbooks of Education,. Dordrecht.

Stufflebeam, D.L., Coryn, C.L., 2014. Research Methods for the Social Sciences : Evaluation Theory, Models, and Applications., 2nd ed. Wiley, Somerset, NJ, USA.

Stufflebeam, D.L., Shinkfield, A.J., 2007. Evaluation Theory, Models, and Applications. Jossey-Bass, San Francisco.

Sutcliffe, H., 2011. A report on responsible research and innovation. MATTER Eur.Comm.

Sutcliffe, H., 2011. A report on responsible research and innovation. MATTER Eur. Comm. Sykes, K., Macnaghten, P., 2013. Responsible Innovation–Opening up Dialogue and Debate.

Sykes, K., Macnaghten, P., 2013. Responsible Innovation–Opening up Dialogue and Debate. Responsible Innov. Manag. Responsible Emergence Sci. Innov. Soc. 85– 107.

Taghian, M., D'Souza, C., Polonsky, M., 2015. A stakeholder approach to corporate social responsibility, reputation and business performance. Soc. Responsib. J. 11, 340–363.

Tan, H., Wilson, A., Olver, I., 2009. Ricoeur's theory of interpretation: An instrument for data interpretation in hermeneutic phenomenology. Int. J. Qual. Methods 8, 1–15.

Tan, J.L., Goh, D.H.-L., Ang, R.P., Huan, V.S., 2013. Participatory evaluation of an educational game for social skills acquisition. Comput. Educ. 64, 70–80. https://doi.org/10.1016/j.compedu.2013.01.006

Taplin, D.H., Clark, H., Collins, E., Colby, D.C., 2013. Theory of Change.

Tarutė, A., Gatautis, R., 2014. ICT Impact on SMEs Performance. Procedia - Soc. Behav. Sci. 110, 1218–1225. https://doi.org/10.1016/j.sbspro.2013.12.968

Turner, J.R., Müller, R., 2003. On the nature of the project as a temporary organization. Int. J. Proj. Manag. 21, 1–8. https://doi.org/10.1016/S0263-7863(02)00020-0

Van den Hoven, J., 2013. Value Sensitive Design and Responsible Innovation, in (eds R. Owen, J. Bessant and M. Heintz), John Wiley & Sons, Ltd, Chichester, UK., in: Owen, R., Bessant, J., Heintz, M. (Eds.), Responsible Innovation: Managing the Responsible Emergence of Science and Innovation in Society. John Wiley & Sons, Chichester, UK.

Vandekerckhove, W., Dentchev, N.A., 2005. A Network Perspective on Stakeholder Management: Facilitating Entrepreneurs in the Discovery of Opportunities. J. Bus. Ethics 60, 221–232. https://doi.org/10.1007/s10551-005-0130-7

Von Schomberg, R. von., European Commission., Directorate-General for Research and Innovation., 2011. Towards responsible research and innovation in the information and communication technologies and security technologies fields. EUR-OP, Luxembourg.

Von Schomberg, R., 2012. Prospects for Technology Assessment in a framework of responsible research and innovation, in: M. Dusseldorp, R. Beecroft

(Eds.), Technikfolgen Abschätzen Lehren: Bildungspotenziale Transdisziplinärer Methoden,. Wiesbaden, pp. 39–61.

Von Schomberg, R., 2013. A vision of Responsible Research and Innovation, in: Owen, R., Heintz, M., Bessant, J. (Eds.), Responsible Innovation. John Wiley, London.

Von Schomberg, R., 2013. A vision of Responsible Research and Innovation, in: Owen, R., Heintz, M., Bessant, J. (Eds.), Responsible Innovation. John Wiley, London.

Von Schomberg, R., European Commission, Directorate General for Research, 2007. From the Ethics of Technology towards an Ethics of Knowledge Policy & Knowledge Assessment: a working document from the European Commission Services. EUR-OP, Luxembourg.

Walliman, N., 2006. Social Research Methods. SAGE.

Walsham, G., 1993. Interpreting Information Systems in Organizations, 1st ed. John Wiley & Sons, Inc., New York, NY, USA.

Weiss, C., 1998. Evaluation. Prentice-Hall, Upper Sadle River, NJ.

Weiss, C.H., 1997. How can theory-based evaluation make greater headway? Eval. Rev.21, 501– 524.

Wilford, S., Fisk, M., Stahl, B.C., 2016. Guidelines for Responsible Research and Innovation. De Montfort University.Forsythe, L.P., Ellis, L.E., Edmundson, L., Sabharwal, R., Rein, A., Konopka, K., Frank, L., 2016. Patient and Stakeholder Engagement in the PCORI Pilot Projects: Description and Lessons Learned. J. Gen. Intern. Med. 31, 13–21. https://doi.org/10.1007/s11606-015-3450-z

Wilford, S., Fisk, M., Stahl, B.C., 2016. Guidelines for Responsible Research and Innovation. De Montfort University.

Wilford, S.H., 2015. What is required of requirements? A first stage process towards developing guidelines for responsible research and innovation 45, 8.

William Trochim, James P Donnelly,-The Research Methods Knowledge Base (2006).pdf, n.d.

Williams, I., Phillips, D., Nicholson, C., Shearer, H., 2014. Evaluation of a deliberative approach to citizen involvement in health care priority setting. Leadersh. Health Serv. 27, 5–19. https://doi.org/10.1108/LHS-01-2013-0002

Willis, J., 2007. Foundations of Qualitative Research: Interpretive and Critical Approaches. SAGE Publications Ltd, Thousand Oaks, CA.

Wilmot, A., 2005. Designing sampling strategies for qualitative social research: with particular reference to the Office for National Statistics' Qualitative

Respondent Register. Surv. Methodol. Bull.-Off. Natl. Stat.-56, 53.

Yin, R., 1994. Case study research: Design and methods, 2nd ed. Sage Publishing, Beverly Hills, CA.

Yin, R.K., 2003. Case Study Research Design and Methods, 3rd ed. SAGE Publications, UK.

Zuppo, C.M., 2012. Defining ICT in a Boundaryless World : The Development of a Working Hierarchy. Int. J. Manag. Inf. Technol. 4, 13–22. https://doi.org/10.5121/ijmit.2012.4302

Zwart, H., Landeweerd, L., Van Rooij, A., 2014. Adapt or perish? Assessing the recent shift in the European research funding arena from 'ELSA'to 'RRI.' Life Sci. Soc. Policy 10, 1.

Appendices

Appendix A

A-1 EVALUATION DESIGNS AND APPROACHES

Table A-1: Design Approaches, Variants and Causal Inference (Source: Stern *et al*, 2012)

Evaluation Design	Description	Variant Approach	Author
Pseudo- evaluation	Evaluations with a hidden agenda and often fail to produce and report valid assessments of merit or worth to all stakeholders	• Public relations- inspired studies • Politically controlled studies • Pandering evaluations • Evaluation by pretext • Empowerment under guise of evaluation	Stufflebeam and Coryn, (2014)
Question and methods - oriented evaluations (Quasi-evaluations)	Evaluations that provide evidence that fully assesses the merit and worth with a narrow focus to the questions asked and method employed but miss out on broad assessment	• Object-based studies • Accountability • Success case method • Objective testing programs • Outcome evaluation (Value added assessment) • Performance testing • Experimental studies • Management information systems • Benefit-cost analysis • Clarification hearing 16. • Case study evaluation • Criticism and connoisseurship • Theory-based evaluation • Mixed methods studies	Stufflebeam and Coryn, (2014)

Evaluation Design	Description	Variant Approach	Author
Improvement and accountability-oriented evaluations	Evaluations that employ assessed needs of stakeholders as the foundational criteria for assessing worth, based on democratic principles in assessing the value of a program.	• Decision and accountability oriented studies • Consumer-oriented studies • Accreditation and certification	Stufflebeam and Coryn, (2014)
Social agenda and advocacy evaluations	Evaluations aimed at increasing social justice by advocating affirmative action to give preferential treatment to the disadvantaged.	• Responsive or stakeholder-centred evaluation. • Constructivist evaluation • Deliberative democratic evaluation • Transformative evaluation	Stufflebeam and Coryn, (2014)
Eclectic evaluations	Evaluations that are pragmatic that accommodates the needs and preferences of a wide range of stakeholders and evaluation assignments without constraints of a single model or approach	• Utilization focused evaluation • Participatory evaluation	Stufflebeam and Coryn, (2014)

Table A-2: Design Approaches, Examples and Process Inference (Adapted from Stufflebeam and Shinkfield (2007) and Stufflebeam and Coryn (2014)

Evaluation Approach	Examples	Process Inference
Experimental	RCTs Quasi Experiments Natural Experiments	Counterfactuals; the co-presence of cause and effects
Statistical	Statistical Modelling, Longitudinal Studies Econometrics	Correlation between cause and effect or between variables, influence of (usually) isolatable multiple causes on a single effect Control for 'confounders'
Theory-based	*Causal process designs*: Theory of Change, Process tracing, Contribution Analysis, impact pathways. *Causal mechanism designs*: Realist evaluation, Congruence analysis.	Identification/confirmation of causal processes or 'chains' Supporting factors and mechanisms at work in context

Evaluation Approach	Examples	Process Inference
'Case-based'	*Interpretative:* Naturalistic, Grounded theory, Ethnography *Structured*: Configurations, QCA, Within-Case- Analysis, Simulations and network analysis	Comparison across and within cases of combinations of causal factors Analytic generalisation based on theory
Participatory	*Normative designs*: Participatory or democratic evaluation, Empowerment evaluation Agency designs: Learning by doing, Policy dialogue, Collaborative Action Research	Validation by participants that their actions and experienced effects are 'caused' by programme Adoption, customisation and commitment to a goal
Synthesis studies	Meta-analysis, Narrative synthesis, Realist based synthesis	Accumulation and aggregation within a number of perspectives (statistical, theory based, ethnographic etc.)

A-2 EVALUATION STANDARDS

The following are the programme evaluation standards developed by the American Joint Committee on Standards for Educational Evaluation (AJCSEE) which have increasingly been promoted through professional evaluation associations, including the American and African evaluation associations. The African Evaluation Association has further adapted the original AJCSEE standards. Regardless of the version adopted, these standards can be used both as a guide for managing the evaluation process and to assess an existing evaluation. The standards highlightthe considerations that must be weighed in formulating an evaluation design.

- **Utility:** seek to ensure that an evaluation will serve the information needs of intended users.
- **Feasibility:** seek to ensure that an evaluation will be realistic, prudent, diplomatic, and frugal.
- **Propriety:** seek to ensure that an evaluation will be conducted legally, ethically, and with due regard for the welfare of those involved in the evaluation, as well as those affected by its results.
- **Accuracy:** seek to ensure that an evaluation will reveal and convey

technically adequate information about the features that determine the worth or merit of the programme being evaluated.

Utility

Stakeholder Identification

Persons involved in or affected by the evaluation should be identified so their needs can be addressed.

Evaluator Credibility

Persons conducting the evaluation should be both trustworthy and competent to perform the evaluation, so its findings achieve maximum credibility and acceptance.

Information Scope and Selection

Information collected should be broadly selected to address pertinent questions about the programme and be responsive to the needs and interests of clients and other specified stakeholders.

Values Identification

The perspectives, procedures, and rationale used to interpret the findings should be carefully described so the bases for value judgements are clear.

Report Clarity

Evaluation reports should clearly describe the programme being evaluated, including its context, purposes, procedures, and findings so that essential information is provided and easily understood.

Report Timeliness and Dissemination

Significant interim findings and evaluation reports should be disseminated to intended users, so they can be used in a timely fashion.

Evaluation Impact

Evaluations should be planned, conducted, and reported in ways that encourage follow-through by stakeholders to increase the likelihood that the evaluation will be used.

Feasibility

Practical Procedures

The evaluation procedures should be practical to keep disruption to a minimum while needed information is obtained.

Political Viability

The evaluation should be planned and conducted with anticipation of the different positions of various interest groups, so their co-operation may be obtained, and possible attempts by any of these groups to curtail evaluation operations or to bias or misapply the results can be averted or counteracted.

Cost Effectiveness

The evaluation should be efficient and produce information of sufficient value, so the resources expended can be justified.

Propriety

Service Orientation

Evaluations should be designed to help organisations address and effectively serve the needs of the full range of participants.

Formal Agreement

The obligations of the formal parties to an evaluation (what is to be done, how, by whom, when) should be agreed to in writing to ensure that they adhere to all conditions of the agreement or that they formally renegotiate it.

Rights of Human Subjects

Evaluations should be designed and conducted to respect and protect the rights and welfare of human subjects.

Human Interactions

Evaluators should respect human dignity and worth in their interactions with other persons associated with an evaluation, so participants are not threatened or harmed.

Complete and Fair Assessment

The evaluation should be complete and fair in its examination and recording of strengths and weaknesses of the programme being evaluated so that strengths can be built upon and problem areas addressed.

Disclosure of Findings

The formal parties to an evaluation should ensure that the full set of evaluation findings along with pertinent limitations are made accessible to the persons affected by the evaluation, and any others with expressed legal rights to receive theresults.

Conflict of Interest

Conflict of interest should be dealt with openly and honestly, so it does not compromise the evaluation processes and results.

Fiscal Responsibility

The evaluator's allocation and expenditure of resources should reflect sound accountability procedures, and otherwise be prudent and ethically responsible to ensure they are accounted for and appropriate.

Accuracy

Programme Documentation

The programme being evaluated should be described and documented clearly and accurately.

Context Analysis

The context of the programme should be examined in enough detail so its likely influences can be identified.

Described Purposes and Procedures

The purposes and procedures of the evaluation should be monitored and described in enough detail, so they can be identified and assessed.

Defensible Information Sources

The sources of information used in a programme evaluation should be described in enough detail, so their adequacy can be assessed.

Valid Information

The information-gathering procedures should be chosen or developed and implemented to ensure that the interpretation is valid for the intended use.

Reliable Information

The information-gathering procedures should be chosen or developed and implemented to ensure that the information is sufficiently reliable for the intended use.

Systematic Information

The information collected, processed, and reported in an evaluation should be systematically reviewed, and any errors found should be corrected

Analysis of Quantitative Information

Quantitative information should be appropriately and systematically analysed, so evaluation questions are effectively answered.

Analysis of Qualitative Information

Qualitative information should be appropriately and systematically analysed, so evaluation questions are effectively answered.

Justified Conclusions

The conclusions reached in an evaluation should be explicitly justified so stakeholders can assess them.

Impartial Reporting

Reporting procedures should guard against distortion caused by personal feelings and biases of any party to the evaluation so that evaluation reports fairly reflect the evaluation findings.

Meta-evaluation

The evaluation itself should be formatively and summatively evaluated against these and other pertinent standards so that its conduct is appropriately guided, and, on completion, stakeholders can closely examine its strengths and weaknesses.

A-3 INTERVIEW QUESTIONS

Stakeholder ID …………Gender: Male / Female…….. Project code…………….
Date …………….   Introduction   I am Tilimbe Jiya from De Montfort University   General purpose of the study   Aims of the interview and expected duration   Why the participant's cooperation is important   What will happen with the collected information and how the participant will benefit   Any questions?   Consent   **Warm up**
Can I ask some details about you?   ______________________   Years workedin technology research and/or innovation projects   I___I____Iyrs I_I_I mths   **Now I am going to ask you some questions about your experiences as a stakeholder in this project.**
Guiding Questions
How were you identified to be part of the research project?   At what stage of the research project were you involved?   What is your role in the research project?

What is your background or expertise and how do you think that would contribute towards the research Project 4n terms of responsible innovation? (a document explaining responsible (research) innovation provided)   What do you think is your contribution to the research Project 4n light of responsible innovation that leads to responsible outcomes? (responsible outcomes explained to mean the same as socially desirable outcomes)   What barriers have you ever experienced in relation to your contribution to the research project towards responsible outcomes?   In relation to achieving responsible outcomes, why do you think a project such as XXX should engage different stakeholders?   What sort of outcomes do you think would result from your engagement in the research Project 4n relation to responsible innovation?   Do you think that you are given the opportunity and resources to contribute towards the project with respect to responsible innovation or achieving responsible outcomes? Please, elaborate on your answer?   What are your expectations for your engagement in the research project particularly with respect to responsible innovation or achieving responsible outcomes?

Closing

Is there anything else you think is important in implementing and assessing influence of stakeholders of TRI project that we have not talked about?

Summarise

Thank participant

Provide extra information and contacts to participants

A-4 Consent Form

CONSENT FORM

Study Title: ***Evaluating stakeholder engagement in ICT research projects***

Researcher: Tilimbe Jiya

The study has been explained to me in a language that I comprehend. All the questions I had about the study have been answered. I understand what will happen during the interview and what is expected of me.

I have been informed that it is my right to refuse to take part in the interview today and that if I choose to refuse I do not have to give a reason.

I have been informed that anything I say during the interview today will remain completely confidential; my name will not be used nor any other information that could be used to identify me.

It has been explained that sometimes the researcher find it helpful to use my own words when writing up the findings of this research. I understand that any use of my words would be completely anonymous (without my name). I have been told that I can decide whether I permit my words to be used in this way.

Circle response:

I agree to take part in the study:	Yes
I agree that my own words may be used anonymously in the pilot study report	Yes

Signature of participant:

SIGNATUREDATE OF SIGNATURE

(in capital letters)

(in DD/MM/YYYY)

Signature of study researcher taking consent:

I have discussed the study with the respondent named above, in a language he/she can comprehend.

I believe he/she has understood my explanation and agrees to take part in the interview.

NAME	**SIGNATURE**	**DATE OF SIGNATURE**

A-5 Stakeholder Study Participation Log

Project Code	Stakeholder Study ID	Name	Email	Role	Date Sent	Interview Date & Time
IT	IT01			Researcher	18/11/2015	24/11/2015 10am
	IT02			Researcher	18/11/2015	25/11/2015 1pm
	IT03			Researcher	18/11/2015	Refused
	IT04			Planning Engineer	18/11/2015	Refused
	IT05			Project Sponsor	18/11/2015	Refused
	IT06			Project Manager	18/11/2015	Refused
	IT07			Researcher	18/11/2015	Refused

	IT08			Planning Engineer	18/11/2015	Refused
SS	SS01			Researcher	01/04/2016	
	SS02			Researcher	01/04/2016	11/05/16 2pm (online)
	SS03			Researcher	01/04/2016	06/05/16 11am (online)
	SS04			End user	01/04/2016	Refused
	SS05			End user	01/04/2016	04/05/16 2pm
	SS06			End user	01/04/2016	03/05/16 1.30pm
	SS07			Researcher	01/04/2016	04/05/16 11am
	SS08			Researcher	01/04/2016	03/05/16 1pm

	SS09			Librarian	01/04/2016	Refused
	SS10			Energy expert	01/04/2016	26/04/16 10am
	SS11			Energy expert	01/04/2016	28/04/16 11am
	SS12			Energy expert	01/04/2016	28/04/16 12pm
	SS13			Energy expert	01/04/2016	13/05/16 10am
	SS14			Energy expert	01/04/2016	Refused
	SS15			End user	01/04/2016	Refused
	SS16			End user	01/04/2016	Refused
	SS17			Energy expert	01/04/2016	Refused
	SS18			Librarian	01/04/2016	26/04/16 11am
DL	DL01			ELT Facilitator	11/04/16	03/05/16 10am

	DL02			BSF Facilitator	11/04/16	05/05/16 2pm
	DL03			Researcher	11/04/16	06/05/16 (email)
	DL04			Researcher	11/04/16	Refused
	DL05			Teacher	11/04/16	Refused
	DL06			Teacher	11/04/16	Refused
	DL07			Teacher	11/04/16	Refused
	DL08			Teacher	11/04/16	Refused
	DL09			Teacher	11/04/16	Refused
3TI	3TI01			Audiolgist	10/07/17	13/07/17
	3TI02			Project Manager	10/07/17	17/07/17

	3DTI03			Music Developer	10/07/17	28/07/17
	3DTI04			App Developer	10/07/17	17/07/17
	3DTI05			Researcher	10/07/17	25/07/17
	3DTI06			Researcher	10/02/17	Refused
	3DTI07			App Developer	10/10/17	Refused
	3DTI08			App Developer	12/06/17	Refused
	3DTI09			Project Manager	12/06/17	Refused
	3DTI10			Researcher	10/02/17	Refused
	3DT11			App Developer	10/07/16	Refused

A-6 Pilot Study Timeline

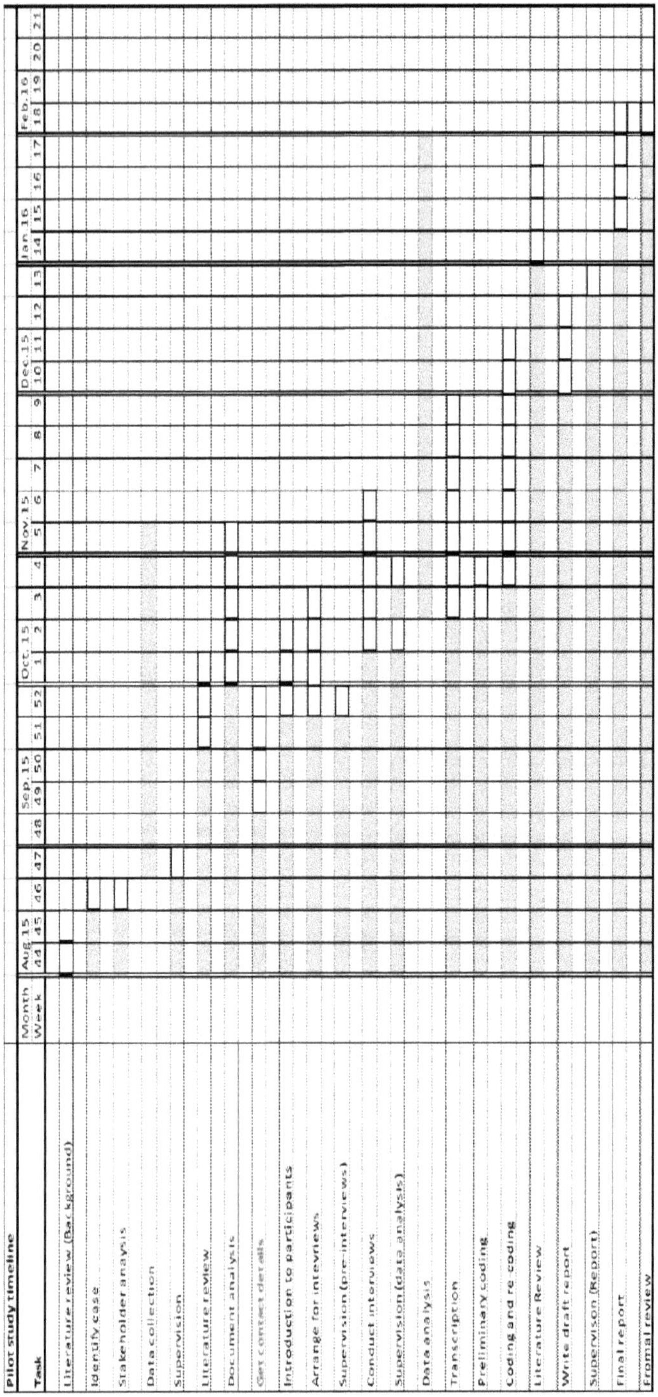

A-7 PRE-DEFINED CODING FRAME

First level coding based on a pre-defined frame (Deductive coding)

Broad categories – Deductive codes	
Code label	**Code description**
Nature of stakeholder engagement	The form and type of stakeholder engagement activities conducted by the stakeholders that were engaged in the ICT research projects.
Rationale for engaging stakeholders	The reason and motive for engaging the stakeholders in the ICT research projects. This includes a look at their role in the research process.
Outcomes of stakeholder engagement	The results for engaging the stakeholders in the projects, particularly those that would relate to RRI
Context of stakeholder engagement	The circumstances that form the setting for the stakeholder engagement in the ICT research projects. These circumstances are those which it can be fully understood and assessed.
Stakeholder	The process and aspects of the stakeholder
identification	Identification process
RRI application	The relevance of the key RRI features as developed in the RRI literature.

First level coding based on a predefined coding frame (deductive coding)

Below is an illustration of how the deductive codes appear in NVivo.

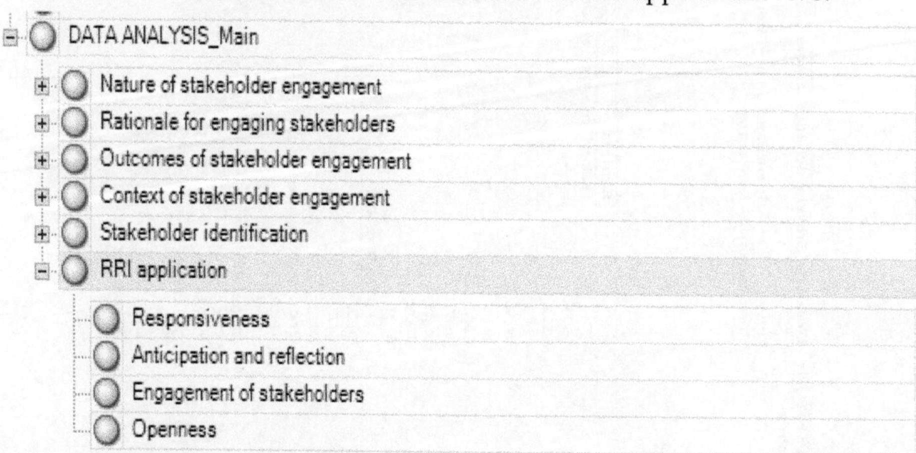

Illustration of pre-defined codes in Nvivo

A-8 Cross-case Analysis: Context of Stakeholder Engagement

Cross case analysis - Context of Stakeholder engagement						
Case project						
	Theme	Identification of	Enough stakehol	Stakeholders'	Research funding	Existing infrastucture for ICT research
	Characteristic:	***Role uptake***			***Resources***	
Project D		x		x	x	x
Project F		x	x		x	x
Project G		x	x		x	
Project I		x		x	x	
		Barriers				
		lack of interest	prioritising	understandin	Lack of capacity	Mind set
Project D	SS01	x				
	SS02					
	SS03		x	x		
	SS04					
	SS05					
	SS06		x		x	
	SS07	x	x			
	SS08					
	SS09					
	SS10					
	Document review					
Project F	DL01					
	DL02			x		x
	DL03					
	Document review					
Project G	3TI01					
	3TI02					
	3TI03	x				
	3TI04		x			
	3TI05	x	x			
	Document review					
Project I	IT01	x		x		
	IT02		x		x	
	Document review					

A-9 Cross-case Analysis: Stakeholder Identification

Cross case analysis - Stakeholder identification											
Case project	Stakeholder	Theme									
			Broad category:				Stakeholder identification				
		Themes:	*process*		*Timing*		*Range*				
		Codes:	ex ante	ad hoc	Past networks	referal	industry	Academia	Local Authority	public	Researcher
Project D	SS01							x			
	SS02			x					x		
	SS03		x					x			x
	SS04										x
	SS05			x						x	
	SS06		x			x				x	
	SS07		x								x
	SS08										x
	SS09								x		
	SS10			x					x		
	Document review						x	x	x	x	x
Project F	DL01		x		x	x		x			
	DL02		x						x		
	DL03			x							x
	Document review							x	x	x	x
Project G	3TI01					x					x
	3TI02		x								x
	3TI03										x
	3TI04			x		x					x
	3TI05		x					x			
	Document review						x	x	x	x	x
Project I	IT01		x			x		x			x
	IT02		x		x			x			x
	Document review						x	x	x	x	x

A-10 Cross-case Analysis: Nature of Stakeholder Engagement

Cross case analysis- Nature of stakeholder engagement

Case project	**Stakeholder**	**Theme**									
						Broad category:		**Nature of stakeholder engagement**			
		Themes:	***Form***					***Barriers***			
			disseminate info	facilitate dailogue	offer expertise	provide feedback	promotion and ownership	lack of interest	prioritising	understanding RI	Lack of capacity	Mind set
Project D	SS01		x	x		x	X	x				
	SS02				x	x	X					
	SS03			x					x	x		
	SS04											
	SS05					x						
	SS06		x			x			x		x	
	SS07			x				x	x			
	SS08			x	x							
	SS09											
	SS10											
	Document review		x		x							
Project F	DL01		x		x	x						
	DL02					x	X			x		x
	DL03			x								
	Document review			x	x	x	x					
Project G	3TI01			x	x							
	3TI02		x				X					
	3TI03					x		x				
	3TI04				x				x			
	3TI05		x	x			X	x	x			
	Document review				x	x						
Project I	IT01		x		x	x		x		x		
	IT02		x		x	x	X		x		x	
	Document review				x		x					

A-11 Cross-case Analysis: Rationale for Stakeholder Engagement

Rationale for stakeholder engagement							
Case project	Stakeholder	Theme					
		Broad category:	Rationale of stakehoder engagement				
		Themes:	consultation	control and direction	mutual learning	resourcing	Social consideration
Project D	SS01						
	SS02			x			
	SS03		x	x	x	x	
	SS04						
	SS05		x		x		
	SS06						
	SS07						
	SS08		x				
	SS09						
	SS10						
	Document review			x		x	
Project F	DL01		x	x			x
	DL02		x	x			x
	DL03				x		
	Document review		x			x	
Project G	3TI01		x	x	x		
	3TI02		x	x	x		
	3TI03		x	x	x		
	3TI04		x	x	x		
	3TI05		x				
	Document review		x	x	x	x	
Project I	IT01		x	x	x		
	IT02		x	x	x		
	Document review			x		x	

A-12 Cross-case Analysis: Outcome of Stakeholder Engagement

Cross case analysis - Outcome of stakeholder engagement

Case project	**Stakeholder**	**Theme**			
		Themes: awareness of responsibility issues	optimal resource utilisation	sustainability of project aims	co-creation
Project D	SS01	x	x	x	
	SS02		x	x	
	SS03	x			
	SS04				
	SS05				x
	SS06	x		x	
	SS07	x	x		
	SS08				
	SS09				
	SS10				
	Document review				
Project F	DL01				
	DL02	x	x	x	
	DL03				x
	Document review				
Project G	3TI01				
	3TI02	x			
	3TI03	x			
	3TI04	x		x	x
	3TI05			x	x
	Document review				
Project I	IT01	x			x
	IT02		x	x	x
	Document review				

Index

www.ingramcontent.com/pod-product-compliance
Ingram Content Group UK Ltd.
Pitfield, Milton Keynes, MK11 3LW, UK
UKHW020048200726
13845UKWH00045B/63

9 789349 964549